Sebastián

E

NCES

France

D0149255

Pamplona

NAVARRE

Huesca

ARAGON

CATALONIA

Gerona

Lérida

Barcelona

Zaragoza

E

Teruel

Castellon

Balearic Isles

nca

Minorca

E

Valencia

Majorca

Albacete

VALENCIA

Ibiza

MURCIA

Alicante

Formentera

Murcia

Mediterranean Sea

a

Miles

0   50   100   150

By Jose Yglesias

Fiction
A WAKE IN YBOR CITY
AN ORDERLY LIFE
THE TRUTH ABOUT THEM
DOUBLE DOUBLE
THE KILL PRICE

Nonfiction
THE GOODBYE LAND
IN THE FIST OF THE REVOLUTION
DOWN THERE

The Franco years

BY

Jose Yglesias

THE BOBBS-MERRILL COMPANY, INC.
Indianapolis/New York

Library of Congress Cataloging in Publication Data

Yglesias, Jose.
    The Franco years.

    1. Spain—History—1939–1975.   2. Franco Bahamonde,
Francisco, 1892–1975. I. Title.
DP270.Y46   946.082   77-76886
    ISBN 0-672-52352-3

For Jaime Gil de Biedma
with affection and admiration

Acknowledgments

I should like to thank the John Simon Guggenheim Memorial Foundation for a Fellowship Grant that made possible much of my research in Spain and at the Widener Library.

My debt to Spanish friends is also great. Pedro Altares, Luis Carandell, Armando Lopez Salinas, Ignacio Martinez, and Jaime Salinas were generous with information and suggestions. Nevertheless, they are to blame for any lacks in this book: they know their country so well that only a slight further effort on their part would have made me a faultless observer of the Spanish scene.

Contents

Foreword

The month during which Franco's life was prolonged, from mid-October, 1975, to November 20, allowed Spanish newspapers to polish their editorials on his death. I spent that time driving throughout most of Spain, and unlike reports in the newspapers, I saw, with only one exception, no public expression of concern for his coming death. I returned late to Madrid the last evening of his life, and went down early the next morning without stopping to speak to the men at my hotel desk. It was at the newspaper stands on Gran Vía that I discovered Franco had died less than four hours earlier. On a street corner I read the editorial in *Ya:* "The hole that Francisco Franco leaves in Spanish life and the space he goes on to fill in history is so great that any superlative would serve only to belittle him. The Chief of State has died, but above all the founder of a State and of an historical era to which his name, in all justice, has been given and which with him ends. During almost half a century his figure has stood at the top national level and his biography and the general history of Spain have been mingled to such an extent that it would be very difficult, if not impossible, to separate." The editorial writers had been unable to find anything new to say. These were well-worn phrases, and they should have gone down as easily as in the past. This time the last sentence did not. I thought: the effort must be made to separate Franco's life from that of the Spanish people.

1

1
By Way of Introduction

In the town of Écija in Andalusia, during the summer of 1976, three young schoolteachers reversed with me the usual order for showing a visitor one's hometown. They did not first take me to see the famous church towers encrusted with *azulejos* nor the baroque chapels nor Roman facades and ruins. They were out to make a point: they led me through winding and climbing narrow streets to Écija's most populous slum, El Picadero. It spread out to the end of town on a promontory overlooking the countryside. Low huts, some no larger than one room, leaned against one another on three sides, so that the door and one window, or two at most, provided the only ventilation and, in some, the only light. Others had a bare bulb hanging from the ceiling. None had a bathroom. In the last five years running water had been installed in some by those who could get the money together, but these had no drains or sewers. The shacks with electricity had two-burner stoves without ovens, but in most the women cooked with wood or coal while the family went outside to get out of the smoke and heat. The ground of the lanes between the huts was baked hard by the sun or paved with a crust of cement; down the middle of the lanes there was a shallow indentation they called the gutter acting as an open sewer. No house had a flush toilet, but a few had primitive privies. At nightfall, a member of each household took the slops and excrement in a pail to a dump some two miles away in the valley.

It was early afternoon, and the women came out and talked and led us inside to show us their places and how they managed. Even when they learned that I was not a bureaucrat who might, with a good word to the mayor, get them running water, they did not cease to tell us their troubles. But now their candor contained no pleading, and they became funny and spirited about their hardships. One pinched her nose between forefinger and thumb and held her other hand far from herself as if carrying a bucket of excrement. "This is the way I go to the dump!" And all of us laughed. Their friendliness made it possible for me to observe that visually El Picadero was lovely.

An unplanned conjunction of various things made it so. The Church's lay charity organization *Caritas* had some time ago donated plaster, tiles, and whitewash to El Picadero's inhabitants, and those old lean-tos built with whatever was at hand had been cast in them like a George Segal sculpture. On that height against the blue sky and the ochre soil and rocks their irregular shapes took on a startling beauty composed of lightness and solidity, artifice and function. Perfect for a tourist poster. I could easily envision a swinging Madison Avenue advertising executive taking over the place as if it were one more tenement in Greenwich Village or a barn in New England, and with electricians, plumbers, and decorators converting El Picadero into a chic place to live. By the time we had walked down from it and could again see it only as a vista, I was able to confess to the young teachers that in truth El Picadero looked beautiful. They agreed. One of them added, "On the outside—like Spain."

That is why if you are out to enjoy yourself it has been best to see Spain as a guided tourist and without knowledge of the language. (I do not scoff at guided tours; if the great relics of the past are what interest you, there is much to be said for them.) This pleasant view of Spain did not obtain during the years of hunger following their Civil War and our World War—then the beggars who appeared out of nowhere, even when you were on a train and it had only paused between towns, destroyed your enjoyment of the country's beauty. Of course, in those days not much of Europe was a pleasure to see either. But in Spain to this day it is best, if you have only a couple of weeks, to stay at the Ritz in Madrid and cross the street to the Prado;

or at the Franciscan convent in Granada, converted into a *parador*, which puts you next to the Alhambra and the gardens of the Generalife; or at the Hotel Colón in Barcelona directly across from the Cathedral and a few quaint blocks from the Ramblas, the Picasso Museum, and the very *típico* seafood restaurant Los Caracoles. I must not forget my own favorite, the Hostal de los Reyes Católicos in Santiago de Compostela, which sits in centuries-old splendor on the Plaza del Obradouiro, one of the great plazas of this world, at a right angle to a cathedral that is one of the few which must be seen. All of Spain could have been toured in this way in the depressing days of the Franco regime, and you could have easily converted the pleasure you were bound to feel into some gratefulness to the regime that had set up a Ministry of Tourism to help make it possible.

Tourists took some twenty years to come see Franco's Spain in substantial numbers. Scarely anyone who had been an adult during the 1936–39 Civil War had the stomach for it. True, the World War immediately intervened, but it was less the physical difficulties than the emotive ones that kept almost everyone from visiting Spain. Or even thinking about it. Spain was a blasted country for which there seemed no possibility of renewal. Indeed, with the fall of the Republic it became, as Camus put it, a square of darkness. The light that left it was ours and the Spaniards' hopes that the great injustices of our time would there be solved and that the grave menace of fascism would there lose its impetus. As one Republican slogan said, "Madrid will be the tomb of fascism." For a few desperate years it seemed possible that men of good will in and out of Spain—liberals and radicals, libertarians and conservative republicans, Protestants and Jews—would bring it off. Although the fight for the Spanish Republic was mined with anguish, hopefulness always supervened, for its supporters moved in the clean light of youth that seems to make right and wrong easily distinguishable.

We are now less innocent about what took place. That war has been as intensely studied as our own Civil War, both from its national and international aspects, and very likely will continue to be. It is fascinating, after all, even from a dispassionate historical point of view, to observe Spain in the twentieth century once more climb the spiral of its past. The forces that with the Counter-

Reformation kept Spain from entering the modern age and manipulated during the Napoleonic era the nationalist sentiments of the Spaniards to thwart democratic development consolidated themselves again in the 1930's. In other centuries these forces—the aristocracy, military, and Church—could count on substantial support or simple indifference from the Spanish people, but it was a different matter now. The Spaniards had shown in elections and mass actions their support of the Republic and its idealistic reforms, and the old guard had to look elsewhere for sustenance.

It was thus out of practical necessity that at first the group of generals who began the uprising turned to the German and Italian fascist governments for help. For Hitler and Mussolini, Spain not only offered an ally at a strategic point in Europe but a fine rehearsal ground for their major war plans. They were unstinting in their military participation, and this support inspired the Spanish generals to adopt the ideology of its allies as the organizing political force of their movement. Without this development, there would still have been many in the West who would have been drawn to aid the Republic, but the presence of Italians and Germans in Spain and the fascist pretensions of Franco's leadership ineluctably drew an entire generation of anti-fascists throughout the world to the Republic's side. Never were political lines so encompassingly drawn in this century; nor was there ever to be so bitter a defeat.

Just as the Spanish fascists boasted that there was a fifth column within Madrid that would help them win that city, so could they have claimed friends in the West who saw to it that the Republic could buy almost no military supplies—the only crucial necessity for victory it lacked. The English and French governments, intent on appeasing Hitler and Mussolini, entered into a non-intervention pact with them which the fascists, of course, did not honor. The American Congress hurriedly passed an embargo on sales of arms to the Republic, with the rationale that this would contain the war in Spain. Only Mexico and the Soviet Union did not follow their lead, but ships bringing such aid had to run the gauntlet of German submarines. In any case, the Soviet Union, already well down its Stalinist path, never gave the Republic decisive help. The apologies for and denunciations of this configuration of forces and the internal

6

differences of the Popular Front government can still turn any discussion of the Civil War into shouting, passionate dissension.

I simplify and gloss this extraordinary war to make the point, about which no one disagrees, that as geography, as well as ideological setting, Spain suffered devastation. Only Vietnam was as badly punished by war. With this bleak image as their last recollection of Spain, the tourists, who like everyone else had averted their eyes from what followed the Republic's defeat, might well have found reasonable the claims that Franco made for this thirty-seven-year-long regime. Unlike most Western nations, Spain had been at peace throughout his reign, and the country was not internally rent by strikes and government crises. He had taken command when Spain was devastated and developed it into a modern, affluent nation—everywhere in the country you could not have avoided seeing the new factories and high-rises nor have been unaware of the Spanish-made cars clogging traffic as significantly as in any European nation. Spain's had been an agricultural economy; Franco made it one of the leading industrial nations. Best of all, no one went hungry. The only beggars you saw were the incorrigible gypsies, but that was a way of life with them: their presence gave a certain piquancy to your stay in Ronda, Granada, and Seville.

If you were a tourist for whom the political arrangements for governing a country had some importance, the replies of Franco's spokesmen to your questions about this may have seemed more abstract than their economic argument, but not without weight. They had suffered obloquy and been ostracized and proscribed by the nascent United Nations for being premature anti-communists. Franco had kept Spain neutral during the World War and had demonstrated under difficult conditions the real thrust of his ideological posture by helping the Axis only with one division sent specifically to fight on the Russian front. Indeed, time had brought the greatest of democracies—the United States—to a belated yet timely recognition of Franco's long-suffering gallantry on this issue. We Americans found no more stable nor strategic a location for our military bases for containing Soviet imperialism than those Franco allowed us to establish in Spain. The photograph of Eisenhower and Franco holding each other in the traditional

Spanish *abrazo* was the lightning rod on which old misunderstandings were dissipated. Spain was our friend and now also an organic democracy. There was Eisenhower in our stead—arms about Franco and smiling and looking warmly into his face.

No one punctured most of these claims for me more coolly or cogently than did Blas Calzada, a prominent young economist who is, among other things, an adviser to the Huarte brothers. The Huarte name is most visible in construction—one cannot avoid it anywhere in the peninsula—but they have many other interests, and Calzada like them belongs to the group that prospered enormously in the last two decades of the Franco regime. His refutation of the Francoists' boasts came about indirectly. It was January, 1976, and I knew that the Huartes had long been eager for a democratization of the country. I asked Calzada why capitalists who had done so well under Franco would want to change the status quo. Why should they, as was said, want free trade unions and a legal Communist Party when these were bound to bring them only headaches?

"One of the many false claims of the government is that we have had social peace here," he began, "and that it was good for economic development." There had been strikes all along, just as that week under the king's more tolerant rule there were 100,000 workers out in Madrid alone; and in the atmosphere of illegality and repression the capitalists were unable to deal rationally and efficiently with them. Calzada liked using the phrase *capitalistas militantes*, deploying the adjective *militante* in the same manner as left-wingers to mean an activist in an opposition political party, to describe those like the Huartes who opposed the Franco regime. Such capitalists want a productive not a repressed, restive labor force, and neither the illegality in which the workers' real unions existed nor the legality of the official trade unions made it possible for them to solve labor problems.

The official trade unions particularly irked him. "Think of it, there are only twenty-seven to represent all the workers in the many industries and places of work in the country!" These are vertical, corporate trade unions in which at all levels the employers and government appointees far outnumber the workers' representatives, and these last were in only the previous two decades elected by workers through a system that made it almost impossible for any discussion of the issues or nominees involved. For militant capitalists, Calzada said, this lack of democracy means that groups within them, even though hated by the regime, can exercise undue influence, as he believed the Communists were doing through the illegal Workers Commissions.

"For example, I have no fears of the Communist Party," he said. "What worries me is the role it plays in the present official unions. Without open elections, without contending interests openly expressed, they can control the workers." If things were out in the open, industrial strife could be worked out. "True, the first couple of years—when there will be opposing labor interests expressed in strikes and stoppages—will be difficult, but there is no reason to suppose that Spain cannot reach the kind of stability that other democratic nations have in this sphere."

Nor did Franco bring Spain industrial growth. "Franco did not have an economic idea in his head," Calzada said. "Neither good ones nor bad ones. What happened was that Spain suddenly found itself in the early fifties with a reserve of $55,000,000 as a result of the military bases agreement with the United States. What to do with it? The pressure then began from militant capitalists to let industry get at these reserves—not as before, through personal and corrupt connections but, well, more fairly, to help industry expand."

"With capital accumulation and a larger consumer market came the pressure to allow foreign investment. The regime simply ceded on these matters—it did not lead or plan them. Franco had nothing to do with it. It was as simple as that."

Indeed, the lack of representative government in Spain has helped hold back the economy. The undemocratic political structure of Spain kept it out of the Common Market, and according to Calzada, who speaks with authority, there cannot be any further industrial development in Spain without membership in it. There are simply no other options, and until there is internal democracy in Spain, they will be kept out of it. It is the only way, to put it in Calzada's words, that militant capitalists can get past the tyranny of patents. The Spaniards can only obtain by membership in the Common Market the technological advances the European nations now have; Spanish industry cannot afford the long-term research that would break new ground for them. Besides, the Spaniards need that market as well for their production. An example: the Huarte brothers now command ninety-four percent of the Spanish market for an auto part of their manufacture; if they cannot sell it in Europe, they have nowhere to go with this operation.

The economic history of the Franco years is, of course, more complicated than this. One possible reason (emotive) that Calzada speaks of the Huartes as militant capitalists is that they are that new breed of Spanish bourgeois who wants to break out of the immobilist position of an upper class that for centuries feared expansion of any sort or the letting down of geographical barriers; for the latter Franco was a godsend who would hold to the status quo—indeed, erase the Republican internationalist experience. That Spanish upper class had neither created jobs nor founded museums. They never learned the lesson of the squandered plunder of the Americas. The colonies and the slave trade financed the industrial revolution for England and France, but the Spanish kings and the Church used their gains to hold back the coming of the Enlightenment. One of the few interesting things Franco ever said (his speeches are abysmally boring) was that he meant to eradicate the Encyclopedia and the Enlightenment in Spain.

But if democratic capitalists like the Huartes have won the fight against such a point of view, they must also find a way of operating abroad, to find there a market that has been lost at home. The 1959 law allowing foreign investment in Spain has gained almost total control for foreign corporations in industries as important as automobiles, tractors, aluminum, glass, synthetic fabrics, telephone, electrical equipment, chemicals, ball bearings, mining. Some economists say that ninety percent of Spanish industry pays royalties for foreign technical licenses, and the foreign investment law allows them unlimited repatriation of profits, quick amortization, no price control on imported materials from the mother company. It is true that all businesses enjoy the benefits of the double and triple bookkeeping common in Spain, the pro-forma personal income-tax laws, and low salaries; but the new Spanish capitalists, who by abandoning the old protectionist policies helped create what left-wingers call the colonization of Spain, are, nevertheless, at a great disadvantage and are forced to confront the most guarded battlement in their country—the political dictatorship.

It should not be necessary to refute the political claims of the Franco regime that their neutrality during the second World War showed that their sympathies were with the Allies—which is its way of saying that Spain was never fascist—were there not so many foreign observers who have fallen for it. Franco kept Spain out of that war because he simply could not have waged it and kept the Spanish people under control. Where his sympathies and that of his supporters lay is obvious. He could not have won the Civil War without the help of Hitler and Mussolini, and the aims and aspirations (ideology) to which the masses were expected to rally and the structure of the state he set up were clearly fascist.

Of course, there were differences with the way things were in Italy and Germany, and it is in the discussion of these differences—for example, the Catholicism that would not yield to the ideology of the Falange—that some arrive at the conclusion that the Franco regime was never fascist and, indeed, could not have been. It does not occur to such political analysts to come to a similar conclusion when comparing Italian and German fascism between which there were many minor differences. There was, I must confess, one major difference: in Spain fascism lived out its biological life. Had the Allies with the help of the Spanish exiles crossed the Pyrenees, as all who believed in the anti-fascist nature of that war reasonably expected, these political analysts would have been left with only differences in kind. They would not have elevated the subsequent maneuvers of the Franco regime to stay afloat in a world without allies to the dignity of an anomalous political system suitable to the peculiarities of the Spanish character.

True, there was in Spain a more cynical use of fascist ideology than in, certainly, Germany. That is, Franco was not the head of a fascist movement when the uprising came but a traditional, ambitious Army general who used the ideology of a recently born fascist movement—the Falange—with which to appeal to those not naturally drawn to the old triumvirate of the military, Church, and upper classes. (He allowed the founder of that movement, José Antonio Primo de Rivera, to die before a Republican firing squad, and he then named himself Chief of State, of the Army and the Falange.) There is a funny apocryphal story about Franco (all such stories about this mediocre man are usually apocryphal because they require an unsubstantiated belief in his wit) advising a new bureaucrat he has just sworn in. "Follow my example," Franco says. "Don't get into trouble—be apolitical." That was the fate of fascism-in-one-country: first the toning down of ideology, then ambiguity of aims, and finally, apoliticism. There were only two constants: an implacable hatred of socialism and democratic institutions, and an unquenchable thirst for power.

Franco failed in everything he set out to do. Apropos of the jailing and subsequent release of an opposition political leader in 1976, a Catalan said to me, "In this country everything begins brutally and ends grotesquely." It could be said about the entire Franco era. The man who waged a cruel war against his country touts himself as the leader who brought it peace, the man who devastated the economy of the nation claims to have eradicated hunger, and the man who destroyed the Republic boasts that he has instituted organic democracy. The historian who sets out to write a definitive account of that era will need a strong stomach.

Many partial studies have been done of Franco's reign. Those friendly to him have, of course, mostly been published in Spain, but economic studies, like those by Ramón Tamames, a Marxist who teaches at the University of Madrid, have also been published there. In Paris the exile publishing house Ruedo Ibérico issued for many years a continuing critique of Franco Spain in a yearly anthology called *Horizonte*. None has an overall view, although the Francoist historian Ricardo de la Cierva has begun a lively but obtuse narrative of the period, if only because the regime had not yet lived out its life. The task is formidable, more formidable than this cliché suggests, because hardly any public statement can be taken at face value, and the truth will have to be searched for in gossip and unreliable statistics. (What weight should one give political leaders whose only electorate was Franco?) And the job will be enervating and discouraging because the enormous literature that exists—the newspapers, memoirs, speeches, government documents—is boring beyond belief. I spent months groaning under its dead weight.

It did not take this to convince me that I would not write such a book. When I went to Spain this time, I knew that the history of the period I wanted to write would have to be told me by Spaniards. I had my prejudices and I had my theories, but they would have to take second place to what Spaniards had to tell me, for it is a belief of mine that what people remember and talk about are the major factors in their history. The most illuminating too, and I suspected that only they could make the gray landscape of those years, which from a distance has made us all look away in distaste, as vivid and full of heroes as their Civil War.

An example. Like many Americans, particularly literary ones, I love the bullfight. I have theories—not lightly held—about the symbolic and cathartic nature of those marvelous, romantic, *macho* rituals. I knew, of course, that for modern Spanish intellectuals the bullfight has no interest. They liked to joke as early as 1964 that only Americans went to it, and in 1976 the best of their jokes dealt with two Americans at a *corrida* complaining like any Spaniard that the sport had gone to the dogs—the stands were full of Japanese! Nevertheless, despite a bad cold I went late one night (everything in Madrid happens late) to hear a two-hour lecture by the art critic Santiago Amón, who is also one of the few literary Spanish buffs on bullfighting, on the closely related subject of García Lorca's *Lament for Ignacio Sanchez Mejías*, the matador who was fatally gored in the early thirties. Amón's lecture consisted not only of a close textual examination of the elegy but also of the personal and professional history of Sanchez Mejías, particularly of his last *corrida*.

I learned a great deal from that lecture, and I came away so excited that after chatting with Amón I still had to talk more about it to the first person I met. That was my taxi driver. And he turned out to be a *banderillero!* From spring through early fall, that is. In winter, to earn a living for his wife and children, Antonio Maeso drives a taxi in Madrid. "Oh, Ignacio!" he exclaimed with a mixture of mourning and admiration, although Sanchez Mejías died long before he was born, "he was gored in my hometown—Manzanares. He began as a *banderillero*, you know. Ah, what a beautiful way that is to spend an evening, with persons who are knowledgeable and appreciate what the *corrida* is all about." We sat in the taxi in front of my hotel and talked of the beauty of the bullfight when all goes well, and he urged me to drop by the bar where he went each morning before he started work.

The bar is a small place on a street behind the Puerta del Sol, and during the mornings and afternoons it is always full of *picadores*, *banderilleros, peones*, even an occasional *rejoneador*. The stars of the bullring seldom come here; they meet at a fancier bar on Veláz-quez in the rich Salamanca area. Still, these men promised the kind of talk that would feed my own notions of the bullfight. And so Maeso began. How he had had to leave Manzanares because in a Castilian town they only take Andalusians seriously as bullfighters. He was thirty-eight and had had a career of bad breaks but so full of courage that he fitted perfectly in the literary tradition. "Fear does not really enter into it when you are in the arena," he said. "It is a lack of confidence, *desconfianza*, that defeats you. Bullfighting is all up here—" and he touched his forehead. "If you do not know enough about that bull in the ring, *desconfianza* arises and you go in and make errors."

But Maeso did not continue in this vein. It was the economics of bullfighting that was most on his mind. The men who came over to our table were there, like him, to talk but also hoping to make contacts for the coming season. Three *empresas*, business com-panies, had gotten control of the sport. Only a half dozen or even fewer matadors now could afford to maintain their own *caudrillas* of *picadores, banderilleros*, and *peones*. Everyone else was hired indi-vidually by an *empresa* who for each meet picked up a *cuadrilla* for the matador. There is thus no continuity of working together with his men, so important for a matador. Also, the matadors now earn little, and even the bull breeders are being squeezed. Only the three major *empresas* and the town governments who rent the arenas make any money out of the *corridas*.

Everyone in the *cuadrilla* has to have other jobs to carry him through six months of the year. There is an official government trade union for them, but it does little, like all official trade unions. The *picadores* and *banderilleros* have been forced to set up a cooperative that makes and repairs their costumes. This was a struggle; at first the fabric wholesalers would not supply them material. Only love of bullfighting keeps the bullfighters going. "You have to have *afición*, vocation, for it is a terrible life much of the time. It is like an addiction. You travel all the way to the south of France, go through a bad afternoon in the arena, and you say to yourself in that car with all your tired colleagues on the way back and all of them having the same thoughts—I shall never go to France again to work. What do those Frenchmen know about bullfighting? (Actually, they are a good public for the bulls, the French.) But you get back, get a good sleep, and when you awake the phone rings and an impresario makes you an offer—and again you are off in a crowded car to work in France."

An old man who had once been a *banderillero* sat with us awhile. He showed us pictures of a young man he believes will make a great matador. He hopes to help him but there is no official arrangement between them. The young man works as a used-car salesman and he can borrow a car with which they drive to the *corridas* in the small towns and this cuts down expenses. The old *banderillero* cannot expect to become a rich manager. If the young man makes it, the *empresas* take over, and even at the *corridas* in Madrid, the most difficult and highest paying, he will receive four hundred dollars per *corrida* at most.

And so it was that Antonio Maeso set the limits for me in what I could write about bullfighting. He said, "The government has encouraged *fútbol*. They want Spaniards to waste their Sundays watching it and the rest of the week in discussing it. *Fútbol*—you do not need to think to get all of that game, there is no art in it." There is room there, perhaps, for interpolating my theories of the bullfight, but I know they would be gratuitous. Worse, they would blur the portrait of Antonio Maeso and distort the Spanish bullfighting scene during the Franco era.

I should have, in any case, quoted Maeso on the comparative values of *fútbol* and bullfighting, for it is an opinion that others, including sociologists, share. Using this criteria I shall quote many other Spaniards I met and searched out—not because they are unique in their experiences or opinions or beliefs, though they are unique and irreplaceable as individuals, but because they speak for others too. They are the ones who guided me through the Franco years, and I have let them take first place in this book.

2
Remedios:
A Survivor

Remedios and her Italian-American husband live in one of the many new housing developments encircling Madrid. They are proud that theirs is not the usual scene of modernity and rubble: between the buildings there are grass and bushes and little winding streets. On the door of their fourth-floor apartment, bought with their earnings in New York, a neat brass plaque says "*Los Señores Riccio.*" From their narrow terrace already crowded with flowering plants they can see beyond their development. The view is no longer a Castilian landscape: highways to the airport; infertile land awaiting new buildings; stretches of trampled weeds between the roads where, on Sundays, young men on their one day off play *fútbol.* Remedios is sixty-one, her husband Steve sixty-eight, and she knows it is luck—she calls it "my good luck," and raises her eyebrows and smiles each time she repeats the phrase— that she has ended here.

"Who would have thought that there would be a happy ending?" she says. "Think of it! Such luck, mine. Nine of us, two twin brothers and seven sisters, and each one still alive and now doing well. Even my brother Rafa who spent eleven years in jail—he now owns the largest vineyard in Cavares and is prosperous and well. No, he is not really well." She points to her head and then moves it from side to side. "Neither is his twin who spent much less time than Rafa in jail after the war. But it is to be expected. They went through too much. Still, we are well in other ways—we have survived. Here we are. I have only one fear now. Can it last? Can it last with Spaniards working less and less and asking for more and more?"

In addition to this apartment between the airport and the city, she and Steve own another in the section of Madrid called La Estrella, bought while they still worked in New York ten years earlier. Buying it was Remedios' idea, and she does not mind that its first tenant is still there, paying a rental that inflation has depressed. It helps pay for this one, she says, and then confesses, as if it were shameful, that they also own a piece of land in Cavares. The old farmhouse on it had gone to ruin, but with the help of two local carpenters they have turned it into a summer home. "In New York I never thought I would go back to Cavares to live," she says, "but the war is forgotten now and except for a nephew here in Madrid all my family is down in Cavares. So we spend six months of the year there."

Cavares is a country town in the province of Toledo, and when Remedios was a young woman—indeed, until about fifteen years ago—its men walked miles each day to work on the farmlands and vineyards surrounding it. It is not until recently that those who worked the lands owned any of it. Remedios' father and two brothers never worked at anything else, and the seven girls when they could not find jobs as maids or cooks or seamstresses went out with the men. They learned these jobs early. Remedios first worked outside the home when she was nine, caring for the child of a couple who owned a store in Cavares. She arrived at their home in the early afternoon, after the family had lunched, and stayed until nine, leaving before they had dinner. Her pay was the afternoon *merienda*, a snack which consisted of bread with one layer of thinly sliced sausage and a cup of coffee, and also three pesetas a month, which was worth then about fifty cents.

From then on Remedios never stopped working. "I can *not* be without work," she says. "I am wearing out the floors in this apartment because this man will not let me go out to work." She points to Steve with her right arm and then lifts it to indicate that his opposition cannot be overcome. "After he retired and we came here from New York and I had fixed this apartment well, I found myself a job. As a seamstress for a rich Madrid family. Oh, there are still families in Madrid as rich as in the old days—a car and chauffeur each for the husband and wife, and a seamstress just for the children.

"After the way I have worked in my day, it was more a hobby than a job for me. The mistress sat with me and talked while I sewed. But this man did not let me stay after three weeks. I made several pretty dresses for the two girls. The mistress hoped I would stay and make a robe for her, but she understood. I know, Remedios, she said, you do not need to work. But I do need to work—look at these poor floors. I have always trusted in hard work and my good luck, but work was not ever something I did to keep busy. For years it was only to find food for my family."

Cavares remained in Republican hands until the Civil War ended in 1939. From the start of the war food was scarce. Remedios was twenty, and she immediately lost her job as maid and cook for a middle-class family. Those who once hired servants now could either not afford them or feared to show they still could. They closed their doors and lived to themselves. Her father continued to work as a farm laborer, but at sixteen her brothers were conscripted in the Republican Army. So was her *novio*, her sweetheart to whom she was already engaged. In his first days at the front, a grenade went off in his hand and killed him.

Remedios made her first bold move from the life that until the start of the war had been marked out for her. She went to work voluntarily for the *Casa del Pueblo*, the Home of the People, as the Socialists called their party headquarters in all the towns of Spain. During the last years of the Republic they became the cultural and political centers of town life. Remedios was not a leader of the one in Cavares, nor even a militant of the Socialist Party; she simply helped the two women Socialist functionaries keep the place clean and prepare it for meetings and fiestas. She still smiles when she thinks of the speeches and songs at those gatherings.

"Of course, I was for the Republic," she says. "I was caught up in the enthusiasm. So was my father, but when I think about it, I must say he was not a political man. I believe that if he had lived in the Nationalist zone he would have been for them. And I? Well, the real reason I went to the *Casa del Pueblo* was that I could go with those two women on their trips to the countryside and other towns to bring back food for Cavares. I could thus get food for my family. That was when I began to feel a responsibility to feed them. It was to rule my life for many years. But I owe it to my luck that when the war ended they jailed those two women and never touched me."

It *was* luck: simply to be found on the *Casa del Pueblo*'s rolls often meant jail or summary execution for people less compromised than Remedios. This was the fate of workers who signed up for the food distribution that the *Casa del Pueblo* organized or of those who went there for jobs that the party's trade union, the CNT, might assign. Her father was jailed; she does not remember the charge—for being a Republican, she supposes. So were the twins when they returned from the front, and so was Remedios' one brother-in-law, Ciprian. Ciprian had volunteered for the Army, and when he came home, the baker for whom he had once worked accused Ciprian at a mass trial of having denounced his son to the Reds, thus being responsible for his death. Ciprian was sentenced to death. He was innocent, and the commutation of the sentence to thirty years imprisonment arrived an hour after he was executed.

"Both my brothers were wounded in the war, but both stayed at the front until the very end. I do not suppose that helped them at their mass trial. But Rafa was wounded three times and at the trial had worse luck than his brother. He had been a militiaman in the first days of the uprising and he was sent to arrest a man who had been denounced as a fascist. His widow showed up at the trial and said Rafa killed her husband. My poor brother said, 'I arrested him, I did not kill him.' But she replied, 'You took him from our home, you as good as killed him.' I suppose there was some justice to what she said."

Remedios waves her arms ahead of herself as if moving aside the dense thicket of those terrible days after the war. "The Republicans had done many dreadful things in Cavares, many stupid things; it was awful. And there was much foolishness too. But my poor brother Rafa was sentenced to many years and served eleven and he has never been right since. If you should ask him, he would not talk about those years. He never has. And I would not let anyone ask him."

A Falangist family in Cavares gave Remedios her first job after the war, to clean house, wash and iron and sew the family's clothes, and cook the meals. She was unhappy with it but not because of the work. All the men in her family were in jail: she needed a job that paid more than her own keep. Her second bold step: one morning early she went out to the road that she was told led to Aranjuez, carrying only a small bundle since all she owned was on her back. She would find another job. She had not told her mother, and it took an effort to explain to the two men in the first car that stopped what she was doing. They gave her a ride, and in an hour she was in Aranjuez.

"I went straight to the marketplace. I did not know where it was, of course—I had to ask. I went to it because that is where the women would be. You ask women, they always know. I went from woman to woman asking if they knew of a family that needed a servant. Such was my good luck that one of them told me she thought Doña Rosa needed a girl. Just a bit earlier that morning Doña Rosa had been marketing and had still been complaining that she had not found someone suitable. This woman told me where the house was and told me too that Doña Rosa was married to a man who was a member of Franco's family and that they had just come to Aranjuez, which was why there was a place in their home for a girl. Franco's family! But I did not hesitate.

"But then I saw the house. It was a seignorial house, as there are in Aranjuez—all those palaces, those grand houses. I did not know where to enter, but a man asked me what I wanted when he saw me loitering and he turned out to be the caretaker. His wife took me inside after she saw me waiting in the courtyard giving myself courage, while the caretaker went in to ask Doña Rosa. Inside her house it was beautiful too, but I looked only at Doña Rosa and answered her without fear. Since then I have always been that way, answering straight out, never hesitating."

Doña Rosa was very taken with Remedios. Remedios could clean, sew, cook, and make her life simpler. Doña Rosa was a young woman, she had two youngsters, and this was the first time she had to see to the management of a house without the advice and help of her family. She asked Remedios for her papers and explained that in these times one could not, particularly in a city new to her and to her husband, hire someone without references. Again Remedios replied without hesitation. She said she had not brought any letters of recommendation, but this would be no problem, for she could return another day with them. "Very well," Doña Rosa said, and that was the way it was left.

"It was a lie about the letters, my first big one to get a job," Remedios says, and then remembers that she had said it to Doña Rosa only to get away from there, not in hopes that she could find someone to recommend her. "Imagine, with my father and brothers in jail there was not a single person in Cavares who would have written a word in my favor. Especially to a member of Franco's family. I went down the steps thinking of this and hurrying, but I had only gone a few steps down the street when the caretaker brought me back to Doña Rosa."

Doña Rosa had indeed been taken with her. She waived the references; she did not want to wait the few days it might take Remedios to obtain them. She wanted her to start that day. It took Remedios some minutes to convince her that she had to return to Cavares and both inform her mother and ask her permission to take the job, for she had only come to Aranjuez on an errand. This was proof to Doña Rosa that Remedios was a good girl, but she made Remedios promise she would return the following day. Remedios walked most of the way home and got there before she was due to return from her regular job in Cavares. She was out of work only one day—what luck!

Doña Rosa was very happy with Remedios and never again asked her for references from Cavares. There would not have been time, in any case, for Remedios lived in and she had no days off. She made dresses for the two little girls and for Doña Rosa and shirts for the husband; she also cooked and washed and ironed. She put the children to bed and got them up in the morning. But she did not do all the cleaning; a local woman came in to do most of that. She was paid forty pesetas a month, worth then about four dollars, and Remedios thought that was fine. She was near enough to Cavares to get news of her family and to smuggle to them packages, mostly of food, that she robbed from her employers. "It was from them that I first robbed," she says without shame and nods her head sharply.

Each morning after breakfast she and Doña Rosa went out together to do the marketing. Doña Rosa liked doing that; it was an outing for her. She thought she was being helpful to Remedios, but it only made it more difficult for Remedios to put food aside for her family. The moment they were out in the street, Doña Rosa would say eagerly, "Let us not forget to find out how many they did away with today!" She meant Republicans executed, for this was the summer of 1939 and the purge was still going on.

"It was especially terrible in Aranjuez," Remedios says, meaning that Aranjuez was marked as a Red town; it had been the training headquarters for the International Brigades. "There were not executions every day, of course, but I went in terror of what we might hear. My father and brothers were still in jail, and although they were not in Aranjuez, it seemed to me in my nervous confusion that it might be they. Doña Rosa did not know of my worry, and no matter how friendly we were to become when she sat with me while I sewed and made suggestions about the dresses, I never told her, never."

Doña Rosa's husband was an engineer, and he had been assigned to Aranjuez to oversee the repair of irrigation canals and reservoirs that had been badly damaged nearby during the Battle of Jarama in January–February, 1937. His was a prize assignment, for Aranjuez was a lovely city and the home set aside for them one of the grand old houses. He owed it to his connection to Franco, Remedios believes, and Doña Rosa was very happy there. Still, it was not Madrid, and when her husband got himself reassigned to headquarters in the Ministry of Public Works, she gladly left and took Remedios with her.

"I had been with them for more than a year and when I told them that my mother was very ill and wanted to see me, Doña Rosa said I could go for a week. It was not entirely a lie—my mother was very upset because one of my brothers had been released and then arrested again. I had to stay longer than I had thought—my father was let go during that time—and when I got back to Doña Rosa, she said that she had hired someone else because one of the girls had been sick. She did not have any job for me, but she gave me a good letter of recommendation."

It was no use returning to Cavares; there were no jobs there. No food either. She walked up and down the broad Paseo de la Castellana in Madrid stopping the middle-class ladies and telling them she needed a job. This time she had papers from a member of Franco's family. One lady took her along to a family she was visiting who

needed a maid. Remedios could tell that it was something of a joke
to the lady to be arriving at her friend's home with her in tow, but
they took her. The Suarezes were highly placed; although he was a
civilian, his position in the Falange had gotten him the job of
managing an Army warehouse which also carried supplies for other
government ministries. All receipts and disbursements were signed
by him, and his signature on a chit for any goods in the warehouse
was unquestioned.

"They stole, not just for themselves but for their rich friends as
well. The manservant and the maid with whom I was first sent to the
warehouse were so well known there that they scarcely looked at the
chits that we brought signed by Don Joaquín. They gave us whatever
the manservant asked for!" Remedios laughs nervously at the recollection. "I believe the men working there added things to those
orders and kept them for themselves. The manservant himself said
to me the first day, Here, this is for you—a can of sardines! And
when Don Joaquín's wife discovered that I was a good cook and
turned over the kitchen to me, I often went to the warehouse alone
to get things for the table. I believe that nothing which came into
that house was paid for.

"After a while, I did not even need to bring a chit or a list of things
they were to give me. But I only stole food. I made them into small
packages with cloth wrappings and closed them tight with needle
and thread and I ran down to Atocha Station and put them on a
train that each day stopped at Cavares. I did not have a package for
each train, only for two or three a week, but I alerted my family and
to be sure, one of them met the Madrid train every day. The
Suarezes paid me forty-five pesetas a month, five more than Doña
Rosa, but there is no estimating the worth of the food I robbed.
Those were the years of hunger. Not only because people had no
money and no jobs but because there was also a scarcity of food that
even money could not always buy. A gallon of olive oil on the black
market cost my month's salary!"

She worked for the Suarezes in a kind of frenzy. It was a harden-
ing experience, calculating what she could steal, packaging it and
running down to Atocha Station, and convincing herself that what
she did was right. When the luckier of her brothers got out of jail, he
told her that she should find another job, that she must not lower

herself by working for Falangists. "He did not understand," Remedios explains and brings a hand to her mouth with the tips of her fingers bunched together, an eating motion. "I did not listen to him, but I said I would look for another job."

It was then, more than a year after she began working for the Suarezes, that Señor San Martín showed up in Madrid looking for her. He was an engineer who had also worked on the Jarama reservoir and he had known Remedios in Doña Rosa's household in Aranjuez. He was a bachelor, lived with his elderly widowed mother, and now that he too was assigned to Madrid needed a housekeeper. He was so eager to hire Remedios that he had gone down to Cavares and searched out her family to obtain her address. Whenever she names him, Remedios pauses and her voice turns soft. "He was a saint, that man," she says.

Remedios believes that unlike Doña Rosa's husband, Señor San Martín was not an *enchufado*—literally, someone plugged into an electrical outlet—and that he was so often invited to her employers' home in Aranjuez because he was the engineer who really worked on the job. "He was not a Franquista, he was a liberal man who sympathized with the people." She sighs, recollecting the difficulties that the offer to take over his household had presented to her. "I tried to refuse—I said his job was harder than my present one, I exaggerated what the Suarezes paid me, but he replied that I could hire a girl to help me, that he would pay me more, in fact, double."

With people above her station Remedios was not used to speaking the truth about important matters. Even now her eyes water at the dilemma. "I finally told him why my job with the Suarezes was so important," she says and squares her shoulders. "I told him I robbed food for my family. It made me cry. All he replied was, 'Ay, Remedios, Remedios,' and he shook his head from side to side repeating 'Ay, Remedios.' I never met another man like him—he was a saint."

Remedios worked for him for fifteen years. He helped her family. He found a job in one of the reservoirs for the brother who was out of jail. The sister whose husband had been hurriedly executed by the fascists came to Madrid to take a job, which Señor San Martín found for her, as a chambermaid at the Hotel Florida on the Plaza del Callao. (Remedios does not know that the Hotel Florida is the setting for Hemingway's *The Fifth Column* nor that most of the romantic, and sinister, literary figures of the Civil War stayed there.) Another sister married and San Martín got her husband a job on a reservoir also. Remedios adds, "From Señor San Martín I never had to steal."

His mother was no problem to Remedios. The Señora was glad to have her take over the management of the old apartment. It was a large place, but with only two persons to care for Remedios found it easy to do all the work herself. She never hired a cleaning woman; that had been an excuse of hers to put off Señor San Martín. The Señora urged her to do less work; she preferred to have Remedios sit with her and talk. Remedios knew how to make talk—she has the indefatigable propensity of Castilians for small talk that has always made the *paseo* time in Madrid lively, even noisy—but if she sat she also sewed. There was much to report to the Señora about her daily errands—the prices on the black market alone was a good subject for years—and in time she talked about Cavares and her family, though the things that weighed seriously on her heart she saved for her meetings with her sister, now in Madrid.

Remedios did not know how much Señor San Martín had told his mother about her and her family, but it became necessary to tell her some things. "My brother Rafa who was to spend eleven years in jail was transferred to Prolies, the temporary prison for war prisoners here in Madrid, and I had to go see him every day. I could not actually see him every day, only once a week, but they allowed me to take him food every day. I took him a basket after lunch, once the Señora had finished hers—she would sometimes say, 'Take him some of this, Remedios, he will like it.' After a while the guards used to joke about what a comfortable home the jail was for Rafa—he ate off china plates with utensils and the clean cloth that covered the basket was a fine serviette! My poor brother.

"You may well ask why I should leave such a good situation," Remedios comments and pauses in order to explain what happened with the delicacy it deserves. "I never thought of it myself. When the Señora died, Señor San Martín's friends found him a young wife, although he was advanced in years. He was not only a saint, he had the intelligence to foresee that there might be trouble with the young wife. He came to me and said, 'Remedios, you have been the mistress of this house. I would not want you now to begin anew here under the orders of another—you would not be happy and it would not be just.' "

He set up Remedios in a small three-room apartment in Madrid. He did not want her to go out to work. As a seamstress she had the beginnings of a clientele. From the first she had done all the Señora's dresses, and the Señora's friends had soon begun to bring her work, which Remedios did as a favor until the Señora insisted that she charge. Señor San Martín convinced her that in a short time she would be entirely independent. He would help her. And so it was: soon besides the private clients there were shops that gave her alteration work and special orders. "I had as much work as I could attend to.

"The apartment was a tiny one but it was comfortable," she says while trying to remember why her life had not pleased her then. She does not say that she was forty-four and had not married. "What I earned was entirely mine. Even the more unfortunate of my brothers, Rafa, was long out of jail and back in Cavares working hard. My sister in Madrid had remarried and Juan María, the son who had been orphaned as an infant and for whom I had looked out all these years, was a grown man of twenty-one. I had made two or three good women friends of the shopkeepers with whom I dealt every day. I should have been happy."

No one needed her. "I do not know what came over me as the months passed. It was a kind of fever—I wanted to do something new, go work in another country as others were doing, break away. One day one of my friends said to me that there was a want ad in the newspaper *ABC* for a woman to work outside the country for an American family. I went to the apartment the ad gave and there were others there before me waiting, but they took me. I said I had experience as a maid. I did not say that I had been a housekeeper and for two years now a seamstress, for a maid was what they had asked for and I did not want to frighten them with my capabilities. It was a young American woman who gave me the job, but she told me that I was to work for relatives of hers, an elderly couple who lived near the city of Boston."

There was dissembling to be done before she could get to America. The elderly couple would pay her fare and someone would meet her in Boston, but she had to get a visa from the Americans on her own. She was instructed to say that she wanted a six-month permit to visit friends. It was like the old days: lying to get a job. "I hoped that when I went to the American Consulate that it would not be a Spaniard I had to talk to," Remedios says laughing. "A Spaniard would take one look at me and know I was no tourist. Still, they must have suspected something, for the American there asked me if I was paying for the trip myself and I was not thinking and said no, that American friends were. I was very encouraged, however, and I told all the shops and my clients that I could take no more work and began to pack."

The visa was denied. She went to visit her clients again. It did not please them that she expected their patronage back, but it seemed to gratify some that her hopes had been cut off. The Consulate called her again and this time asked her how she had met her American friends. She was unprepared for the question, her reply was vague, but she added with some heat, "Look, I should like to visit your country, but do as you like—it is no trouble to me if I do not and it is not important." In a few days the visa arrived.

She did not speak a word of English, but it was all as easy as the young American woman in Madrid had said. A man met her at the Boston airport and drove her through the city and out of it. She looked out the window of the big American car and asked herself, What have I gotten into? He ended up at a residential suburb. "No shops, no public buildings, just chalets, very pretty ones to be sure, but there was nothing like it in Spain. Not then." The elderly couple knew no Spanish, but for that first day a daughter who had studied it was there to show Remedios her room and to explain, with many gestures, what they expected her to do for them. The elderly couple lived alone in the house, and it was full of modern conveniences. Remedios wondered how she would fill her days.

Remedios was surprised, shocked, and curious to find out that her employers were Jews. She did not think she had ever seen any. Later, in New York, she was to learn that Jews were not what she had been taught to expect but for the moment her new knowledge called for wariness. "The old man was not bad, but the wife—a terrible Jewess!" Remedios remembers. "And the bane of my life was a nine-year-old grandson who often stayed with them. He must have spent much time peeking through the keyhole of my room, for whenever I was undressed—the first time I was totally nude—he would quickly open the door. A terrible child. I called him such names!—but it was all in Spanish, so he did not know what I said, poor child."

She cooked, cleaned, washed, and ironed; and when they found out about her special talent, sewed also. She was paid five dollars a week. The old couple began to entertain, and she helped out with that too. "They would call me into the parlor and she would say to her friends, 'Our Spanish girl,' and there I stood, a monument, a sculpture to them. Still, I had no trouble with the work—Jewish cooking is so simple—and I did not have enough to do for seven days a week. I had one day off a week, but they told me not to go into the city, that I would get lost. So I cooked on that day too—what did it matter to me? I was so lonely. I used to walk around the neighborhood wishing I could make friends."

The old man began to bring her a Spanish language newspaper when he went into Boston. He and his wife communicated with Remedios mostly with gestures and much pointing to objects in the house, but when Remedios saw the want ads for maids in the newspaper he brought her, she was able to point to something she had suspected—ads listing jobs like hers at fifty dollars a week. "From the expression on the old woman's face I could tell she was saying to her husband, 'That is what you get for bringing her newspapers!' " They sent for the daughter who spoke Spanish and she went through the house with Remedios with paper and pencil adding to the cost of her air-fare, her meals, the rent of her room, the washing machine she used for her own laundry, to prove to Remedios that in fact she owed them money. "Still, they raised my pay to six dollars a week."

On her walks in the neighborhood, a woman would wave to her from one of the houses. When she motioned Remedios to her door one day, Remedios turned up the walk: she knew it was her good luck beckoning. Mrs. Nichols was Greek—"In America no one is American," Remedios says—and could speak a little Spanish. She was outraged at the salary that Remedios' employers paid, and hired her to work for her on her day off, and on days when the old couple was away visiting, at ten dollars a day. "I robbed the old Jews in that way, but when I think of the things I did for Mrs. Nichols, I see that I was still being exploited."

But Remedios, nevertheless, remembers Mrs. Nichols as a good friend: she took Remedios to Boston to see the Spanish Consul because she was sure that he would help extricate Remedios from her situation. Remedios was ready to return to Spain rather than go on with her desolate life among the pretty chalets. The Consul listened to her story and immediately hired her to work for his own family. No need for her to worry any longer about six-month visas, and when he was transferred to the Spanish delegation at the United Nations, they took her with them. The United States became very interesting now and provided her with the different life she had wanted.

When the Spanish diplomat was assigned to another country, Remedios was passed on to a Spanish-American woman who lived alone with a young daughter. "She was lively, funny, she did not have a penny other than her salary and she spent it all—oh, what craziness! We lived on top of one another in that tiny three-room apartment in a building which from the outside looked very elegant. But I might as well have been back in Cavares when we were so many brothers and sisters in the small house." They were on a first-name basis, but the woman often could not pay Remedios. Instead, she helped her find a job as a seamstress at Bloomingdale's, a job of such steadiness that she was never again tempted to look for another.

"And so I settled into New York City and I got my prize—this man," Remedios says and points to Steve with a deprecating wave of her hand. "My friends told me, 'We have just the man for you.' "

Steve says, "They told me, 'We have just the woman for you.' "

Two years after they were married, they came to Spain during Remedios' second vacation from Bloomingdale's—the first ones she had ever had—and they bought the apartment they now let in Madrid. An investment, she told Steve, but it was the first step in her campaign to get him to retire there. In New York Steve worked as superintendent for one of the old staid apartment buildings on Park Avenue, and the job brought with it a rent-free, three-room apartment. It was on a semi-basement level and looked out on a cement courtyard to the back, but they knew from the apartments of their Spanish and Italian friends that its spaciousness and the neighborhood were a luxury they could never duplicate when it came time to give it up. Each visit to Steve's brother in a Puerto Rican section of the Bronx was an object lesson.

Steve's one real tie to the States was a daughter by a previous marriage. She married and went to Florida, and Steve decided that trips to see her when he retired would simply take a few hours longer. Ten years after Remedios left for Boston she brought Steve back to Spain for good. She has no friends in Madrid. "We live here like people in New York. We say to the neighbors, Good day, how are you, the weather is fine or it is bad. I like it that way."

There are a million more people in Madrid now than when she went there with Doña Rosa. During the time she was out of the country, Spain became an industrial nation. Country towns are empty, the cities are swollen, and there are always one million Spaniards working abroad saving their money like Remedios. They come back to Spain too but seldom to their hometowns. Remedios has one foot in, one foot out—six months in Madrid, six months in Cavares. She loves her apartment in Madrid, but her family is all back home. The brothers and sister who left Cavares to find jobs have all returned.

"Only Juan María who is like a son to me is here," she says. "He has a regular job, a wife, and two children. Like the rest of us he does not talk about the past. His and the rest of the other children's lives have not been as bad as ours. What would be the use of talking to them about the past? What would there be to say that is good?"

In his home, when Remedios is not there, Juan María says, "Politics is a very dirty thing. I can understand that many people want to forget the Civil War and the things that happened. That is the way it should be, and there are those whom it hardly touched, anyway—neither sorrow nor glory for them—but those whom it bruised in the flesh cannot forget as easily. At home I was told the bare facts—that my father was executed, that he was innocent, that I look like him—and I knew from as long ago as I can remember that I was not to talk about it. Never outside the home. Right now, the men who have worked with me for years in my shop do not know how my father died. What am I to feel? No one outside my family has ever come to me to explain it or to make amends. I have been told nothing and given nothing."

Remedios does not know that Juan María feels this way. She never retraces her steps. "All those many people I have known in my work," she says, "but I have never gone back to see them. And why get in touch with those I worked for? They did not know me. I robbed from them, and half of what I told them was lies. Anyway, I believe that what is important is what is to come, not what once was."

Remedios worries that like other Spaniards she does not work enough. That is why she is glad that she and Steve put in as much time as the carpenters on the falling-down farmhouse they bought in Cavares. Steve does not understand this about her; he has no guilt feelings about not working. He sits out on the balcony a great deal and reports to her when a neighbor shows up on the winding street with a new car. "Some of them have two," she says, scandalized, "and this Christmas the store here ran out of color television sets."

It is January 1976 and there are one hundred thousand workers on strike illegally in Madrid. Railway, postal, and subway workers have been militarized or they too would be out on strike. "Tell me that it is not all going to go bad," Remedios says clapping her palms together in a vigorous praying gesture. "I fear it, I fear it. What can come of all this unrest?"

Even her dream of returning to Madrid to live has not come true in the way she envisioned. "Madrid is not nice anymore," she says. "But I must not complain. It is a pretty apartment, isn't it? Still, I used to long in New York for fruit and vegetables to taste as God made them. Now in Spain they also pick them before they ripen and they freeze them and they lose their savor. And we do not go into Madrid itself—it is ugly with traffic and smog; I do not like it."

Steve shrugs.

She tries once more to explain it to him. "I remember how beautiful, how exhilarating it was to walk in the early morning along the Paseo de la Castellana, those first days when I went out to do the marketing for Doña Rosa. How beautiful were the flowers and trees in the center island of Castellana! The gardeners were already out watering the plants and damping the paths to keep the dust down. There was such freshness and purity then!"

3

Asturias:
A Life in the Party

I must first explain about Asturias and its capital Oviedo before introducing the miner Arcadio whose name and looks were the same as of a great-uncle's of mine. The province lies north of the Cantabrian range, and until Iberia Airlines began flights there, the shortest route to it from the center of power in Spain had to navigate Puerto de Pajares, a mountain pass in the second highest peaks in Europe. Asturias is a natural fortress, and from the ninth century when the Moors were stopped in those mountains until the present day when this geographical position has lost most of its strategic advantage, the Asturians have provided Spain with its most dramatic struggles for national liberation and working-class revolution. In 1934, during the Republic, it was only in Asturias that there was a fighting response to the call by socialists throughout Spain for a revolt against the newly elected right-wing government, which to them signified a major step towards fascism. In Asturias, under the slogan "Unite, Proletarian Brothers," the Socialists, Anarchists, and Communists with exemplary unity held Oviedo for several days, the province for two weeks. A short enough period, but historians report with a surprise approaching amazement the efficiency with which all communities were organized and the humane measures of the revolutionary committees that ruled them. But it was an isolated uprising—the general strike expected throughout the peninsula failed—and the General Staff assigned Franco to put down the revolt. He brought in, as he was to do again in the Civil War, merciless Moorish troops. "The last days were characterized by acts of desperate bravado," writes the American historian Gabriel Jackson, "with unarmed miners baring their breasts defiantly at the advancing troops."

Many left-wingers and Republicans have never forgiven the Socialists and Communists the policy that led to this uprising. It polarized all Spain and, in their belief, made impossible the avoidance of civil war when the Popular Front won the elections two years later. The victors in 1934 wrote their version of what occurred, of course, and disseminated many accounts of atrocities by the Reds, the great majority of which were proved later to be fabricated. But the harm was done, and for the good Spanish bourgeois the Asturian revolt was the chilling specter that drove them into Franco's arms. Or so many believed. (I do not: the Spanish upper class and what was called the traditional middle class have shown at every juncture that they know just where their interests lie.) In any case, Asturian workers, whose militant core is in the mining region immediately south of Oviedo, always have been dogged in the connections they make between their working conditions and the politics of a bourgeoisie whom the gradualists more often prefer to woo than confront. A good example of this attitude comes from Manuel Grossi, a leader of the 1934 uprising. In the book he wrote a year later in a Madrid jail, he says, "Our surrender is simply a halt on the road where we correct our mistakes, preparing for the next battle which must end in final victory for the exploited."

The Asturian miners went on to fight as desperately and heroically in the Civil War, when its *dinamiteros*, expert in the use of explosives, gained worldwide admiration from sympathizers of the Republican cause. They continued the guerrilla struggle under Franco longer than any province in Spain, and their general strike in the mining region in 1957 was, perhaps, the first of any consequence during the Franco era. It is no surprise that they vied with the Catalans and Basques for Franco's enmity without ever having committed the sin, as the Basques and Catalans do, of demanding regional autonomy. Theirs has been a class goal, and of course not all Asturians have shared it. For example, Oviedo. Although the last ten years of industrialization have transformed most of the country, Oviedo remains a provincial capital dominated by a group of families still aghast at the ideas of the nineteenth-century European bourgeoisie.

From their ranks came Leopoldo Alas, a great literary critic and novelist of the late nineteenth century, and his apostasy has never been forgiven. His novel *La Regenta*, little known in the English-speaking world outside university Spanish departments, occupies the place in Spanish literature that Eliot's *Middlemarch* does in English. It is a vividly detailed account of the destruction of a woman by the priest-ridden, reactionary society of Oviedo, and it is written with a mixture of compassion and cold fury that makes it subversive to this day. Not until the late sixties, when the censorship relaxed somewhat, was it available anywhere in Spain. In 1964 when I asked for it everywhere (except Oviedo where I did not dare), the request stamped me with booksellers as a good person to be trusted—or as an agent provocateur.

One of the first actions of Franco's followers in 1936 was to raze the still controversial monument to Clarín, which was the name Alas wrote under, in Oviedo's park. It had been erected only five years earlier during the first year of the Republic. Clarín's son was rector of the university in Oviedo when the Nationalist uprising came, and he was immediately arrested. He was not executed until a few months later, and while he was in jail there were appeals from cultural figures and groups throughout the world. They made the mistake, however, of reminding his jailers that he was Clarín's son: it only served to harden their hearts. I talked about these things with José Cueto Alas, a great-nephew of his who is a witty journalist and screenwriter responsible for the charming *Secret Guide to Asturias*. He is a young man who has lived all his life under the Franco regime, in that old ambience of upper-class Oviedo, and his family kept from him as long as it could any knowledge of his famous great-uncle. He was in his teens before he heard of *La Regenta*, and he was only able to read it when an old bookseller gave him a copy he had kept hidden. He considers all this the supreme irony of Clarín's achievement—that his own family should be ashamed of him. The tradition continues: the *Secret Guide to Asturias* was out two months and Cueto Alas told me his mother was still away from the city trying to live down the disgrace.

The base of Clarín's monument is in the Campo de San Francisco, as Oviedo's lovely park is called, and to stand there looking at its neglected nudity felt like a risky action even in the relaxed national atmosphere of the summer of 1976. José Cueto Alas had told me there was now talk of restoring it, and only that year the mayor finally got around to commemorating the anniversary of Clarín's death by a visit to his grave. This came at a time when homage, official and nonofficial, had been done elsewhere to writers closer in time and clearly known as enemies of Franco's cause—Federico García Lorca, Miguel Hernandez, Antonio Machado. In 1976, too, there was greater tolerance throughout Spain for left-wing political parties and trade unions—a week earlier I had attended a huge public meeting of the new Socialist Party of Catalonia and a week later I was to attend a similar one of the Communist Party of Catalonia—but in Asturias such liberality had yet to be exercised. I was to learn this during the next forty-eight hours from the miner Arcadio and his friends.

I met Arcadio when I left the park for Calle Uria, which borders one end of it and is Oviedo's main business street, to keep an appointment with a businessman who must remain anonymous. The businessman had not wanted to meet me at my hotel. Across the street from it is *Seguridad*, the police headquarters, and he had been questioned in its basement several times during the last twenty years. He had never been charged or served time, he had always been released after a few days, but the interrogations had left him with an uncontrollable physical distaste for that street. He was not wary of me; I had come with an introduction from a mutual friend who was a member of the Central Committee of the Spanish Communist Party. We had just shaken hands on Calle Uria and turned to watch a legal demonstration by sales clerks on the opposite sidewalk when Arcadio broke from the group there and came over to us. "Isn't it wonderful!" Arcadio exclaimed. "It is a success!"

The demonstration's objectives were not subversive: the clerks were protesting that their employers were making them work longer hours with fewer days off in order to keep up with the new department stores, subsidiaries of national chains, which were open at all hours, including the siesta. "I wish I could demonstrate with them, Arcadio," the businessman said, "but I am too well known."

"I could not resist it," Arcadio replied happily. "Some of the young people asked me what a retired worker was doing marching with them, and I told them it is the duty of every worker to support his brothers in their struggles."

As soon as the businessman introduced us, Arcadio said, "What can we do? How can I help you? To begin with, let me offer you my home. We have an empty bedroom and it is your home as long as you are in Oviedo." I told Arcadio that I was not so much interested in Oviedo as in the mining area—*la cuenca minera*—because what I really wanted to do in Asturias was talk to a Communist miner.

The businessman pointed to Arcadio. "There you are," he said. "You have already reached your goal." Then he shook his head. "You see the difference between a worker and a bourgeois—I did not think to offer you my home."

Arcadio said he was only a retired miner but that he could introduce me to young ones in the mines today. I said I was primarily interested in someone like him who had lived through all of the post-Civil War period. "Oh, I can tell you about those days, you need not worry," he said quickly, and for the rest of the afternoon and evening and all of the next day he did not cease to do so with unabating energy and an insistence on details and on the moral and political significance of every incident that both moved me and exhausted me.

"He is retired," the businessman said to me, "but as you can see from this demonstration, Arcadio is involved in everything going on." Arcadio shrugged, as if to say that it was one's duty. Then he said that we could see that he was physically vigorous still and asked us to guess his age, expecting that we thought he was younger than he was. The businessman said Arcadio looked fifty-two, and since that disappointed Arcadio, I said forty-eight, although I believed he was at least sixty. He was forty-six. That was how I learned that he had retired early because he had been diagnosed to have silicosis when he was twenty-seven. "I am in the third stage of it now," he said, "and that means I am supposed to have one foot in the funeral parlor. But look at me—I have fooled them."

The businessman and I were on our way to meet a lawyer friend of his at a restaurant. Arcadio agreed to join us for dinner. He joked that the years of hunger had left him with the bad habit of accepting every invitation that involved eating. The businessman laughed: his lower-middle-class family had been plunged into want by the Civil War and as a boy he had taken first communion in two different parishes in order to get the afternoon snack given free to those preparing for it. Indeed, when he was an altar boy, he used to break into the cabinet where the holy wafers and wine were kept. Arcadio said, "I became an expert at knowing just when some young *señorito* was going to discard the fruit he was eating. I used to follow them in the streets, for I knew that there would still be two or three good bites left in it when it landed in the gutter."

Arcadio acquired this expertise on the occasions when he went down from his country village into the large towns along the river Nalón where most of the pitheads are. And once or twice in Oviedo. In his village most houses had tiny gardens every inch of which were cultivated. People mainly planted vegetables and would sleep out in the garden as soon as the fruit began to form or the greens to head. A cornpatch had to be watched twenty-four hours, even when the kernels were green. Those who did not sleep out in the garden lost everything. "Hunger is a terrible thing," Arcadio said.

He and the businessman and the lawyer fought over who would pay the dinner bill. I did not have a chance, but the lawyer and the businessman had to be careful not to offend Arcadio. "I have a pension," he pleaded. "It is one of our few victories." The waiter settled the argument by saying he could not afford to bypass the lawyer who was a frequent client. I was used to this scene with Asturians in my hometown, the latin section of Tampa, Florida. I felt at home. The fact that they were all three militants, as the Spaniards say, of the Communist Party made no difference. We left together full of good feeling, and the others allowed Arcadio to walk me to my hotel. It was late and they knew Arcadio and I had yet to decide when we would next meet.

A block away from my hotel I told Arcadio that he could leave me now. He looked puzzled. I explained that the security police headquarters might have bad memories for him. "I do not care if they see me," he said. "In fact, let them see me—let them see that they have not put me out of commission." I was to learn how close "they" came to it, but for the moment I was more aware that he was eager to see my hotel. It was the Hotel de la Reconquista, an expensive, luxury hotel opened only a couple of years earlier. I walked him

37

through its huge lobby and the cafeteria and the dining rooms and the bar and its special corners for listening to music and television. He was impressed but reserved. He asked to sit down in one corner of the lobby. "Just for a moment," he said. "I am not used to so much smoking as I did tonight. Have I told you about my silicosis?"

I said yes. He asked, "Do you know what it is?" I said I knew about it in general, that in the United States miners call it black lung. "An apt name," he said. "You may then know that it is a progressive illness. Powder and dust accumulate in the lungs and then get hard. Of course, working in coal, chipping away at it as I did for years and then the dynamiting that in my time was done at least twice a day meant that you were working in coal dust, breathing it in all day long. There is such a thing too as rock silicosis—that is worse than mine. Let me explain. The lungs are very similar to a sponge; they contract and expand with air instead of water. The hard deposits that form eventually cut the insides of the lungs. They cause little lesions at first, and the only way to counteract this is to give them a chance to heal. You have to rest and not work hard because the faster you breathe because of exertions the more lesions you cut. You have to lead a normal life, by which I mean no drinking and staying out. You should not smoke either. It has not given me too much trouble, because, as I said, I have a strong constitution, and anyway I have spirit.

"That is enough rest," he said, and got up. I apologized for dragging him up and down the hilly city, and suggested I get a cab and drive him home. "No, no, no, I always walk all over this city. I never take a bus except to go to the mining towns as we shall do tomorrow. I go to the university to listen to lectures, I have many things to do, I have my Party obligations. I thank God that Oviedo has such little pollution. The walk home is good for me—it airs out my lungs."

The next morning, a Saturday, I learned how fast Arcadio could walk while talking. It was some twenty blocks to the modest new apartment building where he lived—in an area whose character had not yet jelled—and he filled me in on everything we saw and gave me bits of its history. We passed the hospital where silicosis victims are treated. "They are supposed to keep track of how we are doing and give us regular checkups, but they do not. I keep after them, too." Their apartment building had no elevator, and five years earlier he had bought a flat on the first floor, so that he need not climb more than one set of stairs. He seemed ashamed that he lived so well. Just before we entered, he said, "Do you know that in only five years we could now sell this apartment for fifteen thousand dollars! That is a disgrace."

Along a narrow hall there were three small bedrooms and a bath, and at its end a kitchen and living room, equally small. Everything—the floors, walls, furniture—had been cleaned and polished to a shine that robbed the cheap furniture and cramped space of its tackiness and sadness. His wife Onelia and his thirteen-year-old daughter María were like the apartment, trim and fair and expectant. We had a small altercation when I saw from the preparations in the kitchen that they were not going to let me take them out to lunch. Arcadio ignored me and motioned me into the living room. Onelia followed with bottles of beer for us and then left us alone to talk. No matter that she, too, was a member of the Party: first of all she was a proper Asturian wife.

Arcadio sat down and started at the beginning. He was born in the mountains of the mining area, in a village called Coto Raso whose name described it exactly—a level mesa that had once been a seignorial estate. Coto Raso was far from the pitheads; for his first job, when he was fourteen, he used to walk six miles to work and six miles home each day. But that was usual; no one thought to complain about it, though in Coto Raso you got up at four to be at the pitheads at seven. Indeed, for adolescents there was a certain wonder and pride in joining the dark stir in the lanes and roads on the way to the mines in the early morning. It was your coming of age.

Arcadio, born in 1930, was the older of two children, and the year the Civil War broke out, 1936, was also the year his mother died of cancer. His father was a miner and a member of the Socialist Workers Party (it was the major left-wing party in Asturias then) and he immediately volunteered, which meant simply that he was given a rifle and assigned to a company that fought on a fluid front, which is what Asturias was for the first four months of the war—securing the mining towns, besieging Oviedo, turning back to defend the region from the advancing Nationalists proceeding from Galicia. Arcadio's father was back in Coto Raso by January of 1937 because his company was cut off from escape, and he was immediately arrested, like the others, but not executed, unlike the others. He owed his life to the village priest.

"I do not want you to think that the priest in Coto Raso was a progressive priest, like the ones you find nowadays," Arcadio said. "He was as reactionary as they came, but he was a serviceable man, he did not deny the sacraments to the poor. Still, during the first day, before my father had gone off to the front and everyone was wild with rage at the uprising of the fascists, my father saved his life from the hotheads who wanted to shoot him. My father was a disciplined Socialist. The priest stayed on in Coto Raso, he did not try to join the fascists, but of course he took off his soutane. He was there when my father was sentenced to death, and he intervened and saved his life."

Because the Nationalists needed coal, his father was allowed to work in the mines. He was a *piquero*, a pickman working at the end of the tunnel at the wall of coal, the best-paid and most dangerous job in the mines. Dangerous because there you breathed in coal dust all day and were most subject to cave-ins. In 1941, when Arcadio was eleven and his sister seven, his father died in a cave-in. There was little protection for the miners then—the managers stinted on timber for the pickmen to erect sustaining beams as they lengthened the tunnels with their picks and dynamite charges—and there were no pensions or insurance. Arcadio and his sister moved in with a maiden aunt who, because she had not married, had inherited the grandparents' old house. She cultivated the two small plots around the house and kept two cows and thus fed herself and the two children.

Long before this, Arcadio had been helping her raise vegetables. There was no school in the village. The miners had set one up in a barn where a volunteer teacher taught the children in the early evening, but during the war there was none. It was sometime later that people were sufficiently fearless and the authorities lax enough to permit it to start again. That is where Arcadio learned to read and write, but he does not think that he owes his class consciousness to the school. He believes he inherited his *conciencia*, as he calls it, from his father. His awakening came from the guerrillas and his determination from the Party.

He met the guerrillas while taking care of his aunt's two cows. He would take them away from the village to pasture and sometimes go a little way into the woods where there were bushes and juniper for the cows to chew on. He made a good cover for the guerrillas: a boy shepherding cows would not be suspected of taking the guerrillas food or carrying messages for them. His aunt was of course anti-Franco, but she did not have much *conciencia*, so he did not often tell her what he was doing. She was frightened for him: guerrillas were not arrested or tried; the *Guardia Civil* shot them on the spot. Anyone helping them enjoyed the same status, and Arcadio's age would not have mattered. Still, there were many people in the village, like his aunt, who even in those years of hunger spared them food, and some of them sent it with Arcadio.

The guerrillas operated at night mostly, and they had time during the day to sit with Arcadio and talk about what they were doing. They explained to him about socialism and the system of justice that they would someday institute that would change the life of the miners. Because he knew the area he began to act as a guide too for those assigned to different bands or simply to show them the best way of going from one place to the other without walking into the open. The mountains of Asturias were patrolled all those years by Civil Guards, and once while acting as guide, Arcadio and a guerrilla came upon a detachment of Civil Guards at the moment when it opened fire on a band of guerrillas to whom Arcadio was taking his friend. Had they arrived a moment earlier they too would have been ambushed. The rifle-fire alerted them, and they turned and ran. It was his closest call.

On his fourteenth birthday Arcadio got his first job in a mine. He was lucky—the job was given him because his father had died in that cave-in and there had been no compensation. He worked at a small open pit mine in the *lavadero*, a shed where the day's coal production was washed. Only women and children worked there, and the pay was perhaps only enough to feed him, though poorly. Nevertheless, it was something, the only cash income at home, a supplement to their vegetable garden and their cows. One morning during his first year there they found that the guerrillas had placed dynamite charges during the night that had only partially gone off. The Civil Guards were already there and they joined with the company guards in beating the women and children, for no work could be done that day and someone must pay.

They were unable to defend themselves. They took the beating as best they could and ran home when the guards tired or chance got them out of their reach. Arcadio remembers breaking away by himself and hearing the screams resounding in his ears during the first of the six miles home. "I was wild with indignation," Arcadio said. "I quit the job, I never went back. I wanted to be gone from Coto Raso forever, to go to the city, do anything but be treated the way we were in the mines. But there was nothing else. There was no escape, and in a short time I found a job in the big mine in Sama de Langreo. It paid better, some ten dollars a month, and I had only to walk three miles to it instead of six to that other miserable place where the guards beat us."

Sama lies alongside the river Nalón which winds through the beautiful lush vegetation of the mountains of the *cuenca minera*, and the city has grown around the pithead, for the mining here is underground. Arcadio worked above ground unloading coal with young men like him and with old-timers. It was here that he met real Party men and began to see them after work in discussion groups. It was his introduction to Marxism, and Sama is his ideological home. Except for the times he had to flee or was away in military service or in jail, Sama was where he worked or touched base. Later that Saturday, Arcadio took me to the workers' club two blocks from the pithead to meet the two generations of activists that have followed him.

"When I was sixteen, they told me I was ready to join the Party, and I did. It has been my life ever since." The war in Europe was long over, but the Party was still oriented mainly towards the guerrilla struggle. They had so long hoped that with the fall of France the Spanish exiles in the Maquis would be supported in an invasion of Spain that it was difficult to give up this political line. Armed exiles had crossed the border, in any case, and they were hunted down as far south as the mountains between Málaga and Granada. In the north they were everywhere, and the local Party organization worked mostly as its civilian arm. The first years of Arcadio's life in the Party were for him an extension of the activities that he had undertaken on his own when he tended his aunt's cows.

In 1947, the guerrillas in their area suffered a defeat from which they never quite recovered. They were infiltrated by a government agent whose references they never checked. He said he had served in Málaga and had had to flee when he was denounced there. They tested him, however, and assigned him with two others to take an outpost of the Civil Guards. In the course of this action he killed two guards. "That seemed proof enough," Arcadio said, "but it was only proof that he was a cold-blooded beast. He was able to kill anyone without a twitch." The man was therefore privy to the news of the arrival of a shipment of rifles and ammunition from France and the time and place where it was to be distributed to the different bands. Arcadio acted as courier to the guerrilla group near Coto Raso, but he only brought them the information about the shipment and was not there for its distribution, when they were all caught.

In 1948, the Party in Sama was visited by an emissary from the leadership in exile. He explained that guerrilla warfare must be given up; it no longer had any chance, given the European context of the cold war. The Party must return to the masses; it must begin to organize the workers on the basis of their day-to-day problems. "We must start from the base, no matter how long that makes the struggle," is the political line that Arcadio has recommended since then for any objective. He himself decided that year to apply for the job of *piquero*, though the rate of accidents and silicosis were highest among them, because it was with them that he could do the most effective political work. The knowledge of silicosis was new, but the dangers of the job had always made *piqueros* the most militant among the miners.

"They try you out for the job first, to see if you are strong and apt, and they gave me a chance because I was not yet identified as a malcontent. I have always been good at learning things and so in two weeks I was doing the job. From the age of eighteen until thirty-two I worked at the end of the tunnel at the coal face, with time out for the *mili* and jail. I married when I was twenty-five and at twenty-seven they diagnosed me as having first-degree silicosis. But I stayed on, as you shall see, for political reasons."

The Party had called off the guerrillas, but many continued to operate until 1952. By then a lot of them were *bandoleros* but so courageous that people could not help admiring them. Arcadio paid

43

no more attention to them. Arcadio concentrated on the men at work. Without doubt, it was the *casa de aseo* that most troubled them. This was the dressing room where they changed into work-clothes mornings and showered after their shift was done. It was filthy and neglected, and there were only two showers for the more than a thousand men on his shift. Since it took some an hour and a half after work to finish changing and cleaning up, the *casa de aseo* was a natural meeting place, for it was illegal to meet anywhere. It was there they came to the decision to elect three men, Arcadio among them, to go as delegates to the plant manager to demand a new *casa de aseo* with better facilities.

The plant manager said he had been thinking about the problem himself. But he stalled them with various excuses: he was making a study of its costs, he was conferring with the owners (this was before nationalization of the mines), he was drawing up designs. Sometimes he was simply unavailable. Finally, on a Friday, Arcadio and the two other delegates gave him an ultimatum. On Monday work must begin on a new *casa de aseo* or the miners would not dig coal. When they came in Monday, they could see that the foundations had been laid and a crew of carpenters was at work. The new *casa* not only had many more showers but also hot running water. "We had won," Arcadio said, "and the miners felt their strength."

Until then Arcadio was not known to the authorities or the management of the mines. He had never been arrested or questioned. He had been a well-behaved, hard-working young man. There were no permanent committees of workers in the mines (the Workers Commissions did not begin until 1964); as in the case just won they were elected only to take care of a particular problem and then dissolved. But during the next four years there were as many actions of this type taken, and each time Arcadio was elected as a delegate to deal with the plant manager. Indeed, it was not yet propitious to have a standing committee: the repression was too harsh and it simply created targets for the Civil Guards.

"From that very first action they called me in to the police commissariat in Coto Raso and questioned me. The first time they could see that I was an innocent young man and they only advised me to be careful, that I had been in bad company and the Reds were using me. The next time they were less friendly. (We were asking for more supporting beams in the tunnels.) How come I again was a delegate? I said that it was not my idea, that the men were simply asking me to report what they felt and that since what they felt did not seem wrong to me that it would not look right to refuse. At the mine I was offered better jobs to buy me off. They asked me to report individual workers who were unhappy. I acted the innocent—I did not snap at any of the bait, as if I did not understand that an offer was being made."

They began to watch Arcadio. He knew it. It was confirmation to him that the Party was pursuing the right line, but it made his life narrow and less fulfilling. He had loved the discussion groups after work which deepened his knowledge of the class struggle, and loved as much talking to his friends and neighbors in Coto Raso, passing on to them the ideas he had gained from the Party and winning recruits. He had to give up all this and make contact with the Party organization as surreptitiously as possible. It did not help. During the last action at Sama before he was drafted for regular military duty at twenty-two (this time they were demanding less and more careful dynamiting at the coal face) he was arrested.

"It was not an unofficial talk like the other times. I was under arrest. They told me I was a Red. They told me the names of the Party people I met with. They kept me there overnight, but they did not touch me and they did not send me to Oviedo. I was lucky. They let me go, but now I had antecedents and this record went with me to the *mili*. I know because the Army captain under whom I served in Salamanca told me. I had been talking to some *compañeros* in my Army unit about the Party and one of them reported me, I do not know who.

"The Captain was a good man. He read me the report from the Civil Guard that was part of my record. If only I had been as dangerous as they said! The Captain told me that with such a record plus the denunciation that I was engaged in illegal activity in the Army I could be sent to jail for many years. Let me advise you, he said, I do not ask you to change your ideas or to do anything that would go against them, I simply want you to wait until you are out of the Army to pursue them—it will then be, at least, less dangerous for you. That Captain was so kind that he gave me a three-month leave, unauthorized by the Colonel, on his say-so alone, to let the whole thing blow over. He warned me, however, that if I received a message through the police commissariat while I was in Coto Raso to return to Salamanca, I must do so at once. I was not to be frightened; it simply meant that my absence had been noticed by the Colonel's office and he would have reported that he had only given me emergency leave. So it happened, but at least I had nine days back home."

When Arcadio returned to Salamanca, the Captain assigned him to duty in company headquarters. To this day he has no explanation for the Captain's behavior other than that he was a good man. Their relations remained formal, and Arcadio did not speak openly to him until just before his *mili* was up, when the Captain suggested to him that he make the Army his career. He promised Arcadio that he would see to it that he got sent to officers' school. At first, Arcadio simply replied no. "Finally, I honored him by showing my confidence in him: I told him that my political beliefs did not allow me. He said that perhaps I could keep them separate from my career in the Army, and was very disappointed when I still said no. I had not, of course, had an opportunity to discuss it with the Party, and sometimes I wonder if I made a mistake. Could I have been more useful to the Party by remaining in the Army?"

A digression: I asked Arcadio when he met his wife Onelia. I knew he had married when he was twenty-five and that he finished his military service when he was twenty-four. Yet he had still to mention her. When she had brought us the beer earlier, I asked her what she thought of Arcadio's ideas. She had placed her hands at her hips and said, "Oh, they are chronic now—we shall have to stick by them." She was hardly out of the living room when Arcadio said, "She is very loyal, but she never thinks for herself. I wish it were different."

I had not understood then and did not say so until now.

"Remember last night when you asked us at the restaurant how we had felt when our Party criticized the Soviet Union on the invasion of Czechoslovakia? We were living in Brussels then and went to Party meetings regularly. She approved of the Red Army going in because all the comrades did, but as soon as our Party declared its opposition she did too, because the Party said so. She also always goes along with what I say, but I want her to think for herself. You know what a shame it has been for me to see her sit through meetings and never say a word?"

They had grown up together in Coto Raso; there had never been a time when they did not know each other. After he finished his military service, he proposed to her in earnest. In those days he used to devote one hour each day to develop her *conciencia*. She joined the Party, but she did not grow intellectually. In marriage and the Party she was a follower; she said and did what was expected of her. She did not read books; she did not initiate discussions or add to them. He shook his head with disappointment; she was like a political assignment he had not successfully completed. "She is a good woman," he said sadly.

The new Party line of organizing the masses around issues that they themselves raised yielded results over the years. Their little victories throughout the mining region over showers, dynamiting in the tunnels, injections of water in the coal face to hold down the dust—all this gave the miners *conciencia* and a fighting, angry morale. When Arcadio returned from military service, he again became a *piquero* and a militant; the authorities knew damn well now he was no innocent. When his son was still an infant, the Party tried for the unthinkable—a general strike of the whole *cuenca minera*. They were the only organization in the area; the miners who had once been predominantly Socialist were now solidly Communist. There were Party committees in every mine, and it was still in the *casas de aseo*, while they undressed and showered and dressed, that they held their trade-union meetings. Delegates and strike committees sneaked away to the woods at night to meet and plan.

In the *casas de aseo* it was decided that they would strike, but it was left to the delegates in touch with the other mines to set the day when they would not report to work. The issues were higher pay and better working conditions, but the impact could not help but be political. There would be no advance notice. Two or three men in each mine had the job on the day decided upon of alerting the others while on their way to work. Arcadio was up all that night, and the first man he met on the lanes down to Sama was a company foreman. "Arcadio, he said to me, what are you doing up so early? And I told him. He was not a stool pigeon—he helped alert the others." No one went inside the pithead at Sama, and as the day progressed, the news began to come in from everywhere by courier that the whole mining region was closed down.

The strike lasted two months. Hunger ended it. All they gained was knowledge of their own power to close the mines. They were also an example to the rest of the country that the Franco regime was not impregnable. Before the strike was over, some 1,200 men were arrested. Arcadio was one. They were treated brutally. After the first evening, some were let go from the *comisarías*, the local police headquarters, with a beating and a warning; but most were transported to Seguridad in Oviedo. There were three days of questioning there, and although they all acquired police records, most were let go. Thirty-three were kept; again, Arcadio among them. With these the real tortures began. Some broke down and confessed, at the instigation of the security police, that Arcadio had *captado* them into the Party, which carries the sense that they had been coerced to join. They were all incommunicado. With the majority of those first arrested the police had complied with the law that required that a prisoner be brought before a magistrate seventy-two hours after his arrest. But with these thirty-three they were taking no chances: they were the hard core, with whom threats and light beatings would not work.

During the first three days, Arcadio was questioned once each day and routinely beaten, but he had stuck to his old story that he had only been a spokesman because his fellow miners had asked him. The security police at the first interview proposed that he work for them; they would keep it all secret. Each time the tone of the questioning changed whenever Arcadio did not respond: his chair would be suddenly pulled out from under him and thrown at him, obscenities yelled, his face resoundingly slapped. But after the others implicated him, Arcadio's interrogators became serious. They made him undress and went at him with paddles two feet long. They told him that more courageous men than he had been brought to that room and they had left their *cojones* there. And it was his genitals he most worried about; his whole body was a mass of hurt, but every other blow aimed for his testicles. He does not know how long that first serious session lasted—he concentrated on saying nothing because there was so much he knew that must not be revealed—but he remembers coming to each time when doused with a bucket of water.

At the start of the next session they told him that they wanted him to countersign the others' confessions that he, Arcadio, had forced them to join the Party. The beating began once more. "I remember thinking as the blows fell on me that if the others had broken under such treatment, I also might, but that if I countersigned their statements I got only myself in trouble and no one else, for they had already admitted their guilt. I feared that I might be so broken that I would reveal other things which I carried under my arm, so to speak, the details of the Party's organization in the mines that they do not know to this day."

Arcadio also thought with anguish about his good friend Caín who had been one of those who named him. (Arcadio did not know of the biblical Cain and I did not tell him.) Caín had been his friend from childhood though his father had been a hit-man for the fascists, and Arcadio had been proud to have recruited him into the Party: a sign of how *conciencia* can transform a man. And yet they had made Caín talk.

"Is that what you want me to sign? I asked them. That I recruited those men? And they said yes, that I might as well do it while I still had my *cojones*. So I signed before they suspected I knew more important matters, and they threw me back in my cell. It meant years in jail for me but a good price to keep my secrets. I bled in many spots and my genitals were swollen and untouchable and, it seemed to me, impaired for good—for many months I had trouble with them—but they did not send me to the hospital. I lay on the floor in my cell and every couple of days a doctor looked in on me and treated my lesions. I had seen no one in all those days, but there turned out to be a guard who was a good man. He passed messages among us and he even took notes to our families outside. From him I learned that I had been treated relatively well and that many had been released. I thought until then that there were still hundreds of us there in Seguridad."

One day he heard that some who had been released were called back to answer new questions and to provide more information about the thirty-three of them still in jail. What if the police learned that there was much more to be gotten out of him? "It was then I

49

decided to kill myself. I had a tiny bit of mirror, which we miners are used to carrying with us in order to check after the showers that we have scrubbed off all the grime, and although I had been searched, they had not noticed it, small and flat as it was. I worked to turn it into a sharp sliver. First, I cut my wrists. See the scars? But the blood did not flow strongly from them, so I started on my neck, searching for the aorta."

Arcadio turned his face away from me and lifted his chin to show me that scar, too, high on his neck. "I hit a vein there that spurted blood straight out, and I was working the sliver lower down and towards the front when a guard looked in and discovered me. I fainted. I must admit that I was not thinking of anyone when I did this—not of my wife, not even of my little son who still did not walk—nor of my life ending. I was thinking of the Party. I was doing it to save my Party. I was unconscious for two days. I seemed to be thinking through it all, I am dead, I am dead, and suddenly I was not. I was not in the basement at police headquarters anymore, I was in jail, and they must have got their case completed against all thirty-three of us, for they did not touch us again. I shall never forget the day I was allowed to leave my individual cell and go out for an hour into the prison yard. There they were—all my comrades! We embraced one another and we talked and talked. For two months we had talked only to beasts."

I asked Arcadio if Caín was in the prison yard too and if he had talked to him. He was puzzled by my question. "Yes, I was especially eager to see Caín. He had been my recruit and I had brought this on him. I knew what they must have done to him to get him to say that I had brought him into the Party and I wanted—well, I wanted to tell him he was my comrade. We were all going to be in jail for a long time now and you need your comrades then more than ever. The mines were working again, the strike was over, but all Spain knew what we had done. They tried us in Madrid, and they gave us one of their lawyers to defend us. He was not a bad man, he tried his best, but all we could hope for was to set a good example. We knew there would be people waiting to see us when we got to Madrid, and there were—some two thousand showing solidarity with us—and as they led us out we sang revolutionary songs. I wanted to sing 'The Internationale,' but that would have been going too far."

The prosecution asked for 1,600 years for the thirty-three of them. Arcadio was sentenced to six and served two. He volunteered for work in order to reduce his time, and they placed him in the *colonias*, the prison encampments in the mines, and he worked again as a pickman. Sometimes he worked on the roads, as had the prisoners of the Civil War, and there, while building viaducts, he often spent the day in water up to his chest. Civil War prisoners had been allowed in their day to walk out of the *colonias* in the evenings and mix with the people of the village, but Arcadio's group was never allowed to leave the encampment. But on Sundays Onelia and the little boy were permitted to visit him. He does not think of those two years as a particularly bad time.

He was released on very strict parole: he had to live in Coto Raso and report to the Civil Guards' *comisaría* each day. He spent a year looking for work. Sometimes he was hired, but he was always let go immediately when the company checked his name with the police or when the police on their own notified the company. Finally, he took his wife and child with him to the *comisaría* and told them, "You will have to feed us if you keep me from working." Arcadio believes that they must have been touched by the sight of Onelia and the little boy. The next day they sent him to a *mina del monte*, a small isolated strip-mining operation in the woods where they dug the coal off the surface. There were only seventeen men working there, and Arcadio began talking to them as he had once when he first went to work in the tunnel in Sama.

There was no *casa de aseo* at the strip mine, only a single faucet with a thin stream of cold water. The men elected him to go speak to the engineer. Except for a guard, the engineer was the only person in charge. "He was a good fellow. 'Arcadio,' he said, 'you are right and so are the others, but you must know that I am obliged—it is the rules—to report demands like this to the administration and give them all details. From them it goes straight to the police. Now, you have just been in jail—you know what would happen to you.' I tried my old ultimatum: three days for a *casa de aseo* or we do not work. Well, he got it built in three days, a good little *casa de aseo*, and I do not know how he managed it, but he never reported me."

"It was not long before the men had other demands and each time they elected me as their delegate. Finally, the engineer called us all together and said to us, What do you think you are doing always selecting Arcadio to talk up for you? Do you want to see him in jail again? I almost had to laugh right there. Anyway, that little mine was an uneconomical operation and was soon closed down—the yield was too inferior."

Arcadio had not, of course, left the Party, even throughout the period when he reported to the Civil Guards in Coto Raso each day. When he worked in the mines as a prisoner, he learned that he had silicosis, but there was no other work for him than the mines. He was young and strong, and in any case, his presence in the mines was essential to his Party work. The mine in Sama hired him again at a time when the Party was planning another general strike in the mining region. The inflation that began in Spain towards the end of the fifties with industrialization and foreign investments made another strike both possible and necessary. The Party told him he would be most useful down at the coal face where his experience made him known and trusted, and he once more took the now doubly dangerous job of pickman.

"In 1962 we did it again—we closed the whole *cuenca minera*. It was on the basis of real work demands, of course, but it had its political effect too. Franco had so often boasted that he had cleaned out Communism in Spain. All through the cold war he had been telling the capitalist countries that he had done what they were now trying to do. Well, our strike showed them. We organized it with great secrecy. Since the last one, the repression had been severe, and our organization, I must admit, had suffered when so many were arrested and went to jail. It meant working by oneself a lot, to a certain extent in isolation, and that is why I got out of Sama the moment someone came to tell me the arrests had begun. A year earlier I had taken out a passport on the advice of the Party, and now I took the next train out of Oviedo and left the country."

Arcadio still feels guilty for having run. He believes that if he had not been thrown back on himself so much, if he had been meeting with his comrades, that he would not have left. He went straight to the Party in Brussels, and they told him he had done right. They informed him that one day after he left for Oviedo the police had gone for him in Coto Raso. Still, he is convinced that he should have stayed and faced them. For the first five years of the nine he lived in Brussels he was too ill to work at a regular job. The work as pickman and the nights of contact work during the organization of the strike had worsened his silicosis and left him breathless and weak. Onelia joined him in Brussels with their two children. She worked as a domestic, he at Party duties, selling the Party newspaper and organizing the forty thousand Spaniards on work contracts there. He admires the Belgians and will always be grateful to them for the freedom and mobility they extended to the Spaniards. It was his first experience of democracy.

The Belgians even allowed the Party to organize openly and hold public meetings. In Brussels, he was able, for the first time, to sing "The Internationale" with hundreds of workers around him, in full voice, fists raised, with the hope of final victory which that song always gave him when he whispered it to himself in Spain, now magnified and shared and made real. Singing "The Internationale" is for Arcadio a battle won. He sold so many copies of the Party newspaper that he was given the prize of a trip to Moscow. "There we met Dolores," he said, and for the first time with me he was at a loss for words. Dolores is Dolores Ibarruri, La Pasionaria, the miner's wife from Asturias, the Communist deputy to the Cortes from Oviedo during the Republic; her impassioned speeches during the Civil War had made her a legend. "She was everything one expected."

There were many things he did not like about Moscow, but there was as much that he admired as achievements of socialism. Both reactions were to help him in the aftermath of the Soviet invasion of Czechoslovakia. He resisted the Spanish Communist Party's condemnation of it. He listened, but he felt that they would be proven wrong. Like most of the rank and file of the Spanish Party he did not agree, but like them he did not leave the Party. It was a period of anguish for him.

"I saw old-timers cry to hear their Party leaders criticizing our workers' state. I said to myself, it takes time to make these matters clear. In six months the truth of the necessity for the intervention to save the country from the capitalists will be undeniable. But six months went by and I knew that thousands of Party militants in Czechoslovakia had thrown away their Party cards. Even then I still hoped that our own leaders would be proven wrong. The inner Party discussions on Czechoslovakia went on for two years. At the end of a year, our general secretary Santiago Carrillo spoke to the delegates of the Party in a closed session in Brussels. The Soviet bureaucracy had feared the democratic example of the Czechs. He said also that not until now could the leadership—*our* leadership—really speak openly and give the full reasons for their stand. He spoke to us in confidence about certain possible dangerous consequences at the time of the invasion. Even now I cannot repeat some of this to you." It was understood between Arcadio and me that the Spanish Party had to achieve more than ideological independence in order to speak openly and its leaders survive.

Our conversation had gone on all morning, with Arcadio's daughter joining us occasionally and laughing in anticipation at some of the old stories. Arcadio is full of hopes for her; she is bright and studious. His son married at nineteen and lives in an apartment for which he is paying with his carpenter's job. He did not want to go on studying; it was not for him. Arcadio did not insist, no more than he tried to recruit him into the Party, but he believes that the boy is now achieving a *conciencia* that in part comes from his parents' example, but more from his working experience. That is as it should be, for the inner Party discussions that started with Czechoslovakia have convinced Arcadio that one must always listen to people and help them with what they want. This must be particularly true of the Party in its relations with the masses—it must go back on every point to the base and fight for its needs. That is why democracy is important.

At lunch, I praised Onelia's cooking, especially a potato salad made with eggs, pimiento, and tiny peas. She said that she too had learned something in Belgium—to eschew the grease and sausages of Asturian dishes that made them so heavy and unhealthy. She explained that she prefers French cooking. "No wonder it is famous—it never disagrees with you," she concluded, and I did not take issue with her, for it had been her longest speech of the day. I suspected that they did not always have steak and French fries as a second course, and felt sorry that they had gone to that expenditure for me. I said, "You are being too good to me," and Arcadio and Onelia knew what I meant. "We live like privileged people now," Arcadio said apologetically, and explained that the Socialist Mutual

Aid Society of Brussels paid him a pension of almost three hundred dollars a month, and Spanish social security another two hundred dollars because of his silicosis: these rewards were a burden to his *conciencia*.

Arcadio was unaware that this life story of his which he had been recounting since the previous evening was what I had hoped for from him. He had talked about himself because he thus offered his friendship and because he could not, in any case, help himself. He was generous with himself as a matter of course, but he believed that to take me to Sama to meet the militants there was his true Party duty and the real object of my interest. Once more I hurried after him down the streets to catch a bus a few blocks away. As it slowed down for our corner, he gestured at a man sitting by a window towards the back and whispered to me that he was going to introduce me to *un cura progre*, short in Spanish for a progressive priest. "You are in luck," he said.

The priest was dressed in a worn jacket and a turtleneck shirt, and he was pleased when I told him that he did not look like a priest to me. He had come to Asturias some fifteen years earlier as a worker priest, and until recently he had driven a truck for a living. His church was in the city on the other side of the river Nalón from Sama, and the old parishioners were not very happy with him. He must not have been their idea of a priest either. He was returning from a trip to Madrid, and on his lap were all the latest issues of liberal magazines and newspapers. One was open to an article by a member of the *Opus Dei* whom I had met, and he gave it to me for my files. "I do not understand people like that and especially their notion of the evangel," he said.

He knew that Arcadio was taking me to the Friends of Nalón Club in Sama, and he recommended the kind of people I would meet there. "Not the people of the *Opus*. I have always said of them that they are Catholics and sectarians and non-Christian. I believe in the sacraments—they are important in bringing us together with our fellow men and God—but that is not all there is to Christianity. The young people from the *Amigos de Nalón Club* come to me to marry them although they do not believe in the sacraments, and I marry them because it is a satisfaction to them to be married in church. I tell them it is a civil marriage I perform for them, since I know it is not the sacraments they want. It is enough for me that they are saying to their friends and neighbors and the world that they are going to live together in love."

In the sixties, when Franco began to speak of instituting organic democracy, the regime allowed a minority of representatives in the Cortes and the town councils to be elected by heads of families. The process was hardly democratic, and there was no rush to elect their own representatives by those qualified to vote. But at the same time the regime committed the error of permitting for the first time cultural and neighborhood associations, and in many places they became disguised political headquarters of the opposition. Throughout the mining region every town set up a cultural club that was a center of trade-union organization, where small meetings could be held and contacts made. Indeed, in Sama we found the street door of the Friends of Nalón closed because a meeting of leaders of the Workers Commissions was taking place inside.

It was Saturday afternoon, a time to be out seeing one's friends, and there were men out on the sidewalk chatting and waiting for the meeting to end so that they could go inside to the bar. All of them were friends of Arcadio's. They must have recently finished work and come from home, for they were scrubbed and shining, their neatly combed hair still wet, and their shirts and cotton pants starched and pressed. Their looks and the tone of the place, as well as the accents of their speech, reminded me of the *Centro Español* and *Centro Asturiano* in my hometown. Only these were miners not cigarmakers.

I asked an old man wearing a beret and carrying a cane if like Arcadio he had been here during the 1957 strike. "I was here during the war," he said, and began to tell me about it. He suddenly turned away from us, contracted his shoulders spasmodically, and started off across the street. One of the two strapping, happy fellows who had introduced me to him grimaced and explained, "He does not want us to see him cry. He had a slight stroke last winter and now he cannot talk about old times without breaking down." We watched him make his way home slowly on the opposite sidewalk.

I said to the two of them, who looked no more than thirty-five, that one must have to be young and strong like them to work in the mines. "Oh we? We are retired," one said, and both laughed. I thought it was a joke—that they had only finished their day's work; a pleasantry cigarmakers engaged in at the end of each day's stint— and I laughed with them. Then one of them added, "We have silicosis." I must have looked dismayed, for he continued, "Oh, just second-degree silicosis, and we are getting our pension. It is not much, but with light work we pick up here and there we get along. The government will tell you that it is kind of them to give us a pension, but it was the strikes that got it for us."

Someone urged Arcadio and me to go inside. "They have been meeting all day, they should soon be finished. Anyway, you are persons of trust." Inside was a large room with a bar along one side and an open door next to it showing a small office. Tightly packed, the large room might accommodate one hundred persons. There were some thirty men there now sitting in folding chairs in a semicircle facing a table at which sat three young men. The others were young too, in their early twenties at most, wearing tight, flared jeans, form-fitting T-shirts or sports shirts unbuttoned most of the way down their chests. Their necks and arms bulged with muscles, and their bodies were so supple that they managed to lounge and slouch in the uncomfortable, rigid chairs. They looked like a crowd of young bucks whom on a Saturday afternoon you expected to find at the town square chasing girls.

They were not all miners. They were delegates from representa- tive work centers, including the mines, in the southern region of Asturias, and some would have to drive a couple of hours to get home after the meeting. There were still two points left on the agenda, but no one was hurrying the meeting to a conclusion by keeping quiet. The first point dealt with some statement to be made by *Coordinación Democrática*, and one young man asked how the Workers Commissions in their area could pass on this or support it when no workers' meetings had been held to ratify the decision of their leaders to participate in the *Coordinación*. This requires expla- nation: the Workers Commissions is a strictly trade-union organiza- tion begun in the early sixties by the Communists with the support of the Christian Democrats; it had in the last few years become part of the *Junta Democrática*, which was a loose federation of anti- Franco parties that included almost the entire Left; in the past few months the Junta was expanded to include center and liberal groups,

57

its objective being to unite all forces to create "the democratic rupture" that the king at the moment seemed loath to initiate; this new grouping took the name of *Coordinación Democrática*. All these organizations, of course, had been and still were illegal.

The chairman replied to the young man who raised the question that such meetings had been held and the workers had supported the new *Coordinación*. The young man protested that no directives of the sort had come down to his group and that no one knew about the *Coordinación* and that therefore ratification had not been discussed at his work center.

Another young man read to him from a two-month-old newspaper of the Workers Commissions in which all this had been announced and meetings called for. "If some people do not know about the *Coordinación*," this second young man added, "it is because they do not want to." The first young man was still unconvinced, and said it was too important a political decision for workers to take without sufficient discussion. The second young man replied in a mocking tone, "I think there is someone here who is a member of a political party and not of the Commissions." The Chairman interrupted to say that everyone had the democratic right to speak and argue in a Commissions meeting, and he advised the first young man that his work center should soon discuss the *Coordinación* in meeting and decide about it one way or the other.

What had actually surfaced, though it was never quite in the open, was the tip of the old disagreement between Communists and Trotskyists about popular front tactics. The young man who injected the issue did not like the inclusion in the Junta of bourgeois parties, especially since to his mind that coalition was already insufficiently oriented towards socialism. Later, Arcadio whispered to me, "I know that fellow who raised the question. He represents sales clerks. He is a Trot and a good boy but immature and new to the Commissions."

The planning of the next meeting presented an important problem. The Commissions of the whole province were to be represented and by more than one delegate. At that meeting they hoped to start a major push to force the government to legislate free trade unions. But where to meet? No church large enough was available, and anyway, in Asturias there was such little toleration that they had to meet more secretly than that. Someone suggested the forest, but there were many practical objections to that. Finally, the chairman asked for reasons of security that everyone there who was not a delegate leave the meeting while they decided where the next would be held. Even the man tending bar went outside.

After the meeting broke up, Arcadio told me that some of the men agreed to stay to talk to me. There were about six who remained, and they warned me that since they had been meeting all day, they could not stay long. Some of the old-timers stood around too. The setup was too formal; it was not my kind of scene: the questions and answers of press interviews do not interest me. I tried to be casual and personal; I told them a bit about myself and said it was a wonder to someone like me to find that people in a country like Spain which had been isolated and repressed for almost forty years had achieved such a high level of political consciousness. I turned to the younger ones and asked if they could remember when they became conscious of their opposition to the regime. They were silent. They were a courteous group, they wanted to reply, but they did not seem to know what to do with such a question.

Finally, one young man said there was no particular moment when he decided that he was anti-Franco. "I was just a little boy when I saw my aunt and her daughter beaten by Civil Guards because they wanted to find out where my uncle was. And then the woman next door too, because her husband also was hiding from them." One of the old-timers interrupted to tell me, in general, impersonal terms, about the repressive measures of the Franco regime, and by the time he finished I feared I would not be able to get the conversation back to the tone I wanted. I tried again. I said that in Madrid I found that much of the younger generation was sick of hearing about the old days. Since many of these young people were middle class, they were, in effect, rejecting parents who had supported and gained from the Franco regime. There was a phrase for their rebellion—*no me cuentes tu batallita*, don't tell me about your little battle, a response to parents who attempted censoriously to tell them how much they had done to bring them their present prosperity. I had heard too that the sons and daughters of Republicans and left-wingers responded to their parents' stories in the same way. That did not seem to be the case here, I said, and waited.

Again, one of the old-timers replied, and again, impersonally. Here the struggle did not pass from generation to generation, it went on all the time, young and old together. Another said that I had to remember that in places like Madrid the new generation had been almost entirely cut off from the previous one. Here, they all went to work at the mines. The chairman was bothered by these replies. "Oh, I remember when people were fearful and did nothing, when—I might as well say it—only the Communists were doing something. But when we Communists began to respond to their work problems and they saw they could make some gains, then there was unity and they moved."

Earlier I had seen him take some notes when I first introduced myself, and he now looked at them and continued talking. "There are some points I want to make before I go." He began with a mild criticism of the United States for the role it had played in bolstering the Franco regime, and went on to explain why all progressive forces in Spain wanted a democratic rupture in Spain in order to tackle, in political freedom, the serious economic problems the people suffered. He ended with a description of the goals of the Workers Commissions, and in a burst of rhetorical confidence said they would lead the country through mass action to socialism.

I did not interrupt him. I had given up trying to get their personal stories. I did not even tell him that in Madrid I had spoken on two or three occasions with a member of the Central Committee of the Communist Party about the Party's position on trade unions. The Party wanted a single, united trade union in which plurality of political representation would be assured by complete democracy within it. He knew that others, particularly the Socialists, were hesitant about this—they really wanted the old days back when the Socialist Workers Party had its own trade union, the UGT. He knew also that they worried that the Communist Party really wanted to dominate the single union they proposed, but in fact, the Party had no such interest, because they had learned from the recent history of the developed capitalist nations that the great monopolies knew how to manipulate the most powerful of trade unions and limit their goals to bread and butter issues.

I was tempted to tell the chairman this because I had succumbed in my writer's frustration to my old impatience with the dogmatism and arrogance and ideological complacency of Communists. The chairman and the old-timers had aroused in me an old ambivalence, more acute here because I was in the presence of real fighters, men who, as the old cliché of the Left puts it, had laid their lives on the line. Everything in my background led me inexorably to love and admire them, but I could not surrender my intelligence nor resent their narrow-mindedness any less.

Then a wonderful thing happened. A young man who was the chairman's friend and had stayed only to go home with him decided to answer me. "I cannot tell you when I began to learn from my parents, for my father died before I was five," he began calmly. "He died of silicosis in the days when silicosis did not exist. Which means that it did exist but they did not acknowledge it. So there was no retirement and no pension for him. I knew that was wrong." Then loudly: "We had to scramble for food. And I went to work in the mines when I was a boy and I did not last long. I did not last because I would not take mistreatment. I left. I made the rounds of Europe—Holland, England, Belgium, Sweden, Germany, Switzerland, France. And always I was in trouble. Because of this!" He leaned towards me, his eyes brilliant with anger, and pointed to his mouth. "I would not be silent. I did not have to be taught. Fascism taught me. The capitalists are bastards. The system made me. So I came home and I went to work in the mines again, and again I was in trouble. But now I am in the Commissions and in the Commissions I am fine. I can be myself." He shrugged his shoulders and clamped his mouth shut as if to make an end of that, and then decided to add, "That is what I have to tell you."

Everyone was silent. They all looked at me, and I did not mind that my eyes were moist. Arcadio was supremely happy with the young man's speech. He expressed it in words the Party had taught him. He said, "There you have an example of the spontaneity of the working class."

At first I thought I would end this account of Asturian Communists with Arcadio's statement. At the time he said it, it seemed to round off everything perfectly. Now I fear that it undercuts the anguish of their lives under Franco by its eloquence and that it glosses over the human cost of their struggle by the young man's undefeated stance. As an ending it also sounds inspirational, and we

American writers are always urged to avoid that. I should, therefore, end with Arcadio becoming ill in the car ride back to Oviedo. He had talked too much and smoked too many cigarettes during the last two days. He opened the car window and said, "I get nauseated when I do not have enough air in my lungs." He turned his head towards the draft of cool night air and breathed as deep as he could, then slumped back and shuddered. "Oh, José, José, I am very sick."

That ending also has the merit that Arcadio, my protagonist, returns to the center of the story. Nevertheless, I shall end with the two fellows outside the Friends of Nalón Club, the ones who looked so vigorous but were already in the second degree of silicosis. The last time I stepped out of the club they were still on the sidewalk. They now greeted me as if I were one of them. One had been leaning against a car, and when he saw me, he straightened up and said, "Oh my friend, my friend, when shall we be free?"

4

Amparo and Gabriel: A Basque Love Story

During my first visit to Madrid, in 1965, I tried to phone the poet Gabriel Celaya. I had his address but that did not help: telephone directories were neither current nor reliable. The only solution was to show up at his apartment without warning. The taxi driver was not sure where the street was; it turned out to be a sidestreet in the Madrid equivalent of the Bronx. On the way, I remembered his wife was a poet too and had collaborated with him on two books. I made an effort to recall her name: Amparo Gastón. A good thing it came to mind, for it was she who opened the door. She was a pretty woman—not more than forty, I thought—and she stared at me with big, alert eyes. I greeted her by name and began to explain that I was the *yanqui* who three years earlier had translated four of Gabriel's poems. She called out my name before I got to it. "How wonderful that you have come! I have been sitting inside sulking. I am alone. Gabriel and I had a terrible fight. He is out somewhere, damn him. He slammed out of the house. You may never see him and I do not care if I do."

I laughed because she laughed.

"He does not have to come back," she explained. "There is nothing I can do about it. I have no recourse. We are not married, you know."

I did not know. She led me down the corridor lined with paintings. My mind raced to come up with the person who had told me they were married or the occasion from which I had gathered it—there were his love poems, the many dedications to Amparitxu, the Basque diminutive of her name. She sat me at a small dining table in a living room whose walls were covered with jammed bookshelves and more paintings, and poured me red wine from a decanter. She told me that Gabriel had long ago left his wife and two children for her, and that since divorce was impossible in Spain, the authorities or any unfriendly neighbor could, and did, consider her his mistress.

"When they want to rub it in, they can call me his whore." It gave her pleasure to tell me about her compromised situation, for she could thus curse the regime and, along the way, Gabriel too. She sipped her wine with enjoyment. "He is out walking, I am sure, and he will return when he is tired out and it has all blown over. He has terrible outbursts, but you can see I am calmness itself."

When we heard the front door open and close, she called out, "Gabriel, there is a surprise here for you." In a moment, he appeared at the door of the living room and stopped there. He was shorter than I expected; stocky like a Basque, his face large and round with ample room for his big features. He was half bald and his graying hair unruly—hardly a romantic figure. He looked at Amparo from under his brows, with suspicion and caution. She told him who I was and added, "He knows all about our fight." His mouth opened wide in a smile, his eyes narrowed happily, and his body shook to keep from laughing unceremoniously—what happiness that the fight was all over!

Gabriel has written a poem which tells his side of these quarrels. Even in so personal a poem he uses the vocabulary of social protest. He calls it *I Accuse Love:*

> She told me what she wanted. Anything now could happen.
> I drank my coffee slowly, very slowly.
> When I finished, there would be nothing left.
> I should have to leave. Put on my walking shoes.
> Begin once more to invent a life for myself.
> I placed the cup on the saucer, folded the napkin.
> I lit a cigarette. I looked at the teaspoon.
> The world and everything in it fell away from me.
> And suddenly she said, "How about a little drink?"

Amparo and Gabriel: A Basque Love Story

Oh, happiness! says the refrain that follows. *Let the birds sing!* The quarrel is done, and he does not have to invent a new life for himself. He does not mean by this the prosaic new arrangements that in other countries and with other couples take place after broken affairs and divorce. Hurtful though they can be, they are not as devastating. Perhaps only in Spain can Gabriel feel as he does. He left not only his wife and children but the life style of the Basque industrial upper class when, in 1946, he picked up the working-class girl that Amparo was then. Nor did he leave for a quiet life of enjoyment of their love. He became one of Spain's leading poets, and his personal life provided him with the metaphors of his politically charged verse, always, of course, in opposition to the regime. The happy ending of a lovers' quarrel keeps more than his daily life intact, but for Amparo it is always dubious, inseparable though each quarrel proves them to be, because her relationship with him receives no recognition in Spanish law or with her countrymen.

She laughs happily, but she can also say, "Oh, the things this man has put me through—his rages, his drinking."

"I have to admit, she saved my life," Grabriel replies, sounding like one of his poems to her: *It was Amparito/ suddenly real, suddenly prodigious/ who saved me from chaos when I was lost . . . / and that is why, since then/ we feel so secure, so united/ Amparito and this old repentant bourgeois.* "I first saw her in a bookstore in San Sebastián. She was reflected in the mirror of one of the columns. She was reading and then she looked up and I saw her enormous eyes."

He was thirty-five. He was the manager of the family factory. He and a cousin his age together ran the family business. They had both been sent in their teens to the *Residencia* of Madrid University before the Civil War. The *Residencia* had inherited the liberal ideas of education introduced in Spain at the end of the nineteenth century by the Free Institute of Education, and although it was reformist only in education and was apolitical otherwise, there was still a strong prejudice against it in Church and conservative circles. That his family sent him there, and to study engineering not law, is proof, as political analysts say, of the progressive nature of the Basque bourgeoisie.

Many of the intellectual and liberal political leaders of Spain had stayed at the *Residencia*. Gabriel's room had been shared in the early twenties by Federico García Lorca and Salvador Dali. Gabriel enjoyed all this. Indeed, simply to live in Madrid was a grand intellectual adventure for a young man from the north who was already writing surrealist poetry. It was no surprise while reading García Lorca's *El romancero gitano* in a trolley to be interrupted by another occupant wanting to know his opinion of it. "I like it, but it is fake," Gabriel told the man. "It is not genuine gypsy poetry." The man laughed and introduced himself. He was Lorca—*that* was a surprise.

But not a shock. After all, to the *Residencia* came people like Le Corbusier, Valéry, Calder, Milhaud, Stravinsky, Jules Romains. Nor was it unusual nearby to run into Juan Ramón Jiménez, Ortega y Gasset, and Unamuno. Being in Madrid was worth going along with his father's desire that he major in industrial engineering instead of the humanities at the College of Philosophy and Letters. His father promised him that he would not have to practice the engineering that bored him; he could immediately go into the family business. Obtaining the engineering degree was no problem, but what really interested him were, as he recalls, "painting, at which I failed, despite my enthusiasm for it, for lack of technical training, and poetry, in which self-teaching yields better results."

In 1935, he published his first book of poetry. That year, too, his studies completed, he came home to San Sebastián and the family business. The next year the Civil War broke out and he enlisted as an engineer in the Republican Army. There was no problem about that with his family; like the peasants and industrial workers, the Basque upper class was solidly Republican. In 1937, the north fell and he was jailed. The father of one of the girls whom he had been courting became civil governor of the province, and he got Gabriel released. He is not sure now whether that was the reason he married her. "I cannot disentangle it from the things I was feeling then, but it was not love," he says, and Amparo reminds him, "You had two children with her."

But there is the testimony of the poetry he was writing at the time. It is full of words like silences, absences, anguish, solitude; phrases like "in my breast a caged bird," "drowning in myself," "man is too small for his yearnings"; and the epigraphs are from St. John of the Cross. He did not publish them until 1947, a year after he met Amparo, but he did not revise or change them; he has published more than fifty collections of poems; his notions about the nature of poetry have changed often, his attitude towards life even more; but he respects the man he was and lets the poetry be. It is a record of his emotional life. Sometimes as exact as in *Biography*, published in 1975:

> Don't pick up your spoon with the left hand.
> Don't lean your elbows on the table.
> Fold your napkin neatly.
> That, to start.
>
> What is the square root of three thousand three hundred
>   thirteen?
> Where is Tanganyika? What year was Cervantes born?
> You will get zero in conduct if you talk in class.
> That, to obey.
>
> Do you think it right for an engineer to write poetry?
> Culture is an adornment and business is business.
> If you carry on with that girl, we will close all doors.
> That, to live.
>
> Don't be so crazy. Be educated. Be correct.
> Don't drink. Don't smoke. Don't cough. Don't breathe.
> Ah yes, don't breathe! Say no to all the no's.
> And rest: die.

The family appointed his cousin to speak to him. "She is gorgeous," he said, "but can't you be more discreet?" Gabriel thought he had been. Not for his own sake but for Amparo's: she was a good girl of a decent working-class family. She went to the bookstore for its rental library; she could not afford to buy books. There were no other occasions for them to meet, until he hit upon a perfect arrangement that allowed him to keep her and still live at home playing the role of husband and father. He started a small publishing house, so small that Amparo was its only editorial employee, himself editor-in-chief and sole owner. They called it Norte and set it up in a two-room office in San Sebastián. They published only slim collections of poetry.

Love and poetry. But they were serious about the need for such a house. They wanted to help break the intellectual isolation of Spain: they published Blake, Rimbaud, Rilke, Eluard; also, some of the new Spanish poets who did not write official poetry. In their first year they brought out two collections of Gabriel's, poems written during the previous decade, which he signed, as he had his first book in 1935, with a shortened version of his real name, Rafael Mugica. It surprised him that this caused his first troubles with his family—their suspicions about his relationship with Amparo came out in the open later. Now that he was an engineer-executive, they said, it was improper for him to publish poetry, particularly under the name by which the family business was known. Indeed, as the Board of Directors of the company, they informed him that it would impair the firm's credit standing.

There was a solution to that. From his other Christian and surnames he picked Gabriel Celaya, as he did later Juan Leceta when he believed that he had evolved a style that signified a complete break with his past. (Eventually Gabriel became his only persona.) But there was no satisfactory resolution to the problem of Amparo. He was not about to give her up: he was living for the first time. She symbolized everything he wanted his life and his poetry to be. *Oh, my sweet little animal with bright eyes*, said one of his poems to her, *I know that I cannot, I must not hoard for myself these delights* . . . He quotes her on his poems: *I come from the common people, I do not understand you, señorito. Señorito*, that word of address that a social inferior uses with the young gentleman of the house— out of their hearing, always in the pejorative—today is invariably used to mean privileged, parasitical.

Amparo's father was a factory worker and a Socialist. He was literate, and for this reason his neighbors had elected him president of a neighborhood association in the days of the Republic. Only because he could keep the association's books, Amparo emphasizes in order to explain how unjust his jailing had been when San Sebastián fell to the Nationalists in September, 1936. A good deed had been the worst evidence against him at his trial. In the first days of the generals' uprising, local Falangists were rounded up and held at a hotel under arrest. The wife of one of them who lived nearby came to Amparo's father to ask him to speak up for her husband, expecting that a character reference from a Socialist might obtain his release. It did, and this was used later at his trial to prove that he was an influential Red. There was also the fact that he owned books and read the novelist Pío Baroja.

Their home was confiscated, as could happen with political prisoners, and some para-official group took away the furnishings during the days of looting. None of the five children were sufficiently grown to help the mother. The two youngest were boys and they had been sent abroad in the first year of the war with a large group of children for temporary refuge in the Soviet Union. (They ended up with a family in Belgium and Amparo's parents had no news of them for years.) But another good deed of Amparo's father saved them now. He had brought into their home years earlier two teen-aged boys who had been orphaned, and they now were heads of families able to take into their homes what was left of Amparo's.

Amparo's mother got a job as a cook and stole food to bring home. One of the girls was a good enough seamstress to find work occasionally to do at home. The father spent only six of his thirty-year sentence in jail. When it seemed clear that Germany would lose the war, many sentences were reviewed and that was when he was released. His first year out he was not allowed to live any closer than two hundred fifty miles from San Sebastián, but his family was now eligible to apply for an apartment to rent, and to claim their furniture at a government warehouse where confiscated property was held. Their home had been ransacked by an unofficial gang, so Amparo's mother did not expect to find their furniture there. She came home with nothing.

Amparo tells these ups and downs laconically. They were ordinary suffering, common to most Spaniards. Only when she was able to talk back or beat the system in some way does she speak with energy. As in the case of the furniture. "You were honest with *them!*" she said to her mother, and went to the warehouse herself the next day, using the excuse that her mother had been too upset to look through the place carefully. "What good was the apartment without a stick of furniture?"

She picked out four beds, a table, and some chairs. They took her word for it, and only made her sign a receipt. She saw a row of sewing machines, and it occurred to her that her sister could use one. "I don't know what made me suspect that it would not be as easy to get a sewing machine, so when they were not looking I reached under the wooden top of one and with my thumbnail I scratched and scratched away. I did not tell them it was a particular one that belonged to us, I said it must be one of several there that looked the same. They said I had to have the factory number. I argued. I said that I was too young to have kept such records, and finally they themselves suggested that I check with my mother and come back another day."

She returned the next day. Middle-aged now, her hair dyed and close-cropped in the latest fashion, her manner as assured as any upper-class Madrid intellectual's, Amparo tries to imitate the innocence of the girl she once was. She had feigned it then too, but she softens her voice and humbly pleads with wide, staring eyes and says, "Señor, my mother has been through too much to remember the factory number, but she begs me to tell you that she recalls that we children had scratched the wood of the machine." They agreed to let Amparo have it if there was one with such scratching, and were so helpful that together they found it.

Gabriel moves his head from side to side and looks up to heaven and announces, "What whorishness she was capable of even then!"

Her father's health was ruined by mistreatment in jail. Even when he was back in San Sebastián he had no peace. Whenever Franco came to the city, which occurred at least once a year when the government summered there, he was incarcerated. Every month he had to report to the Civil Guards. He was too ill to work and, in any case, no one would give him a job. He did not last long. Two Civil Guards came to the house and talked threateningly when Amparo appeared at the door. "Your father has not reported for two months. We know he is in hiding and you must take us to him. Otherwise, it will go bad for you."

"In that case, I will take you there," she replied, and said not another word. She tried to walk ahead of them, and she would only answer, "This way," when they asked her where he was hiding. Finally, one of them said, "But this way there is only the cemetery." The other observed, "She is dressed in mourning." The first explained to Amparo, "They did not tell us he was executed." She turned on them. "He never did anything wrong. He was not executed, but you killed him," she said. "You killed him with your jails." They apologized. They did not know what to do to make amends. They invited her, as Spaniards anxious to show good faith will, to step into a nearby café and have something with them.

"Did she say no? Was she indignant?" Gabriel says. "No—she went in and had a few *tapas* and a glass of wine."

"Of course not, one did not turn down food or drink," Amparo explains. "Those were the years of hunger. Anyway, they were being most correct."

They were so poor that Amparo remembers clearly the clothes that her two brothers wore when they returned from Belgium about this time. They had been raised by a liberal middle-class family, and they arrived with all their things to stay for good. "They were a marvel to me, but we were a shock to them," Amparo says. "What clothes! I studied them closely. I felt them at every opportunity. It was no wonder that they should want to go back to Belgium. They were young men, used to better things. But they were trapped. Still, one of them got away very soon."

He was old enough to be drafted, and his company was assigned to the Pyrenees. The borders were sealed, and their job was to keep exiles in France from crossing to join the guerrilla movement that was still operating inside Spain. Amparo's brother picked up orders that arrived at company headquarters one morning reporting the whereabouts of guerrillas. He left ostensibly as a scout to pinpoint their position, but he crossed over into France and made his way on foot back to Belgium. He is there still, and makes a good living as a master cabinetmaker. The other became a Socialist, was caught with a bundle of leaflets, and spent several years in jail. There he became a Communist.

"You would think that I should have longed for a quiet life and not have taken up with this man," Amparo says. Her father had seen to it, before the war broke out, that his daughters got a primary education, and inspired them, particularly Amparo, with reverence for literature. In time this qualified her to become a doctor's receptionist. That was the job she left to become Gabriel's co-editor in the publishing venture. For Gabriel's bourgeois family the enterprise was suspect not only because poetry was an improper activity but also because it was unprofitable—there must be some other explanation for his behavior. But for Amparo's family the job was a fine career and an unhoped for turn of good luck—they could only rejoice.

It was her grandmother, now living with the family, who first began to worry the others and alert them. What is the matter with this girl! she would exclaim on the many nights when Amparo, who had presumably just finished working late, did not sit down with the family to eat. She was not hungry, she was tired, she explained. But since when did work keep anyone from eating? That she worked long hours did not make them suspicious: everyone lucky enough to have a job worked as long hours as they were asked. Then came the times when she was away overnight. She explained that she had been in Tolosa to deal with printers, but they knew there was an early evening train back from there, one that would have gotten her home in time for dinner. "It is not an easy matter to select the proper paper," she countered, but that did not work for long. They threw her out of the house, and she went to live in the Norte office.

None of this happened suddenly. It was two years since they had met in the bookstore. Gabriel knew by now that his was not simply a passion about which he had to maneuver discreetly; she was indispensable to him: love reinforced by ideology. "Guilt! Guilt!" Amparo says, only half-joking, and Gabriel agrees. Having been born a Mugica has been a sin that he has tried to expiate with his life and his poetry. In the factory the workers knew he was *blando*—softhearted—and they came to him with problems no Spanish boss would have listened to. He always found a way to help them, and now here was Amparo—a pariah, and he was the one to blame.

Rejected and isolated, Amparo knew, nevertheless, that if she lived decently she would win over her family. Working-class morality is less tied to formalities and appearances than that of the bourgeoisie. Gabriel knew that his break might well be irrevocable. He had to consider not only his wife and children, who were blameless, but also his proud and snobbish mother who would never forgive him. From his father he expected only aloofness. It mattered more to his mother that he was their only son. During his childhood she had totally devoted herself to him. He was sickly, and she took

72

him to Pau in France, for months at a time, to help him over his allergies and asthma and poor appetite. She neglected San Sebastián society, her husband, and her daughter for Gabriel. His fears came true: when he left his family and business for Amparo, his mother replaced him in her will with his children and never spoke to him again. A few years ago Amparo persuaded him to go see her when she was dying.

Gabriel wrote a ballad called *Man Overboard* in which he turns this anguished situation on its head by means of jauntily rhyming stanzas. It is dedicated to "Amparito, the siren." A submarine sights a man in the water kissing a siren; they call to him to return and he refuses. He had meant to commit suicide, but he has found a siren and a sea without end. The word goes out in Morse code to the world: *Everything is going wrong,* and ten, then one hundred submarines come to the rescue. *I send a message to my family/ Don't save me. I'm well.* The siren tells him not to heed the rescuers: *We shall play hide and seek/ with our own two hearts.*

> I no longer know what I want.
> I have forgotten who I am.
> I don't know if I live or die.
>
> And yet I send a telegram:
> "Let Marie and Johnny marry.
> They can sleep in my bed."
>
> For I shall not sleep
> ever on earth, ever in peace.
> For I shall never return.

Gabriel signed over his share of the business to his wife and children. From the first the checks went to her directly. He gave up his inheritance. With her common sense, Amparo adds, "And also his job." He set up house with Amparo in San Sebastián. "What audacity!" Amparo says. He now too became a pariah. But—*Hold me suspended in your eyes, never grave/ and let our day to day life always be magical!*

They held out in San Sebastián until 1956. His new life provided him with many themes. One in particular preoccupied him for many years: to lead the ordinary life of the common people, doggedly persisting and losing one's ego in shared experience. In a poem in the form of a letter to a friend of his previous life, he asserts that the complicity between elitist esthetics and the hunger the people suffer invites him *to be poor, banal, mute, any-body . . . . To dress, eat, earn one's bread, die/ are not vulgar mat-ters though you say so.*

For an anthology of the new poets published in 1952, he supplied, as each was requested to do, a poetic credo. It began: "Let us sing as if it were breathing. Let us talk about what we are engaged in doing every day. Let us not make poetry like someone leaving for seventh heaven or posing for posterity. Poetry is not—cannot be—intemporal or, as is said with a little laugh, eternal. We have to bet on *the here and now."* He wanted his poetry to speak for others and it did. He wanted to wipe out the "I" in his poetry and he failed. In the uncountable number of poems he has published there is much that is uneven, but each is distinctly his.

Indeed, he is the most self-conscious of poets. He offers the reader not only a detailed record of his life and the personal and political passions he has felt but also a critique of his own poetry. He can disarm the critics with: *Mine is not a poetry thought out drop by drop./ It is not a beautiful product. Nor a perfect fruit.* His objective was other: to change the Spanish world as he had changed his own. With Blas de Otero, he became the best known of the "social poets" before he left San Sebastián for Madrid. In the years between 1946, when he met Amparo, and 1956 he published fourteen collections of poetry, two in collaboration with her. This was a sign of fecundity and power and also of an ability to manipulate the language adroitly. He managed to be explicit and yet pass the strict censorship of those days.

He had a national reputation, but of course it did not provide him with a living. They had to close down Norte; it had been a luxury. On occasion he got work as an engineer on a freelance basis. Amparo found short-lived jobs. Amparo's family soon decided that Gabriel was a good man and they welcomed both back, but there was still too much feeling against them in San Sebastián. Each time Amparo went out she was snubbed. The authorities kept close watch: they were thought to be members of the Communist Party.

Amparo and Gabriel: A Basque Love Story

"They said I took up with him to get at his money," Amparo remembers, "but life was impossible for us in San Sebastián—we would have starved. I kept insisting we had to try our luck in Madrid, but he would not budge."

Gabriel is not a physically adventurous man. He knew Madrid only as a privileged student. San Sebastián was his hometown, and much as he made Amparo's life his own, Spanish society is more indulgent with men in situations like his. He did get to see his children occasionally and also his father, and although he was always to write in Castilian, Vizcaya was his homeland: he has almost never spent a year entirely away. In any case, all Spain was a prison. As a poem by his friend Blas de Otero said, *Here not even God can be saved/ They assassinated Him.*

"We had terrible quarrels," Amparo says, "and after one such I simply upped and went to Madrid. I found a very cheap apartment for us both and even a *situation* to keep us going. And *then* he came."

The "situation" was as secretaries and caretakers for a rich lady with a country home an hour out of Madrid in the province of Segovia. For years this provided them with a basic income. Gabriel also got freelance engineering jobs. And he wrote. There was never a year when he did not publish one or two books, sometimes three or four. But they barely got by. "And his guilt made him send anything extra to his children," Amparo says.

Three years before I showed up at their apartment in Madrid I had translated some poems by four of the "social poets," several of them by Gabriel, and published them in a literary quarterly. They paid twenty-five dollars for the poems and an introduction, and I thought it might seem less of an affront to the poets if I sent each a new crisp five-dollar bill and announced I was keeping five for myself. I learned later that the five dollars had been a nice windfall for Amparo and Gabriel.

In 1966 both Amparo and Gabriel were arrested at the Puerta del Sol at a demonstration in which only women were to participate. Some two dozen women were held in all. By our standards it was a timid demonstration; by theirs, at the time, audacious. The women who responded to leaflets either mailed or surreptitiously left in bars near the area simply walked in twos and threes about the Puerta del

75

Sol. They did not carry placards or call out slogans, and if they had not been arrested, the usual crowds to be found in Madrid's equivalent of Times Square might not have noticed anything unusual. The organizers of the demonstration—most likely, the Communist Party—wanted only women there, expecting that in a *macho* country the police would tolerate more from them. But Gabriel followed Amparo down there and hung around corners anxiously watching, and since he was well known, the police grabbed him. "The Party should have locked him in at home," a mutual friend later told me. "Everyone knows how he feels about his Amparitxu."

The women were held overnight; Gabriel three days. He was fined about two hundred dollars, and I collected money from New York intellectuals and sent it to him. To thank me he wrote a short piece on García Lorca based on his acquaintance with him during his student days. He expected that I could easily publish it and thus be repaid. Of course, only a literary quarterly took it. They paid forty dollars when they published it a year later, and since I was passing through Madrid at the time, I handed him the money less apologetically than the first time. Amparo cursed. Gabriel explained that a week earlier he had been offered forty-five dollars for an entire book. To this day no Spanish writer makes a living from his books. A few do from their entire output, but that has to include much journalism and some commercial screenplays. It follows that I have been unable to find more than two or three of working-class origin.

As if to emphasize what little resources poets command in Spain, Gabriel told me during my 1967 visit that Yevtushenko had just been there expecting to give a reading in Spain. "He unashamedly proposed that we organize it for him. We had some two dozen persons here at a party for him when he told us. No one said a word—how to explain about police permits and the problem of finding someone who would rent us a suitable hall for such a subversive event? But he persisted, and it came out that he expected to read to multitudes at the *fútbol* stadium. I had had enough to drink by then, so I was the one to tell him—'With the exception of possibly one hundred students at the University, no one has heard of you in Spain. Poets count for nothing.' "

That Amparo and Gabriel only got by in Madrid did not mean that they lived to themselves. The entire intellectual community are their friends. There are few art openings or literary cocktail parties to which they are not invited. Amparo was accepted from the first. Still, one reason I did not find Gabriel's phone in the directory is that it was taken under Amparo's name, as is the modest apartment they have finished paying for. She cannot inherit from him, and if the apartment were in his name, her only possible legal status would be that she is a friend of the owner or renter. "Worse," Amparo adds, "his kept woman."

They have not had children, and that has made things simpler for them. Yet the Spanish expectation that childless bohemians will not remain faithful to one another has been confounded. They have never strayed. In the sixties Gabriel was shocked to have a literary foreigner, at a gathering in Mallorca for the Formentor Prize, suggest to him, after a night of much drinking, that each retire to the other's bedroom. It took him a moment to understand the man's proposal. "I hope you understand that I do not think that your wife is unattractive," he replied. "It is simply that I prefer Amparo."

"No, no, I must say that the friends we have made have always been very respectful," Amparo says. "Of course, it is not very flattering that none of the men has ever made a pass at me." A few years ago, Gabriel's sister, who never married, stopped Amparo in the street in San Sebastián and introduced herself. It made Amparo feel good. "Imagine what it must have cost her to do that."

In the last few years they discovered that Gabriel's father did not entirely disinherit him. He left him a small part of his own share in the family business. Their accountant hopes that it can be arranged for Amparo to receive this when Gabriel dies. Under Spanish law she cannot be willed the copyright to his many works. Not even for his share of the two volumes they co-authored. It must go to his children who, now in their thirties, are proud of his work. "And his royalties," Amparo adds. All this hurts her. During their first years in Madrid she wrote one or two books for children, but she has for a long time devoted all her energies to him—as housewife, hostess, secretary, and unofficial editor.

It may be that she stopped writing because Gabriel appropriates all the material of their lives. In 1965, Amparo told me an affecting incident of the time when they were first in Madrid. She traveled to Burgos each week to see her brother in jail; she was the only one in the family near enough to visit him, so she went regularly. After a while she got to know the other people who went there by the same train, and it bothered her that one working-class woman remained unapproachable. The woman's jailed son looked ill; indeed, worse on each visit. One day Amparo noticed that the woman was not called into the long room where they talked with the prisoners. Amparo saw her on the walk back across town to the railroad station, and she tried to catch up with her. Before she got to her, the woman paused at a short bridge, took out black stockings, and leaning against the side of the bridge, put them on. She squared her shoulders and walked on. Amparo hung back. Two years after she told me about it, this incident appeared as a poem in Gabriel's collection *Lo que faltaba*.

"In the early sixties the so-called social poetry underwent a crisis," Gabriel writes in the introduction to *Itinerario poético*, published in 1975. "I think this was due less to the exhaustion of its possibilities than to the incredible diffusion it attained despite the bad auspices under which it was born. Due also to the weariness that any dominant literary current produces and to the proliferation of epigones that, as always happens, managed to turn into a cliché what had begun as a dazzling discovery. To this must be added that the climate of furor and hope in which it was born had been extinguished with the passage of years during which no other change was produced than our country's first steps towards a consumer society."

He goes on to say, like the good Marxist he had once been, that this demonstrated once more how the cultural superstructure is dependent on the socio-economic base which produces it, and points out that many rebel poets accommodated themselves to the new situation. He himself tried to return to his origins, hoping to find a new poetic vision, and ended by breaking with Marxism and the Party. He adds sadly, "When one is my age it is difficult to overcome certain disillusions. And even when one thinks one is explaining, one may be doing no more than rationalizing vital faults. Nevertheless, this may be more honest than exploiting old positions." He now believes that "as nuclear physics shows us, we are submerged in a world of structures that function beyond what is humanly possible for us to comprehend."

But time has played Gabriel another trick. His old books were reissued, and a new generation has discovered them. At the 1975 Book Fair in Retiro Park in Madrid, a few months after he wrote the above, there were such long lines the day he came to autograph his books that extra police were called to keep them orderly. *Cantos iberos*, published before he left San Sebastián for Madrid, sold 20,000 copies that year. The most famous poem in this militantly political collection—*Poetry Is a Weapon Loaded with the Future*—was put to music in the late sixties by Paco Ibañez, a singer-composer raised in France by his exiled parents, and it has made its way throughout the Spanish-speaking world. A Spanish worker-priest in Uruguay, released from jail at the behest of the Church and the Spanish embassy in Montevideo, brought Gabriel the thrilling news in 1975 that the cells of the political prisoners in that country would resound with Gabriel's lyrics each time one of them was taken away to be tortured: it was their way of telling one another to hold out.

In February 1976, we are together downstairs at José Luis in Madrid, a bar with a tiny dining room in the cellar. It has an urbane maître and a superb chef, and is much in fashion. The previous evening we had all been at a concert that had turned into a political demonstration. It had been the first time in years that Raimon, a Catalan singer and composer of protest songs, had been allowed to perform. The elite of the opposition to the regime was there in the first twenty rows, and the youth everywhere. In the first row were leaders of political parties, some of them men who had been in jail for years and all of them prominent public personalities. Yet it was when Amparo and Gabriel walked in as just two other members of that distinguished audience that the entire arena first got to its feet. They chanted his name.

Such was the crush and the excitement that I had been unable to get to them. I tell them this now at José Luis and ask them how they had felt about the unexpected ovation. (I already knew from the morning's papers that Amparo had responded with a raised fist and that Gabriel had signed autographs even in the men's room.) "How did I feel?" Amparo asks. "I gave them the fist—I have never changed." I turned to Gabriel. "Me? I cried," he says. Amparo laughs. "His big, fat, Basque tears," she says. "The old guilt—it still operates."

Another table at the restaurant has caught Amparo's attention. A man and his young son are having lunch together. Amparo whispers, "See, what I was telling you about separations now being common? It is the father's day with his son. I can tell." She suppresses her first excitement at the sight; she has realized that it is not a matter for rejoicing.

She thinks of something else. "I was putting out the wash this morning when a neighbor, a woman who once barely nodded to me, was doing hers, and she said to me, 'I have a clipping from the newspaper for you. It mentions your husband's name.' She said, 'Your *husband*.'"

5
Woman in the Public Eye

I was not the first Spanish woman to live openly with a man. Perhaps Amparo was," Marisa begins, bending forward to light a cigarette with the silver lighter on the elegant coffee table. "But I may have been the second. Also, I took some steps that others did not—most live with men who cannot divorce their wives, but I left a husband and I have had a child with Rogelio." She sits with her back to the sliding glass doors to the balcony of her apartment in the middle-class Princesa section of Madrid. The draperies are drawn, but the light is diffused by the filmy, floor-length curtains. There is a tray of coffee before us, and the well-appointed furniture, the book-lined walls, the unspoken sense that there are no pressures, that all is ease—these create a strange, incongruous setting for the telling of her story, intense and anguished from early childhood. She talks for three hours.

My family comes from Toledo. Both my mother and father. Their ancestors there go back so far that although their last names were the same and their families were proud of their genealogies, they did not know that they were distantly related. They found out when the Church required, before marrying them, that they come in with their family trees, in case some dispensation were necessary should they turn out to be cousins. It was not necessary. I don't suppose there would have been any real trouble—they belonged to the good families who ran things in Toledo. But this did not help when the Civil War came—it was Toledo, after all.

(Marisa takes for granted that everyone knows what happened in Toledo at the beginning of the war. When the uprising came, the Army and the Falangists were unable to take the city, and retreated into the palace-fortress on the northeast fringe of the city, on a high bluff above the river Tagus, a structure known as the Alcázar since the thirteenth century. About one thousand men holed up there, and they took their families and some hostages with them. The two-month siege by Republican militiamen, during which the defenders of the Alcázar held out bravely against rifle-fire, arson, and dynamiting, was ended when Franco's Army took Toledo towards the end of September 1936, after its swift conquest of Andalusia. The defense and relief of the Alcázar became the symbol of the Nationalists' determination and heroism; the selflessness of its defenders the grand example of Franco's cause. The rights and wrongs on either side have never ceased to be argued; to have chosen the losing side has been judged by the Francoists as so grievous a fault that it is scarcely to be countenanced.)

My father was a liberal Republican. Not the only one of his class to be a Republican, but he was, though mildly so. Still, he was Secretary of the City Council when the war broke out, and remained in this post until the city fell. And he felt strongly enough about the Republic to take his family—my mother, my sister, and me—to Alicante which remained in the Republican zone until the very end. I learned years later—for I was three when the war came, six when it ended—that during the last week of the Republic he spent a terrible twenty-four-hour period when he did not sleep, trying to decide what to do. There were still ships and planes to take us into exile, and it was up to him whether we got on one of them.

He knew about the concentration camps in France and he could imagine what life in exile would be like. Could he take my mother, a provincial upper-middle-class girl, away for good, and rear his girls in an alien country? What had he to fear in his own case? In Toledo he had been a prominent Republican, but in those first angry days after the uprising he had saved many individuals of the upper class from bands of Republican militiamen who attempted to take them out at night for a *paseo*. There would be desperate phonecalls to him at our house and he would order a guard to the home of those threatened. This was bound to be remembered, and with the war over, passions must subside. They should get by. He decided to take us all back to Toledo. He was immediately jailed. Three times he was tried on different charges and three times condemned to death. He spent seven years in jail. Two of them in death row, never knowing if the next morning he was to be executed.

None of the people whose lives he had saved spoke up for him. No one made the slightest gesture on his behalf, much less appeared in court to defend him. Except for a brother-in-law, a doctor who like all his family connections had remained in Toledo with the Nationalists. He wrote a cautious letter to the court—it was too dangerous to do more for a Red—saying that my father had been a man of humane and honest conduct. I remember too that he was the only one to come see us. When we were ill, he treated us free. My grandmother, my father's mother, lived with us, of course, and since my mother's parents were dead, there was no one else who came near us. It was my mother alone who saved father's life.

It was a kind of miracle—not so much that he was saved but that *she* did it. What was she, after all, but a provincial heiress? She had been taught to say *s'il vous plaît, la fenêtre, la maison*, and to tinkle on the piano. She was timid and ignorant—to be frank, dumb. But now she showed a capacity for action and such indefatigable energy that it astounded everyone. She herself contacted lawyers in Toledo and Madrid, she went to anyone with the slightest influence, she followed up every suggestion anyone made, she got past doors that wished to remain closed. Two and three times a month she went to Madrid—leaving us with grandmother—to plead with influential people and to get advice from lawyers. At first she was intent on proving his innocence and getting him freed, but very soon all her efforts were simply bent on delaying his execution. Stop that and then she would think about the next step.

All this was enough to keep her busy, but she also had to work as hard to find us a place to live. The mansion in Toledo had been thoroughly sacked and then confiscated and closed up. They would not let her have it. She pleaded for a year before they finally ceded her the use of one room, but since this dispensation did not include a kitchen or bath, we could not settle there. The farm outside the city which mother inherited from her parents had not only a large house but many small outbuildings, and it was there, in one of those

83

little places, that we spent almost two years. The house and other buildings were turned over to lowly families of the victors—Army sergeants, Civil Guards and such—and I remember playing with their children and always having to repress my feelings. It was hard—I was always very outgoing.

So you see, it was not simple for mother to do what she did. I think of her heading for Toledo each day—on foot most of the time—to see father in jail there, to see lawyers, to plead with the authorities in charge of confiscated property, to catch a train to Madrid—how did she do it? And then getting back, usually at night, through the countryside. It was remarkable, remarkable. Especially since there was such little hope, and people not only did not want to help they did not even want to see her. I must not say that—there were the old tenants on the farm who gave us food. Still, it must have seemed hopeless. But before two years were up she won some victories—father had not been executed and the authorities allowed her the use of another room and the kitchen in the house in Toledo, and so we all moved back there where my sister and I could go to school again.

My sister and I. We reacted in opposite ways to all this. She became withdrawn and quiet and very studious—she grew up to be an important academician in the sciences. I was aggressive and bold. I loved to play, and for a long time I refused to learn to read and write. But I would not compromise to make friends. When the girls asked one another at school what their fathers did—you know how middle-class girls are, concerned with status from childhood on—I always said right out, My father is in jail. Their eyes would open very wide and then they would never come near me again.

Being in Toledo gave mother greater mobility. Also, it made it possible for her or grandmother every day to leave a basket with clean clothes and food at the jail for father, and to visit him as often as they allowed. I was still a youngster, and it was a while before I realized with what anxiety they went there. They had no assurance that he had not been executed at dawn. Twice a week I went with one or the other, sometimes just to leave the basket for him and to pick up the one from the day before. I shall never forget the first time I noticed grandmother crying when she was given the basket with his dirty clothes. I saw them. They were bloody. Later, I overheard that this was not the first time it happened. They knew that he was regularly beaten. Now I knew it too; I do not remember ever looking inside the basket again.

Another vivid memory is of him in death row. I do not know whether that was while we lived in the country or after we were in the house in Toledo. It could have been both, for he was sentenced to death three times. I remember our standing in the corridor outside his cell talking to him. Between us was wiring, bars, and another layer of wiring. I liked visiting him. It was not sorrowful—father always talked cheerfully and asked me many questions about school. One morning I said to the guard—I had not planned to say it, it just came to me there—that I wanted to kiss my father. The guard must have been unprepared for such a request. He allowed father to walk behind the bars and wiring to a cell at the far end that had a tiny window into the corridor. Father crouched and I was able to kiss him.

They got to know us there. The other prisoners would greet me and I would exchange pleasantries with them. Across from father's cell was a prisoner I became most friendly with. He was an ordinary Republican soldier and he had the wonderful old-fashioned name of Cresencio. He was not in his cell one day, and I noticed it immediately. Where is Cresencio? I asked. My father said, Cresencio is not here anymore, and that was all. I do not know if I knew, but I knew enough not to ask for him again. I think it was then I realized that the same thing could happen to father.

That miserable jail. It was an infested hole—rats and vermin of all kinds. Yet every six days we visitors—the children included—were forced to disrobe and be examined and fumigated. As if we could have infested that jail any more than it already was. There were so many prisoners in Toledo, as there were everywhere in the country, that a new jail was built. Rather, improvised out of empty warehouses, in the area between the old city walls and the river. It was especially humid down there and it was the home of armies of rats. Father was in that jail when he was once more tried and for the third time sentenced to death in the notorious case known as the *Expediente del Tesoro de la Catedral*—the Case of the Cathedral's Treasury.

A large group of men were tried together and condemned for

stealing the treasures of the Cathedral, one of them the famous mantle of the Virgin of Sagrario with its one hundred thousand pearls. Santa Rita, she was known as. You can go to the Cathedral now and see all those damn things back in the Treasury. No one knows how they suddenly showed up. But when I think of the number of men who were executed for that accursed Santa Rita! Again, father's sentence was not carried out, all due to mother's appeals. She had found a lawyer in Madrid who was able to move people in various quarters, and she even had hopes the lawyer would get him a new trial.

The last vivid memory I have of father in jail is his removal from that horrible place by the river. We were not, of course, told. The word got out among the relatives of the prisoners one night that they were going to be taken away at four in the morning. No one knew what this meant—everything was always done in ways to cause as much fear and suffering as possible. It was a cold and misty winter morning. I shall always remember the scene at the railroad station. They had expected to do it all secretly and the thick fog seemed to help. Still, we could see—the four of us were there to at least get a look at father and perhaps to be seen by him—that there were here and there little clusters like ours, no one talking for fear of being told to leave, and standing at a distance from the tracks where a freight train waited. How timid that sounds when I tell it now, but in those days it took courage just to be there waiting.

They came out of the mist, the long line of them. They were manacled with their hands behind their backs, and shackled in groups of four, and made to walk two in front and two behind. Slowly, the families began to move closer. There were guards everywhere. The families called out farewells to their men; they did not dare go right up to them. I saw father when grandmother called out his name. I asked a guard to let me kiss him. This time I had thought about it in advance. He let me. The next thing I remember is the prisoners entering the freight train awkwardly, in their chains. In father went, and when you thought the car was full, we saw them squeeze more and more in—we stood there astounded and helpless.

But mother learned that very day that they were being taken to a new jail in Madrid—Carabanchel. Father had the dubious honor of inaugurating that place. God only knows how many political prisoners it has housed until this very day. He was farther away from us now, but at least he was out of that hole by the river. Mother went to Madrid more often, and there began to be hope, real hope for a new trial. The nights when mother returned from a visit to father and the lawyer we would sit up speculating endlessly. We would fall asleep in our chairs, wake up, and start speculating again. Finally, a new trial was scheduled, and the lawyer began to predict that he could at least get the death sentence commuted. It was 1946, the Nazis had lost, and the regime was trying to rid itself of the fascist stigma. After all, there was no evidence against father but that he had been Secretary of the City Council.

None of us could be at the trial, of course. Like the others it was a closed military trial, and the lawyer advised us to stay in Toledo. There was no phone at home. Mother and the rest of us were to go to a public phone and call a friend in Madrid. I do not know how often we called before there was an answer at the other end. And then it was father himself who answered! We got on the first train to Madrid. He was out on *libertad vigilada*, a kind of strict parole, and he was to live no closer than forty miles from Toledo. Father elected to live in Madrid.

It was like a grand holiday to live in Madrid and without the old fear for father. Mother went back to being mother; father a lawyer again, and the properties which had been returned in part provided more income. In the changed atmosphere we even had family friends again. Father found a school for the two of us that was not oppressive, a place called the Gymnasium, as all German schools were called. One term we were inundated with the daughters of Nazis who had fled here, but the next term only five remained, for their parents had realized by then that it was a liberal place with a non-clerical atmosphere. The headmistress was very careful, how-ever; the school passed all the government inspections. I owe a lot to that school, I who once had not wanted to read or write. I know, for example, that its language training was superior to any you got in Spanish schools, state or private. It was their way of opening our minds to other worlds than our miserable one.

From there I went to the University. We were middle-class girls, but our father believed in education for us. I enrolled in law school, as earlier my sister had decided to major in sciences, without any

---

opposition from my parents. Mother was not enthusiastic, but father certainly approved. There I met my first husband. I call him my first husband though Rogelio and I have not been able to marry legally. Still, I consider that marriage is not a matter of laws and that Rogelio is my real husband. The other I divorced when I told him at the time, I divorce you. Indeed, he married again and had children, just as I did. But at the time he did not accept it. He could do nothing about it, however, because he was in jail then.

When I met him he was a teaching assistant working for his doctorate. I was very much in love with him, and I was with him all the time after my classes were done. We had friends, of course. Other university students. We talked endlessly, but like any good Spanish girl I was home at nine in time for dinner. There was no possibility of our going to bed, even if there had been a place or opportunity. With my upbringing it simply could not have happened—it was unthinkable. So the night when we forgot the hour—we had gone on walking and talking after we left the others—we were quite innocent. It was suddenly eleven-thirty. I will take you home, he said, and I will go with you and explain. But I knew it would not be as easy as that.

On my block, I told him we could not just go upstairs to my apartment and walk in on the family. Let me call first, I said, and went into a café on the street and called. Father answered the phone and I told him what had happened, that we had not kept track of the time. Where are you? he asked. Downstairs, I said. He told me to stay at the café and that he would come down. He arrived with a delegation—my godparents had happened to be visiting and they came down with him. We sat at a table as if it were a trial. What has happened? father asked. I repeated what I had said on the phone. Father said I was ruined, my godmother that my reputation was now soiled. The young man protested. There is nothing to worry about, he said, I will marry her. And father said, I should hope so.

Two months later we were properly married. Why should either of us have objected? We were in love—at least, I was—and sex was what we were longing for. Here we were being told that we could now go to bed—why should we say no? Nothing about our lives was going to change—just sex and in the best bedroom in the house. We waited as long as we did to get married—two months—because his family objected. They were a well-to-do provincial family, and perhaps because he was their first-born they cut him off. We had nothing to do with them while we were married. But father supported us. He was to continue to work for his doctorate and I for my degree.

We spent the next four months in bed. I suppose his studies suffered. Certainly mine did. Anyway, there was also trouble at the University. We were, of course, left-wingers, and those were the years when the University was busy with activity against the regime. I suppose it was a combination of things—his views and the stupidity of the courses and professors—that made it seem unlikely he could get a doctorate. It did not faze him. He thought up a plan for studying in Germany. He would work hard there and get his degree. Father agreed to pay for it all—it sounded so grand and ambitious. He went alone. It would have cost too much for both of us. Besides, I was now pregnant—my University career was over after two years of studies. He would return after the first term in time for the baby's birth.

He returned accompanied by German friends. I could see that he had changed. He was out with them a great deal; he was showing them Madrid, and of course, you did not go out with a pregnant wife. He was still leading a student's life, but differently now—it was obvious to all that he had been introduced to fast ways in Germany. He did not change his habits when the baby was born. I was tied to the house with the baby, of course, but I began to hear from friends how he spent his evenings. I would remonstrate with him when he got home late and drunk. He beat me. It happened time and again. One night when father was not home, he became particularly violent. Mother regained her old spirit and took matters in hand—she threw him out of the house.

Our baby girl did not draw him back. He had not the slightest interest in her. I saw him outside—mother would not have him in the house though father did not like it that she had interfered—and I tried to discuss what we were to do. Nothing came of it. He was simply going to return to Germany for the next term. Everything was unresolved between us, and I had managed to become pregnant again. He said to me, I do not care about the children, when I said we had a responsibility towards them. He was always to say, "My children will be raised by others," and that is what happened with our two girls. My sister shared the care of them from the first to help me out, and then came to feel like a mother to them.

Since my then husband was still being supported in Germany by my father, I went to work. I got odd teaching jobs, sometimes just tutoring at home, and after the second girl was born, as a secretary. He did not come back when she was born, and I decided to go see him in Germany to get things straight between us. "Will you come back and be my husband?" I asked him. He said yes, he was ready to come back, but he had conditions. We had to live independently. He did not mean by this that we should support ourselves but that we live by ourselves and the girls with my parents. I agreed. Anything to save the marriage, as I had been taught.

I came ahead to Madrid. I found an apartment, painted and furnished it, and found another job for myself. Then he came and announced that he wanted to take the course for the journalism degree that had just been added to the University of Madrid's curriculum. He had decided that this, not philosophy and teaching, was the career for him, and with such a degree he had a better chance. This was true—with the School of Journalism the regime hoped to turn out newspapermen loyal to it. It made sense, and again father supported him in it. He and mother kept the girls, since my sister was very attached to them and that way I could keep on working and carry our living expenses. Thus we made another start.

I worked, spent some time each day with the girls, and then came home and cooked and cleaned. He was presumably studying, but the apartment was always full of his friends until all hours. There were parties there—orgies, I should say—and I often was obliged to clear them out. It was a scandal. He and his friends were out to *épater les bourgeois*, and I could see in our neighbors' faces just what they thought of us all. It did not seem to me a very useful kind of rebellion but I was too unhappy to think much about anything. I knew he was unfaithful to me, but he was not about to leave such a good situation.

Still, he did finish the journalism course and was offered a job on a newspaper in Bilbao. It meant separation from the girls, but that did not count with him. He would have preferred Madrid, of course, but it was a post on a newspaper, after all, and Bilbao was not exactly a backwater. I went along with him—I found another apartment, set it up, and once more got myself a job to help carry it. And it *was* interesting there. That was the time of the first illegal strikes. We were caught up in this hopeful activity, and we could see by the number of foreign newspapermen who arrived to cover all this that it was important. He began sending news abroad in secret. The newspapermen who came to Bilbao went to him for information, and he started to make a name for himself. My job was only a secretarial one, but my evenings and weekends were full of excitement that was meaningful.

I was in San Sebastián the weekend they arrested him. An old school friend had gone up there for a week and asked me to join her for the weekend. I still had my job and I could not spend much more than a day with her, so I took a late train back and instead of going home, I went to friends in Bilbao closer to the railroad station and to my work, where I should have to be in just a few hours. It was they who told me. He had been arrested with a group of activists on the usual charge of Communist subversion. Some of them were Communists, of course, but he was not. Not then. The group was transferred to Madrid, and although the censorship was so strict that nothing of this was allowed to appear in the newspapers here, there was much publicity abroad and pressure for their release.

I had long ago lost faith in him as a husband—as a person, also, for although I agreed with his politics and would not for a moment have betrayed them, I did not trust his motives. My duty then was to be in Madrid to help. Again I dismantled our apartment and followed him. They were all in jail, but the publicity and pressure had their effect—the government announced that their trial would be an open one. Not only relatives but newspapermen would be permitted; the first time such a thing was allowed since the Republic.

I do not know what the regime hoped to gain by holding one of its summary trials in the presence of foreigners who could publish what they saw. My then husband planned to make a speech in court, but like all the others he was not allowed to make a plea in his own defense. The judge cut him off, but he managed to say something that caused a sensation. He had a gift for that kind of passionate outburst. He called out loudly, "I here and now apply for membership in the Communist Party of Spain!" He was a hero to everyone.

To me too. And I joined the wives of all the other prisoners when we were permitted—such are the contradictions of this regime—to accompany them on the train to Burgos where they were to start serving their long sentences. It was a joyful train ride in its way.

I came back to Madrid to live with my parents and my girls, and I got another of those secretarial jobs for which I was by now well qualified. My parents could not have been more solicitous. My father would go up to Burgos with me to visit him. Sometimes he went on his own. In the eyes of good-hearted people my then husband had turned out to be a good man and consequently a good husband—he was in jail for a good cause. I was a martyr's wife. We had many friends and acquaintances from these years in Madrid and Bilbao, and they made sure to include me in things. Besides, we were all involved in semi-clandestine political activity, and all this kept me occupied.

I met Rogelio at an art opening. My husband had written some art criticism in his last year at the School of Journalism, and so I had met intellectuals and artists who asked me to the galleries. I had heard of Rogelio. He had already written a couple of screenplays for our new serious directors and several that were strictly commercial, and his face looked familiar, so I must have seen him at other openings. We fell in love. Real love. We wanted to live together as husband and wife. I no longer had the foolish moral scruples I had as a student, when for the sake of appearances I was forced to marry, but I had other scruples now. Ideological ones that prevented me from divorcing my husband while he was in jail, and profound moral ones that told me I must not deal with this love for Rogelio as just an affair.

The second one won out. Oh, the immoral advice I received from friends. Sleep with Rogelio—what is there to prevent you?—and remain the other one's wife. That seemed really evil to me. I wanted to marry Rogelio and make a home with him. Rogelio left the decision to me. He would support me in whatever I wanted to do, and he would not pressure me: he would be there whatever I decided. Divorce my first husband, marry Rogelio, these were actions of my own defining—legally neither was possible. I went up to Burgos one visiting day and I said to him, "I divorce you—we are no longer husband and wife." He was outraged, but there was nothing he could do to me. He could not beat me and he could not harass me. He has never forgiven me.

I think I knew that his being in jail was the best occasion for divorcing him. God knows what would have happened if he had been free to carry out his rage. I had done the worst thing you could do to a man of his kind—I had wounded his pride. His left-wing politics did not make him less a *macho*. I had divorced him. He will never forgive me. He has made any kind of amicable settlement impossible. There could have been a legal separation, but he will agree to nothing. Even if I were the kind that were willing to get an annulment through the Church, as has become possible in the last few years, by paying one million pesetas, that too would have been out of the question, though it would have freed him to marry the woman with whom he now has a couple of children.

For two years my father did not speak to me. To make his position clear he went to Burgos frequently to visit my husband in jail. My mother, who for the years father was in jail had been so bold for a woman, also disapproved of me, but she did not stop talking to me. In both cases you could say she played a traditional woman's role— to fight for her husband's life and to remain long-suffering with her daughter. The girls stayed with them or, rather, with my sister, to whom they were closer than to me. I suppose my parents saw it as a way of saving the girls from the scandal, but I did it because it was better for them, less disruptive. I certainly was not going to stop seeing them and I never have. My sister was married by then and unable to have children, so they have been part of a real home where they are wanted. And Charo, my daughter with Rogelio, is close to them.

When Rogelio and I married—we *are* married—and moved in together, I learned who my real friends were. Anytime I left the apartment I walked as if the streets were a large empty space. I looked at no one. I always waited to be greeted first. Very few did greet me, and those were embarrassed. When I was pregnant with Charo, it was worse. It is only recently that you see properly married women out in the street when they are obviously pregnant. You can imagine the scandal that trailed after me! When I went out with Rogelio, my so-called friends acted differently. After all, Rogelio was Rogelio Bermudez, the famous screenwriter, so they would greet me hypocritically. Dear Marisa, one does not see you anymore, what have you been doing with yourself, and so on. The whole experience was like a kind of purgatory. Not for me—it was they who were purged from my affections.

I was immensely happy to have Charo. You can understand that, I am sure. How wonderful to have a child when you are happily married. I had not had that experience, and I lay in the hospital bed glorying in how well everything had turned out. It was then that Luis, my gynecologist, broke the news. He wanted to be the one to tell me. I must explain about Luis. He is the gynecologist for a whole stratum of intellectuals and artists here in Madrid. You will find him at theater and art openings and later at Bocaccio's with people of our set, and Rogelio jokes that he knows all the wives more intimately than the husbands do. I say all this to make it clear that Luis broke the news to me as a friend who thought about things the way we do. I could not, he told me, appear on Charo's birth certificate!

For just a second, I thought Luis was joking with me. Then he explained that since Rogelio's civil status was that of a bachelor that no name could appear on the form as the mother. Put down my name! I cried. Under the law, he insisted, he had to write *Unknown*. It meant, too, that Charo could not carry my surname as is the tradition with us here, only Rogelio's. I was beside myself. What is to prevent you from putting down my name? I said. He not only would be breaking the law himself, he said, but he would be inviting a charge of adultery against me by the authorities. Should they want to harass me or Rogelio, this would be a perfect excuse. Charo would have to appear forever on her birth certificate as a bachelor's child, not even as *my* illegitimate daughter.

I don't know how long I kept Luis there with me answering my questions. It always came back to the same thing—there were no options but what the birth certificate form provided. He pointed out to me, as a kind of consolation, that there was one further blank to fill if the mother is unknown. The form asks, *Signs of Identity of the Mother,* and there he could write *Marisa*. Just Marisa, nothing else. If the authorities could not under these conditions charge me with adultery, my legal husband still could. He was out of jail now—his sentence had been reduced—and there was a period of thirty days after my having given birth when he could effectively denounce me.

It seemed unlikely, but I did experience a certain suspense until the month was up. I am sure his politics did not allow him, for he was a prominent Communist now. That worked in my favor, not his real feelings.

Charo was barely out of her infancy when again I came across a situation in which my identity was denied. We were already living in this apartment. Rogelio had bought it under his name. We had not given that any thought, anymore than I had anticipated problems with the birth certificate. One day a young man came to the door and left us census forms to fill out and said he would return in two or three days to pick them up and to answer any questions we might have. I was reading them quite casually and filling them out when I realized that after listing Rogelio as the head of the family and Charo as daughter of the family, I could only appear under the heading of *Other Tenants*. Under that heading, all I could reply was that I was either a relative or a friend.

I said to Rogelio, "I am not your relative and I do not want it to appear anywhere that I am your friend." We discussed it, and of course Rogelio had no objection to my taking a stand on this matter. We decided that after listing my name I would draw a line through the space where I was supposed to write one or the other of the two categories permitted. When the young man returned—he was just a young fellow hired temporarily to complete the census and anxious to pick up the forms and be gone—I asked him to come in because there was a problem with the form. I told him plainly what my relationship with Rogelio was and showed him what I had done with the form.

He remonstrated. "But it must be completed the way it indicates," he kept repeating. I told him this would be a lie on my part, that since the form did not permit me to write down anything but relative or friend and not, as in more civilized countries, common-law wife, it was quite reasonable of me to draw a line through the space. "But I will get in trouble when they review it at headquarters," he said. I said to him, "You write in the margin that you pointed out my deficiency in filling out this question and that I shall be happy to go to your superiors to explain if they have any questions." He settled for this. He also said, "I admire your courage," for in two or three homes there were women with the same problem but they found the alternatives given convenient. So he turned in the form as I had filled it and we waited and waited, screwing up our courage to fight it legally. Nothing happened.

The next census was a couple of years ago, and I like to think that what I did was done by others, for this time there was a slot for what you call a common-law wife. The fact is that our society has changed so much, despite the regime and the old traditions—there is such an enormous push from below that I think we shall see changes sooner than in other places. Think of it, we still labor under the accursed Napoleonic Code which even the French have given up. Nevertheless, we are on the verge of great changes in the status of women. When it comes, I think we shall go farther than the Italians despite their having had a democracy all these years. We are certainly ready for it.

For practically all of Franco's years the only organization for women was that of the Falange, the one that José Antonio's sister heads. They have talked—talked, that is all—about women being given weight and value in the country's life. But for them divorce and such things are libertinage. The Legally Separated Women's organization is the only feminist group at the moment. And there is the women lawyers' group. There are also radical feminists, and they are beginning to get together, but it is all at a very early stage. In the main, feminists are divided between those who are political and believe social change will free women and those who think women's liberation has to be fought for separately and right now. I lean towards the latter. Equality for women must be fought for everywhere, particularly in the home, and finally women must fight the enemy within themselves.

Still, I do not discount the purely legalistic fight, like that of the women lawyers. Because 1976 is International Women's Year, a few rights have been conceded us. We can now inherit property on our own, which means my mother can now leave me part of the family farm, and Rogelio can make me his heir. Would you believe that until this year my first husband would have got whatever was willed me? We can also now apply for a passport without our husbands' permission, and we can even engage in some business transactions in our own name.

Yes, things have changed and will change a lot more. I do not belong to the women who are organizing. They have come to me and asked me to join them. I approve, I wholeheartedly approve. I tell them so, but I also say I cannot become an activist. I have had enough . . . I am sorry. After all, I am a bit like my mother. I am willing to tell you my story, but I will keep you to your promise to change all the names of persons and places and make me unrecognizable. I do not want to be in the public eye anymore.

6

Young Waiters in Madrid: A Cartoon

I owe to Luis Carandell this particular corner of the maze that the Church has made of sexuality in Spain. The School of Pharmacy in Granada instructs its students, as follows, on obtaining semen specimens for fertility tests: married men are to use a perforated condom, since it will always retain sufficient liquid; bachelors are to wait for spontaneous ejaculation.

Aniano first talked to me on New Year's Day, 1976. He showed up that morning at my apartment in a Madrid hotel to tend the mini-bar, a job usually done by a young woman who was always taciturn, probably out of wariness. He had served me *café con leche* and *churros* at the cafeteria counter on the ground floor a couple of mornings when I was on the run, but we had never more than exchanged greetings. Now Aniano crouched at the small refrigerator stocked with soft drinks, beer, liquor, cocktail nuts, and one bottle of champagne, unlocked it with his passkey, and said, "I see you did not celebrate here last night." I replied that I had been out with friends. "I spent a quiet evening," I added. "But you at your age—you must wish you did not have to work this morning." I chuckled in the accusing and encouraging manner older men have with young bachelors; we like to think that boys like Aniano are disporting themselves in ways we now imagine were usual with us during our own salad days. Aniano stood up, sighed, glanced away from me, and said, "I think it was the saddest day of my life."

"You did not go out?" I said.

He shook his head.

"Then you stayed home with your family?"

Young Waiters in Madrid: A Cartoon

He shook his head again. "They are all back in Zamora," he said. "I live with my sister, but she went home to be with them."

"No friends?" I said.

"It is a long story," he said. Two days later, when he again came to restock the mini-bar—he was working sixteen hours a day that week—I asked him if he would tell me his story. "*Pero yo soy un humilde, no tiene interés,*" he said. "But I am a lowly person, it would not be interesting."

We made a date to meet during the afternoon of his next day off, at a bar on Gran Vía. There were two at that spot, and I headed for the jazzier bar with standard modern décor, which called itself, as new eating places in Spain now do, a *cafetería*. Aniano came out to get me from the bar which, although recently redecorated, was more solidly middle class. Its clients were mostly businessmen, and the only women there were middle-aged ladies with their husbands. Aniano led me to a table with too much energy for a regular of the place but with the sober pleasure of one who wishes to be viewed as such. He also ordered his snifter of a Spanish brandy with the preciseness of someone who long ago settled for that particular brand: he was happy to be a man.

"I am not used to complaining about my lot, as I did the other day," he told me after we were served. "You caught me at an unguarded moment, but I also have to admit that I am a romantic. I was feeling sorry for myself because I was all alone on New Year's Eve. I had called my old sweetheart and she was very courteous, but that was all. I said that I had been thinking of old times and wanted to wish her well for the new year, but I was really hoping that she did not have a date and we could take up our old romance."

I nodded sympathetically. "It is difficult to talk about, isn't it?" I said. He sipped his brandy and nodded manfully. I wondered how best to encourage this stoical young man, but before I could ask another question he was launched on his story. We were there two and a half hours, and we were to talk often again during that month at the hotel's cafeteria when he sometimes served me lunch. It turned out that he loved talking and that when he said that he was a romantic, he meant that he was a *macho*—an old-fashioned Spanish male—in a changed social situation.

I have to admit that I am scarcely out of the eggshell, he began. I

99

am twenty years old and it is only five months since I finished my *mili*, eighteen months in the Army which were very much like everyone else's. But I have been working since I was fourteen and first came to Madrid from Zamora, and there is much in life that I have already suffered. I do not remember my father, for example. He died when I was practically an infant. I was the last of seven, and I am sure that there would have been more if he had not died. Everyone tells me he was a wonderful man. A real man—that is why there would have been more children to follow me. As it is, I have always been under the guidance of my oldest brother who is now forty, and it is with him that I have had all my disagreements— fights, actually.

My father and mother are both from Madridanos in the province of Zamora—that is where we lived until father died. He was an agricultural laborer. He worked for a big farm, but the house we lived in was on land he owned. He did not fight in the Civil War, and I have always heard that it was lucky that they lived in the Nationalist zone. An uncle of mine fought, but I think it was in the Blue Division that went to Russia. I am not sure. I do not know much about that war. Only what I heard, and no one talked much about it—it is ancient history. They say it brought us peace.

What they talked about was the hard times. It was so bad that I heard there were occasions when they cooked the hooves of animals to make stew. Oh, my parents had to make many sacrifices to bring up their children. I believe it. And when father died it was much worse. I do not know what he died of. He had terrible pains in his stomach. Maybe it was appendicitis. Or cancer. There was no hospital. The local doctor saw him and he was a real doctor, but I guess he was not up to it. We had uncles in Madridanos, but with father dead it was hard going.

First my oldest brother went to Zamora and got a job. Then the rest of us followed because it was easier to make a living there. Not easier, there were simply some opportunities for jobs. My brother was the real head of the family. I have quarreled a lot with him, but I respect him the most. He is just old-fashioned, that is all. He thinks a young man needs no more than twenty cents to go out for an evening, when just stepping out the front door costs you that much. But he lives according to his beliefs. When they took him away to do

Young Waiters in Madrid: A Cartoon

his *mili*, mother gave him all she had saved at the time—1,500 pesetas. They sent him out to Morocco, and he went through hell there. The Army food was a starvation diet. It always is—that is why mothers are always sending packages to their sons in the *mili*—but out there in the desert it was worse. And yet when he returned home, the 1,500 pesetas were intact. Isn't that wonderful? It was our family fortune at the time. Twenty-five dollars.

I went to school in Zamora until I was fourteen, and mother took me with her to Madrid, since I was the youngest, when she accompanied my oldest sister who had found a job as a cleaning woman. Not with a family where one always has to be servile, but at offices after they close in the evenings. So at fourteen I went to work and no more school. I had gone through secondary school—I have my papers to prove it, but of course I am practically illiterate. After I was settled in a job and mother saw that sister needed no one to protect her reputation, she went back to Zamora where she could work and take care of her grandchildren. I still live with my sister and a good thing, too, because the money you make in restaurant work when you are at the bottom of the pole is not enough to live by yourself.

Hostelería is what I always wanted to do. Even when I was just starting, when all I did was clearing tables and cleaning up, I watched the waiters to learn to do things with a flourish, not to clunk a dish down on the table but to wing it lightly through the air and settle it carefully in front of the customer the way a good pilot lands a plane. You know how it is when you are a kid. Also, I quickly got the knack of opening a bottle of beer or mineral water with only one hand, leaning into it just enough so as not to topple it but strongly enough to get a grip on the cap. My ambition was to be a waiter and save enough money to start my own bar. That would be very nice, indeed.

I tell you why I like *hostelería*, though I no longer have any hope of owning my own bar. There is talk in *hostelería*—you learn about the world and you make friends. I have made many friends that way. You see so many sides of life and you come into contact with people you would not otherwise. I point this out to friends who work at other jobs. I get to meet and exchange opinions with persons in a higher social strata than mine, whereas my friends can spend a lifetime without meeting a single person who is not of their class. You get to know how to tell the real thing from a phony. At the hotel I can tell who has money and who is putting on airs that he is not entitled to. Yes, it gives you knowledge of life, *hostelería*.

But it is no longer for me. I have lost interest in *hostelería*. I am tired of it. That is a fault of mine—I go into a thing with enthusiasm, even with passion, and then I lose interest. That is the way it was with schooling here in Madrid after I got my first job. In the evenings, I went to a trade school that prepared you to work in a bank. I went to it at first with all my energy, but at the end of the first year the school dropped me. Why? Because I was not studying at all. It is not because I was not intelligent enough to grasp the trade but because I was distracted by other interests. And I guess the time has come to tell you what it is that always distracts me. I am a terrible fellow—I love women!

I began to run after women in Madrid and soon I had a *novia*, a sweetheart of my own. In Zamora, I did not know any girl. We used to talk and talk about them and get so excited that we would all masturbate in a group. Each one of us bragged, of course, but none of us, I believe, had ever gotten close enough to a girl to touch her. But here it was different. After I met my *novia*, I spent every free moment with her. Who had time to think of anything else? But she dropped me when I was doing my *mili*. That is why I was so sad on New Year's Eve that I blurted it out to you the moment you asked if I had had a good time. I do not think I would have told anyone else. Any friend who asked, I said I had been out on the town.

On New Year's Eve I was all alone. I called her and we talked. It was more than a year since I had heard her voice. She thanked me for thinking of her and wishing her a good new year. She told me that she has a *novio* and I said I wished her happiness with him. It was all my fault. I am sentimental, but I am also hard. I used to purposely fight with her to teach her a lesson. She had a lot of pride, too much, and that turned her into a woman who wanted to dominate. That cannot be—I was the man. Once I knew that she was serious about me, that she would not leave me because of a quarrel, I began to punish her for her pride. That is the hard side of me.

Of course, I was punishing myself too, and I was suffering even more than she. I would build up some little disagreement into a big quarrel to make her give in to me, and I would walk out on her.

Then I would rush home and stay by the telephone waiting for her to call. A lot of times, damn it, I called her. That is the sentimental side of me. In fact, if I were not so sentimental, there would not have been so many quarrels and hurt feelings. My feelings, I mean. For example, the weekend when she dropped me for good. My sentiments were hurt that during my weekend pass she was going to spend a half day rehearsing with her church choir.

She was very religious and she was part of that choir at the church she had been going to since she was a child. I told her just what I thought about her spending half a day of my leave from Valladolid singing, and I went home. Home to my sister, that is. My mother and real home was in Zamora, but I did not go there to spend my leaves. I came to Madrid because I am sentimental, and she was putting religion ahead of me. I told her what I thought of religion too while I was at it.

I am a Christian and I believe in God and all that, but I do not believe in priests and going to church and the rest of their hypocrisy. They tell you that making love is a sin! I tell you that I love women and they will never convince me that it is a sin. Not that I ever did it with my *novia*. I loved and respected her, and I was too serious about her to really try to force her to do it. Oh, we did many things together but not that. We kissed and kissed, long kisses that excited her and drove me out of my mind, and we would sit close together and she would hold it throughout an entire movie. Once when we had been like that a whole evening and I tried to persuade her to let me do it, she burst into tears. She told me that the last time that we were alone and I had tried to persuade her that she had felt terrible shame when she got home and saw her mother. She cried some more and talked about her mother and things like that and I knew she was right. Stop crying, woman, I said, I promise, I promise. I will never try it again. And I did not—I had too much respect for her to do it, being as sentimental as I am.

But when she dropped me—for she did not phone and I did not call her—I was hard about it. I did not come to Madrid on my next weekend pass but to Zamora. There I met a girl who in three days let me do what my *novia* had resisted for one and a half years. I met her at a dance in my neighborhood. One of my old friends pointed her out to me. She does it, he said, but I took that with a grain of salt—I knew myself and I knew my old friends. Still, I asked her to dance and walked home with her and since I knew she was a hot one, a *calentona* as we say, I kissed her. That was the first day. She said, "Don't you think it is too soon?" I asked her if she did not like it, and she said, "Yes, but it is too soon."

I did not believe her. What a terrible fellow I am! But I am good at telling what people are really after from the way they react, whatever it is they are saying. The next day I took her to the Arboleda, a beach along the river in Zamora, with only one thing in mind. There is the open area with people bathing. Girls with bare arms and bare legs, they give you ideas. And then woods where people picnic and walk. I took her out there where no one was. And there we began. *Trac, trac, trac!* "No, no," she would say, "I have never done this." Though I was doing practically everything. Oh, her tits! I took them in my hands and ate them like melons. "No, no, no!" She covered up. "What kind of a role do you want me to play?" I asked. "Do you want me to take you out and show no interest in you other than that? You would think I am a fag." Well, she masturbated me, and I told her, when she accused me of being interested in only one thing, that all I wanted was that both of us have a moment of pleasure—what was wrong in that?

I told her that the next day when I again took her to the Arboleda. This time I walked her deep into the trees where you would not think the sun was out at all. It started the same way once more—"No, no, I have never before done this!"—but finally she gave in. I do not believe that it was the first time for her, I do not believe it. When I was talking her into it, I said to her, "Do you think I have not been with girls before?" But the truth was, it was the first time for me and not for her, though she never admitted it. Well, the time has come again to tell *you* the truth—I cannot be sure that it was not the first time for her, because I was so excited that I came before I put it in her and I was in no condition to tell you if there was any obstruction.

That is the way I am—very fast. Probably because of the little experience I have had. What am I saying! I have had no experience at all. That time with her has been the only time. It quivered and quivered and I could not aim. I think it is the carnal touch that does it. I have too much imagination and I go off immediately. These days I come and come every night. I think a woman—*zas!*—and I come. More than once a night. However, I am not complaining.

I did not go back to that girl in Zamora. When I got back to the barracks in Valladolid where, by the way, the purest Castilian is spoken in all of Spain, I told a friend about it. It does me good to talk over my experiences with friends, also to tell them all the sentiments and thoughts that occur to me. In Valladolid we did not do anything but guard duty, so there was plenty of time to philosophize. Anyway, such things you cannot tell to your sister or even your philosophy to your *novia*, right? But with friends I feel better for it. My best friend there in Valladolid right away said, "Whenever you go out with that girl, you make sure that you use a contraceptive, for she could be trying to trap you into marriage." I thought it over, and the more I reflected about the way she had acted with me—on the third day after I first met her she opened up the whole way!—the more I became convinced she was trying to catch me. That is why I did not look her up again.

We are so backward about these things in Spain. We are primitives compared to the United States. I meant it when I told her that it should be pleasurable to both. It was not just propaganda to get her to lower her panties. I kept saying to that girl, "What is the matter, why are you not getting more excited?" I did not want to use the word "come" with her, of course, but she understood what I meant. "I am excited," she said, but she was not shaking the way I was. After a while she said she had been satisfied, but I don't know . . . The other day at the hotel I was joking with the cleaning girls—just joking, you know, for they are not loose—and I said right out that I thought it was quite natural for a woman to suck it and a man to return the compliment. Well, they were scandalized.

All my friends agree with me when I tell them that I really want a girl to have pleasure in me and me in her. They agree, but I don't know how convinced they are. Some of the older ones, like the elevator man at the hotel who could be my father, say there is danger in that. You teach a woman to enjoy it the way we do and they will be falling on their backs for anybody. They have a point there, but if a man is the strong one in the marriage and does not let the woman dominate, she will not stray. Anyway, I want to give pleasure, not just *zas, zas, zas*. That is why I have never gone to a prostitute. I would not pay a woman to let me fuck her. Once an older brother was going to take me to a prostitute when I was thirteen, but he changed his mind. I was too young, he said. I was not—that was when we kids were all masturbating without a stop. I might have gone then for the experience, but not now.

Now one picks and chooses, right? Once when I worked near Bravo Murillo Street I came out of a movie theater close by and a friend said to me that a lot of fags go to that movie house. He asked me if I was letting one service me. I had not noticed any fags there. If you are not looking for a thing, you do not find it. That is my belief. If a fag had come up to me there or at a bar and proposed something to me or tried to feel me, I would give him an *hostia*, a punch, without thinking. I have a way of reacting violently. That is why I try to say nothing when I am angry, because I may say more than I should. Why hit a fag? They cannot help themselves. I have learned to respect them since the time I worked in a cafeteria and my three other colleagues were fags. Except for Alfredo at the hotel, I have never known such good work *compañeros*, and there was never any fooling around. Why should I not respect them despite this weakness of theirs?

Of course, it is easy to be choosy when it comes to fags. Women who take the first step are another thing. At the hotel only once has a woman made an overture to me. She would order breakfast in her apartment and she was always in a robe when I came in with the tray. I could see her tits. I discussed it with the older men running the elevators. They said, "Ho, ho, ho, that is an overture!" The last day she stayed at the hotel she offered me bonbons. I have to finish this box off, she said. I took a bonbon, but I could hardly swallow seeing her breasts almost hanging out. I did not do anything. I have this bold face, but the fact is I am timid.

The elevator operators tell thousands of stories. One of them told me that when he was helping out as a waiter, the way I have been doing with the mini-bar, to make more money, he went into one of the apartments rented by a couple to answer a call for breakfast. He opened the door with his passkey and announced his presence and the man called, "Come in." He found them in the living room doing it dog-fashion. The man told him to put the tray on the table and take the twenty-five pesetas that were there as a tip. He also said, "I hope you do not mind that at the moment I cannot hand them to you myself." Now, that story I do not believe. I am beginning to think that we Spaniards are a lot of *fantasmas*—ghosts who are not the real thing. Sometimes I think that some of my friends who tell me that they have so much experience are just like me, wetting their sheets at night.

Maybe we are so backward about these things because there has been little freedom for a long time . . . In the movies they now show girls naked to the waist at every opportunity. Even if they are just brushing their teeth. It is because after forty years of nothing we want everything we can get. Not that I do not respect Franco for what he did for the nation. There are all those years of peace, which is more than any other country has had. And prosperity such as we have never known. Except in *hostelería*. I earn too little. I have to tell you about that. I get about 11,000 pesetas each month, less than two hundred dollars in your country, and I still do not know what my basic salary is. What I earn is composed of my salary and a percentage of the orders we serve—ten percent. Who can figure that out? Besides, it is not an equal percentage—the headwaiter gets the largest amount of the ten percent and so on and by the time it gets to me it must be very little. I suppose I should ask how it is all calculated, but I do not know how to go about it. *Service compris*, the French customers say, and leave no tip. They do not know we are behind the times—the service is *compris* by the boss.

What was wrong with Franco's time was that there was no freedom of speech and no freedom of the press. I do not know why that was so, for I have not given it much thought. Maybe it was because they were all older men and they like to keep the reins on the young. Younger men is what is needed. That is why I think Juan Carlos will be good. If we had an election, none of those men Juan Carlos had to put in the cabinet would be there. I believe that people would vote in men of thirty-five or so, men young enough to feel the rhythm of life. They would not have to think about what to do, because they would naturally feel the pace of things. That is what was wrong with those old men—they had no natural rhythm.

I talk that way because I love music, all kinds of music except classical. What enthusiasm I have for Bob Dylan and the Beatles and the Rolling Stones! And that wonderful woman who died—Janis Joplin. I especially love *soul*. Oh, *soul!* I had an American friend for a while, a Negro who was doing his *mili* for your country at Torrejón air base just outside the city, and he had wonderful tapes he played for me. I was surprised when he told me I was his first white friend, but I guess I should not talk about that to you. It was from his tapes—he would bring them up to the apartment, for my sister also welcomed him—that I heard the groups I most like. I like them though I do not know the words. He played me the songs I loved most of all. They were not *soul*, they were songs that people in the south of the United States sang while they picked cotton. *Folk*, that is what those songs were called. I loved them most of all. But then I have strange tastes—you would not believe that I like Gregorian chants, but I do.

"Well, I think the time has come for me to go meet my friend," Aniano said, looking at his gold watch, a proud possession. I waved to the waiter and he added, "Since you are not letting me pay for my rounds, the next time we meet it will have to be all on me. That is the way it is with us during the *paseo*—each man pays a round of drinks. This is one custom that the times have not changed. No disrespect intended."

"What are you going to do tonight?" I asked.

"My friend and I are going to a discotheque. Each one of us pays one hundred pesetas and that entitles us to a drink each, but I have had my limit of alcohol tonight. Two snifters of brandy is about all I can handle. I am ready for whatever happens. Not that anything has ever happened at the discotheques. I have never met a girl there with whom I have done more than dance. Anyway, it is the music and the rhythm I like. If a girl gets too close, I get hard, of course. They must notice it, but they act as if they do not. Another thing I do not believe. But I have never come while dancing, never, though some friends say they do. But here I am talking about women again. What a terrible fellow I am!"

Outside on Gran Vía, we paused to breathe in the cool air. On the sidewalk opposite a few hundred workers milled about the building which was the provincial headquarters for the government corporate trade unions. "Why are they demonstrating?" I asked disingenuously: I knew that the representatives of the workers were being allowed upstairs to negotiate with the government-appointed officials in an effort to end the illegal strike of the auto workers going on that month. The workers on the street were there to apply pressure by showing support of their own representatives inside the building.

"They are demonstrating for the same reason everybody is striking," Aniano replied. He lowered his voice and looked at me mischievously. "After forty years of not being able to speak out . . . they are like me tonight, letting it all out." He shook himself a little. "Did the brandy have no effect on you?"

I nodded. I said it had and that I would go back to the hotel and have an early dinner in the dining room of the cafeteria. "The food there is just as good as in the restaurant upstairs," Aniano said, "and my friend Alfredo will wait on you." I asked if Alfredo was the husky fellow with the broad shoulders. "Right, you watch out for him—he can throw you over those shoulders of his the way he does me. He is an athlete—he even skis—and he has a lot up there in his head. I listen to him. He is my good friend although we are so different."

I already had some notion of how different Alfredo was—not simply that he was tall and muscular whereas Aniano was thin and slight, nor that Alfredo looked open and healthy and Aniano sly and pinched. The first time I ate alone on the second floor of the cafeteria, where between seven and nine I could be alone, Alfredo advised me against a particular Spanish wine. "I believe it is adulterated," he said. "For a year and a half it has not tasted right." I changed my order, and when he brought me a wine to which he had no objection, he added, "Do you know what the *Opus Dei* is? It is a combination of the Church and the capitalists, and they have taken over many businesses and banks. They are smart technicians and they use all the modern methods to make more profits. When they are not stuffing our heads, they are emptying our pockets. They have increased the business in that wine so much that they now put some chemicals in it instead of leaving it in the caskets to age properly. So enjoy this wine before they pollute it too."

It was eight-thirty when I left Aniano, and there was no one in the cafeteria dining room but Alfredo. Actually, he followed me up from the street floor where he also waited on diminutive formica tables; he was used to dashing up and down these stairs in two or three light leaps. Although the staircase was open and from the front of the dining room one could look down, as from a broad diving board, on the young couples at the cafeteria bar downstairs (its modern, ersatz sophistication made it popular with the middle-class university students), the din of the pre-dinner crowd was contained below. "This must mean you plan a quiet evening," Alfredo said. "Or are you going to dine after the theater and only want a bite now?"

I decided to surprise him, and said, "No, it is Aniano who is making a big night of it."

He studied me a moment. "Then you are the journalist he was meeting. I thought it was one of those stories of his which he reserves usually for our other colleagues."

When he brought me the soup, he said, "Aniano went to the discotheque, right?" He shook his head. "He should be studying French. In *hostelería* you need to know foreign languages. I take French at the academy every Monday night, my only free one during the week."

He came back before I finished the soup. "Aniano is a good boy. I feel like a father to him. He is only twenty."

"And you?"

"Oh, I am twenty-four," he said, as if that put him in another generation. "I suppose you are here to report on the strikes?" He took my smile for assent. "I have friends at the Chrysler plant and the problem there is more than money. You cannot go by what our newspapers say—they are still hemmed in. The real problem is the number of cars they are forced to turn out each day. On my friends' belt line they have little by little increased the number to twice what they were doing. They put into effect the quotas and work norms of their French plant, although the equipment is ancient here compared to that in France."

I already knew this from striking workers with whom I had met, and I did not pursue the conversation with Alfredo. During the three weeks that were left to me in Madrid, I ate upstairs at the cafeteria at least twice a week. Those times were during the hours when the other tables were empty and Alfredo was free to talk. I did not make an attempt to interview him, but I kept notes on his conversation out of habit. From these I was able to piece out later the extraordinary work schedule he followed all week. I was alerted to it by his talk on my last evening there about what he called his married life. He worked at two full-time jobs, which is not unusual for a Spaniard, and had freed himself from *macho* conventions, which is unusual, particularly for a worker.

From seven in the morning until three in the afternoon, Alfredo was a car mechanic at a motor pool in a government ministry. That left him an hour to travel home, bathe, shave, and get to the hotel cafeteria to work from four until midnight. Every third Saturday he worked a half day at the motor pool, but he was always off on Sundays at that job. At the cafeteria he worked six evenings a week, with Mondays off. On Mondays he attended French class from six to eight in what Spaniards call the afternoon, this being his only unhurried and free evening of the week. It took me a while to realize that there was not a single day in the week when he did not work at one job or the other.

I had never seen him look tired: he had not once trudged up those stairs to the dining room. He had never complained about a schedule that almost never allowed him time for a full night's sleep or lovemaking. I could only recall a certain air of pride in how ingeniously he timed everything he did. I had once asked, "Why do you work at two full-time jobs?" and immediately felt foolish for asking. He replied, "I do it to help my family and still have some money for the things I like to do." His father had died a year earlier and he was the eldest: he then took on his second job.

The new job cut down on his sports activities—swimming, neighborhood *fútbol*, skiing—and the time for girls. "You could say that until the age of twenty-two I was a carefree bachelor," he said. "But it was time I settled down, anyway." Finding an apartment for the family when his father died was his first act as the male head of the family. They had lived in an apartment building that the motor pool's ministry (his father had worked there too since Alfredo was a boy) made available to its employees who were heads of family, but now they were put out in the street. Alfredo did not qualify as a head of family. "Literally thrown out," he said. "They placed the furniture out on the sidewalk. That happened to families whose fathers died or were fired, whatever the reason, and there were seventy-two families in all evicted that year. We got together, went to the Housing Ministry with a priest, and protested. They made available eleven apartments and we drew lots for them. We were one of the lucky ones."

"I learned a great deal from that," Alfredo said, and held up his right hand as if taking an oath. "Not about luck—there is no such thing—but about protesting and organizing and the right way to do it. For example, taking that priest along with us was smart. Without him, they would not have given us an audience at the Ministry. Right now at the motor pool we are talking to one another. That motor pool is such a world apart that there does not even exist an official union for us. Any mechanic gets 20,000 pesetas whereas we get 15,000. We are only a nucleus now—you cannot trust everyone, for many have long thought they are privileged and have not noticed they are as exploited as anyone else. But we have found ourselves a priest—the press. Twice little notices have appeared in the newspapers that six hundred workers at a motor pool in the government are unhappy. That puts pressure on them. We have made a start."

When he brought the dessert, he had only time to say, "It was the poet Machado who said that Spain is divided into those who follow the Cross and those who wield the Axe."

With the coffee, he corrected himself. "No, it was Leon Felipe who wrote that. On one side is the old Church and the aristocracy and on the other those who criticize by destroying, by using the axe. For example, every Spaniard thinks he is king, so he wants to change things immediately—he wants the whole structure of forty years to come down at once. But can it come down slowly? The king's government wants to replace the pillars one by one, and that is what they are doing. By the time they get around to the last pillar, the one they put up first will be very, very old. We never catch up."

When he brought me the bill, he said, "You were surprised that I have read Antonio Machado and Leon Felipe? I have read a lot. I only got a secondary education and had just started college preparatory high school when I had to work, but I have read Freud and that school of psychology, like Jung. I test my ideas against theirs and those of persons I know and then I decide for myself. I come to my beliefs that way, not just from books, because people can be very learned and say stupid things.

"When I have a decision to make I think through my own ideas first and then I go to a friend who I think would know about that particular problem. I select the one among my friends who is most grounded in such matters. I listen to him and then I go over my own ideas once more and then I make up my mind. If it is a deep problem, I do not talk about it. I go off by myself. I become quiet, and there is no expression on my face or even in my eyes. Like this." He let his arms hang down at his sides and tried to stare vacantly. He was too pink-cheeked and robust to succeed. "It frightens people to see me that way."

My last evening in Madrid on that visit fell on Friday. Aniano followed me up the stairs to the dining room to say good-bye. There was no one there but Alfredo. He picked up Aniano and held him on his shoulder with one arm, like a bag of flour. "What did I tell you!" Aniano said while he hung there. He tapped Alfredo on his head and Alfredo put him down. "I am getting out of here," Aniano said, and flew down the stairs. Alfredo watched him with a paternal smile, his breath unhurried: it had been no effort to lift Aniano. "I always feel good on Friday evenings," Alfredo explained to me.

You may well ask why Friday nights are so special, he said when I sat down. You see, tonight my *novia* waits for me downstairs when I finish at midnight. We have not seen each other since Monday night, my evening off. Rather, since Tuesday morning. Friday nights we go to a discotheque for a couple of hours and then we go home. Her home—my other home—where she lives with her sister. We are together all night and tomorrow until four when I come to work here in the afternoon. Not on Saturday night, for it is only right that on Sunday morning I should wake up at my own home and be with my mother and brothers and sisters. But Sunday during the day I am with her again and then Monday afternoon and evening until I get up Tuesday morning at her place and go off to the motor pool.

My *novia* and I are a regular married couple without having gotten mixed up with the Church. I have never believed in that. I told her so when I fell in love with her. She was probably as advanced as I already, but we talked it over and she agreed and we have been like a couple living in matrimony ever since. We are not waiting to have children before we marry. We will only marry when we are ready. It is real love—it grows and grows. I know that is not the rule in Spain. It is a terrible trauma for a girl to lose her virginity. I know what men think, but it makes no difference to me whether a girl I meet is a virgin or not. The men are all tied up in knots about it and it creates terrible complexes in women. Complexes of inferiority if she has lost her virginity. The moment comes when she thinks she has to explain and expects you to reject her.

Sleeping with a woman is not a light matter, though I remember a time when I would have stuck it in anywhere. I would not want a man to come and violate my sister and leave her with nothing. I want my sisters to have really serious relationships. Let them sleep together. It does not matter that they may separate and go their own ways. She will have learned something then. He will not have left her with nothing. She will know for the future what love is and what she is looking for in life. I think I have found it with my *novia*. I do not press her, but I believe she has also found it with me.

Ah, you see why I am so happy tonight. It is the beginning of our weekend together, the time I dedicate to her, even if it is broken up so much by all these jobs. We engage in sports on Saturdays and Sundays, we go to the movies, we have deep conversations, and sometimes we just read books in the same room. But Mondays are my favorites. After I finish my French class, we do the shopping like a perfectly married couple. We go to this shop and that for groceries and to the department stores for clothes and nonsense, arm in arm. Which reminds me, for shopping together gives you knowledge of real life, that the Minister of Economy should not be telling us to tighten our belts to control inflation. These gentlemen want us to tighten our belts while they are loosening theirs.

There are all sorts of economies *they* can practice. If they are having a meeting, it need not include dinner. And servants to bring them refreshments. And why should the queen go to India? Why should she be traveling around at our expense? But that is not what I set out to tell you. I meant to explain why Monday nights are my happiest times. We walk from shop to shop arm in arm, we look at things and decide whether we need them. We are not out for entertainment. We are leading our lives calmly, the life that we have made for ourselves, and anyone looking at us as we go arm in arm doing our shopping must think, There goes a couple in matrimony.

7

Up from the Depths

For some living is stepping on shattered glass with naked feet; for others it is looking at the sun face to face.

—Luis Cernuda

This is Sergio Albert's story, but I cannot leave out of it his lover, Miguel de Iriarte, however selective and circumspect I try to be, for if I feel an obligation to hide their personal identities I must not obscure their social ones. In this lies the interest of Sergio's courtesan career. Without men like Miguel de Iriarte, it is impossible to imagine Sergio, the bastard son of a poor country girl from Murcia, the most impoverished province in Spain, rising into the affluent upper-middle-class world in which he now moves. True, it is mostly among literary and artistic people that he lives—not Miguel de Iriarte's aristocratic family circle and their peers—but despite the predictable penchant among artists for bohemianism, more class snobbery exists in intellectual circles in Spain than in similar ones elsewhere in Europe, and certainly much more than in the United States. As the young anthropologists, Juan Maestre Alfonso and Marisa Rodriguez, often told me, Spain's politics, even under Franco, was always more progressive than its social arrangements. To this must be added that Franco's regime made social mobility impossible for most of its reign. Young men like Sergio Albert, no matter how darkly handsome, usually ended up as hustlers on Las Ramblas in Barcelona and the Puerta del Sol in Madrid. Whenever Sergio contemplates a break with Miguel—and I spent hours with him during the aftermath of a violent quarrel—it occurs to him that a descent into that social abyss may well be the result of such a rupture. Class consciousness colors his most inti-

115

mate feelings, but it would not surface as frequently if Miguel de Iriarte were absent.

Without Miguel I should not have met Sergio. Miguel and I got to know each other in New York in 1960 when he first began to travel abroad for the bank whose management has been in his family's hands since the middle of the nineteenth century. I worked in an international corporation which did some business in Spain, but it was our common literary interests that turned a casual business meeting into a friendship. It was he who introduced me to the Spanish social poets and novelists whose influence was then at its height. He was spiritually allied with them during the hours when he was away from his paneled Victorian office lined with portrait paintings of his predecessors, and he had also published poems, short stories, and literary criticism which were less influenced by Spanish literary tradition than by his undergraduate years at Oxford. I have seen him in the years that have followed, during encounters in New York, Havana, London, and Madrid, drained of the hope for revolutionary change in Spain that had once warmed him.

The change first became perceptible in the greater play that he allowed irony whenever he reviewed what had happened in Spain since the last time we met. I remember laughing with him in the early sixties at a story about the Cuban poet Nicolás Guillen. He had just run into Guillen in Paris and had reminded him that in 1957 in Rome Guillen had said despondently to him, "Ah, you in Spain are on the verge of wonderful things, but we in little Cuba, we shall have to wait on the entire world before we have our revolution." In the fall of 1975, Miguel recited all the jokes about Franco's unending illness, all accompanied by laughter in which there was no pleasure. He was drinking heavily and finished in a bitter mood. "I want him to be dead," he said and did not laugh. "Then I can be my own age. While he is alive we are all a horrible, senile eighty-two."

I saw him several times during the fall and winter that year and again in the early spring of 1976. Franco's death did not make him any happier. Only in talks with sympathetic friends with whom he could take for granted an appreciation of the importance and authority of his literary gifts (little exercised now) could he expand and enjoy himself. Even when hilarious, he was bitterly ironic.

"Let me tell you an anecdote to show you how backward we are," he said. "A poet we all know—a fine poet, though a bit too abstract for me—is in terrible trouble because of his rather unusual sexual preferences. He is not only gay but only likes men in the Air Force, and not simply in the Air Force but only in the ground crew. A factor that is also important is the uniform—even with all the trouble he has been in for months, he told me the last time I saw him that new dress regulations that no longer require them to wear short boots are playing havoc with his sex life.

"But let me start at the beginning. A couple of years ago he managed by hanging around the nearest air base to make contact with one such uniformed man. This contact introduced him to others, and in a short time they were smuggling him into the base on weekends, where he spent his time at the canteen buying everyone drinks and paying for their favors." One weekend a master sergeant, whom the poet had ignored because he was too old for his taste, reported the presence of a civilian at the canteen to the colonel. When carried away, the poet paid as much as five thousand pesetas for a kiss, and the master sergeant, like all the others, was not averse to making money so easily.

The colonel came down to the canteen himself and had the poet thrown in jail on suspicion of espionage. He was to stand military trial, and was held incommunicado. This is where the story gets complicated: the poet held the lucrative position of an *agente de bolsa*, an official job peculiar to Spain; these *agentes* are men whose signatures on all stocks and financial transactions make them valid. There are only some fifty men in the country licensed by the government, and they are guaranteed an enormous income. Every Tuesday each signs the proper papers covering the previous week's transactions and his work is done for the week.

"As Tuesday neared, the poor fellow had to ask to see the colonel urgently, and he confessed, 'Señor Coronel, I am not a spy, I am a fag.' It did not help. The colonel did not release him in time and had him tried sometime later by a military court on various moral charges. His colleagues on the society of *agentes de bolsa* expelled him, and he will soon be impoverished. His lawyers are working up an appeal on the basis that the soldiers inveigled him into the base and fleeced him. And meanwhile he is in dread that he may end up in the jail for homosexuals in the south. There they are separated

117

into queens and so-called males, and the poor poet says he is neither—he only likes to fondle their genitals and if he is lucky to be masturbated in turn."

Miguel likes to point out that every element of this story—the treatment of homosexuals, the position of *agentes de bolsa* in the financial world—shows Spain to be hopelessly anachronistic. "But most of all—that colonel. All they've got on that air base are a few old Mirages, but the colonel decided the poet was a spy. In any really advanced country with real military secrets to protect, any officer would have seen immediately that the poor poet was only a fag. And none of this would have happened."

In the spring I went with Miguel to a poetry reading by a friend of his generation, which Miguel attended only for this reason. Miguel was recognized by university students, and they milled about him when it was all over, so that he was moved to tell them to join us at dinner. It pleased him to hold court, but he did not temper his view of the kind of poetry they wanted him to write. The students wanted literature to be *engagé*. One of them, in effect, asked, "What is to become of you?" He did not mean simply Miguel but rather the social poets and storytellers with whom he classed him.

I saw that it took poise for Miguel to smile away the personal, hurtful element in the student's judgment. He replied with perfect condescension: the students were his inferiors in these matters but only a snob would have denied them their right to question him. He explained carefully, and at greater length than is necessary to this story, that in 1962 it became obvious that what they had hoped for Spain could not happen. The economy had taken a turn that made revolutionary change impossible. To have continued to write as they had would have required falsifying the reality that had given their writing value.

"You see, some of us had made our personal condition—our unhappiness, you might say, as children of the bourgeoisie—operate in our prose and poetry as symbols of Spain's miserable condition," he said. He took a deep breath and went on. "When the economy began to develop into what it is now, these ideas of ours could no longer work in our writing, simply because the relationship between them and the real life of the country, always illusory at best, was now patently false. Anyway, the reasons a poet or novelist or critic writes are usually very personal. You might consequently say that I have stopped writing as I did because these ideas ceased to excite me. Not because I repudiated them but because they no longer engaged me—as a writer."

I expected angry replies or at least a verbal putdown. That is what would have happened with our young radicals in the sixties. None of this occurred. Indeed, one of them invited him to speak at his *escuela mayor*, a kind of dormitory that exists at Spanish universities that is not only a place for students to eat and sleep but also a social and cultural center. Miguel said yes. This student reminded me of Sergio Albert: he was dark, intense, Andalusian. As we left, Miguel said privately to him, "Call me at my office," and gave him the name of his bank. To me he said, "Let's walk," and when we were a few steps away from them added, "Fidelity is so boring."

"There is going to be hell to pay when I get home," he said. "You saw that Sergio was in a mood, didn't you? You were not fooled by his excuse that he needed to rest?"

Before the reading, I had picked up Miguel at the apartment he owns in a luxury building ringed with balconies like tacky flounces. I had gone there because I wanted to fix an appointment with Sergio for the next day, and he and I had agreed that I would show up at the apartment in the morning since it is not far from the center of Madrid. "We can lock ourselves up in Miguel's study while he is away at the bank," Sergio said in the flat, pragmatic manner that is at odds with his romantic good looks. "You can then ask me anything you want and you will stay for lunch when Miguel comes. I shall be very boring, but our housekeeper is a good cook." Then Sergio told us that he was going inside to lie down and not going to the reading with us.

"He wanted to be coaxed," Miguel said on the way home. "I know he has not spent the evening resting. You did not see him on the sidewalk when we came out of the reading, but I did. He made sure that I saw him and then disappeared. He is so primitive, there is going to be a row. He was letting me know he was out cruising—and of course he has had no trouble finding someone to take him to bed. He likes them over thirty-five, and men that age fall over one another to oblige him. I think we are at a dead end."

I reminded Miguel of the last time he and I had been out drinking, four years earlier in New York, and how happy he had been to be returning the next morning to his young new lover. "I remember how lucky I felt about his gerontological obsession," Miguel said, and laughed without, somehow, sounding less weary. "If only I could feel jealous and respond in the way Sergio wants. Little did I know when you last saw me that his ideal of love is the perfect bourgeois marriage—my coming home twice a day to the little woman in the tastefully appointed apartment, watching television together, having friends in occasionally to dinner, weekends at the country home. How boring!"

Miguel has the use of a magnificent family estate in the mountains near Madrid, a place his elderly parents never use and which only a sister sometimes visits. Besides the apartment in Madrid, he also bought a small town house in a farming community in the province of Toledo when he first met Sergio five years ago. It is four hundred years old and faces the town church across a tiny cobbled square. Its last tenants raised pigs on the ground floor and chickens on the third; it had no electricity or plumbing. Miguel designed the restoration of the interior and patios, and Sergio devoted himself for four years to finding the proper décor and furniture. The doors, for example, had all come from various parts of the country—superbly hand-carved antiques of ancient hardwoods. "It took a long time to get this place ready," Miguel said the Sunday I spent there, "because Sergio likes to bargain."

I praised the high-back chairs when we sat down to dinner. "Oh, those are no good," Sergio said. "They are nineteenth century. We must replace them with something genuine."

That day in the country had left me with the impression that Sergio was an interior decorator and that he would soon open an antiques store. Walking Miguel home, I said to Miguel that Sergio did not exactly correspond to the portrait he had just outlined, that he must also be busy with his work. Miguel shook his head. "He helps some of my friends' wives buy things, that's all." The smell of flowering oleanders distracted him; he breathed deeply and sighed. "Oh, a lot of it is my fault, but I have apologized, although I thought we had an understanding that we could sleep with others so long as we told each other."

But apologies did not help, Miguel continued, and their agreement had not been real. "Recently, I asked a man who had shown up at our apartment with an old friend of mine to stay overnight. But first I had asked Sergio if the notion attracted him. He said yes, but apparently he did not mean it, for the last two or three weeks have been hell. He cannot get that night out of his mind and keeps punishing me for it. He may get violent tonight as he did on other occasions . . . He once attacked me with a knife, another time with scissors. One of these days I shall not be able to hold him down. He is stronger than I am."

I said all this had something of the tone of the opera *Carmen*, and he laughed and then said, "I hate bad manners and quarrels and violence. They depress me. Oh, I know you think there is a class difference involved. It is not simply that. The way I am is not just something I picked up from my family—I also won it for myself." He exhaled a loud sigh and it turned into a kind of laugh. He shrugged as if to say it was nonsense for a grown man to be caught in his situation with Sergio.

I said, "Weren't you pleased with tonight's encounter with your admirers?"

"They were sweet, weren't they?" he replied. "I did not tell them that I seldom get any ideas for stories or essays, that I sometimes think of suicide. I have written a couple of poems and some prose that I know are good. That's enough. Ideas no longer come to me the way they used to when I was young. I sometimes start something and put it away, but I not only do not go back to them as I used to, I do not even remember them. A poem needs to sit on my head and not go away."

At the door of his building, I asked him if he thought Sergio would speak to me openly the next morning, but he did not hear me. He said, "I wish I could have another whiskey before I go up." I automatically gave him a paternal, disapproving shake of the head, and he laughed as he was to laugh the next morning when he turned to me, after I expressed surprise to find him still home, and revealed a swollen, battered face with one eye closed. "I fell while taking a shower," he announced, but as soon as the housekeeper and Sergio walked out of the room, he said in English, "We had a fight, just as I predicted," and laughed again.

Miguel wore a business suit. On the marble coffee table were an untouched cup of *café con leche*, and *churros* getting stiff and cold. Next to them was a bowl with boric acid solution the housekeeper had fixed, and he dipped a cotton ball into it and said, "This is deliciously soothing, but I should prefer a whiskey." I said he must go to his doctor not the office, and Sergio, who had returned to the room, spoke for the first time. "Yes," he said. Miguel did not look at him. He explained to me that there was a board of directors meeting that morning and at its close he was expected to speak to the press about some major new credit ventures of the bank. He got up, accepted a towel from the housekeeper, dabbed at his face, and said, "I do not know if I shall be back for lunch." From the foyer he called to me, "In any case, I shall see you before you leave for Barcelona."

Only the housekeeper thought his swollen face was a result of an accident and she was uncomplicatedly concerned for him. "Don Miguel, I shall cook as if you are expected. It will be good for you to come home and rest." He was touched; he hung his head. The housekeeper had won the national lottery a year earlier; enough to retire on, but she still came four hours each day to shop and clean and cook; the other jobs she had she gave up.

When Miguel left, Sergio and I went to Miguel's study. I said it was surprising that Miguel's face had not discolored. He replied in the even, controlled voice usual with him, sounding almost expressionless, that Miguel had kept a raw steak on it for a few hours. The phone at the far end of the room rang and he talked into it with more emotion than he had to me. I strained to hear but caught only phrases. "I do not know what will happen . . . terrible, he looks awful . . . it is all over." He hung up and sat across from me and began to tell me about his mother.

"She was a peasant girl of fourteen when she went to work as a maid for a rich family in Valencia. She came from Murcia, the most backward of provinces, and—" he broke off and said hurriedly, "I do not know if I can talk to you today or if you will want me to when you hear . . . You must suspect that Miguel did not fall in the bathroom. We had a fight. I did that to him with just one blow of my hand. I do not know what is going to happen. He says it is all over. I did not mean to hurt him. I just hit him with an open hand. I feel terrible . . . numb."

Later, I learned from Miguel that Sergio's hand had been open, but he had struck Miguel a karate chop that was worse than a punch with his fist. I did not want to lose the interview with Sergio, and tried to calm him with banalities. He decided that since there was nothing for him to do until he talked to Miguel again that it would perhaps help him if he talked to me. "All he is worrying about," Sergio said, "is whether he will look all right for the press, you heard. But with me—where will I go, what will I do? Still, it is over. I fear what could happen the next time. Look at the result of a simple slap. Anyway, he will never forgive me. Appearances is what he cares about."

It had been Sergio's mother's appearance that had led the rich Valencian family to pluck her out of the countryside after one of their stays at their villa there. She was beautiful. "She is a beauty now," Sergio said. "She is still a relatively young woman." The job was great luck during the years of hunger, even if her cleaning work in that household was the lowliest of the staff, at the beck and call of the other servants. She scarcely got to see the master and mistress. But their only son, an adolescent, did notice her. "It is a commonplace story," Sergio said, "but what is not usual is that she was a beauty and he was a skinny, stunted monkey. He still is. Thank God, I look like her."

Her family, Sergio's grandparents, came to Valencia soon after she started working there, but the few pesetas she earned and the food the housekeeper sometimes spared them was not enough to keep them and their other children. That their daughter got pregnant by the young *señorito* was a boon to them. The *señorito's* rich parents gave her money enough to keep them all, for in her pregnant state she could not remain in the house. And some months after Sergio was born they gave her money enough to enable her and her family to realize an old ambition—to move to Barcelona. The north was always the mecca of the Murcianos: in the economically lively environment that Catalans and Basques create with their industries some jobs fall to those without connections but with sufficient wit or brawn.

Sergio's mother was fifteen when he was born, sixteen when they moved to Barcelona. They did not know Barcelona and they could not find jobs, but they quickly found their way to the squatters' settlement on the lower slopes of Montjuich, the solitary mountain on the southern rim of the city. You did not pay rent there; you built a *chabola*, a lean-to, with whatever was at hand, or if you were lucky, you inherited one. Sergio's mother soon began to walk down into the city to the Barrio Gótico and the Ramblas to look for men. Sergio does not know how long she worked as a street prostitute nor when she met the man, a gypsy as handsome as she was beautiful, with whom, despite quarrels and short separations, she has been until this day. He does not remember her in the squatters' settlement, only the grandparents. About that period he recalls only his wild, free life with a band of kids whose days were full of mischief: stealing was their objective, and they even tried to dig up graves. His mother was someone who visited only long enough to leave them money, often not waiting for Sergio to come in from his wanderings with his gang.

He knows, from information he got years later, that they did not live only from his mother's earnings. She was in touch with his rich Valencian grandparents and they sent money for Sergio's upkeep. How much, he does not know (he never saw any of it), for in the catch-as-can life of his mother and grandparents you were secretive about your assets, a trait Sergio himself exhibits. In any case, he feels no gratitude towards his mother, and only a little towards his poor grandparents who had the care of him during those early years. From clues dropped during backbiting talk and violent quarrels he has deduced that it was he who was crucial to his family's survival during the years of hunger. He knows in his bones that he was exploited, and he looks at all his relationships for danger signals that he is about to play that role again.

"I have lost all the things of value I earned at such a hard cost due to Miguel's infidelities," he blurted out in the study. "My jewelry— rings, cufflinks, bracelets—and my solid-gold DuPont lighter. He brought hustlers here. Once I came home and found him in bed with a black, an ugly monkey that it was an insult to find here asleep. A *chulo* he picked up in a gay bar. His taste for mud, as he calls it. I waked Miguel and he had the temerity to say, 'Sergio, this is not what you think.' I made him wake the monkey and send him off. He paid him right in front of me. But some of the others got up while he was drunkenly asleep and made off with my things. And now he expects me to leave when I have nothing to fall back on."

Up from the Depths

When Sergio was six, his mother came up to the squatters' settlement for him. She was angry that they had to go looking for him, but she did not yell this time. She took him down into the city—the first time since he was an infant that he saw Barcelona—and bought him shoes and clothes, and it was all so dazzling that he does not remember when he changed into them. That very day they took a train to Valencia. His rich grandparents had asked for him. Their only son, his father, had not married, and since they were getting old, they wanted to have their grandson with them. His mother stayed in Valencia only long enough to leave him at their home.

"I hated it. I felt imprisoned. I had to wear shoes and stiff clothes all the time and stay in the house. I wanted to leave as soon as the novelty wore off. I suppose my grandparents were good to me, but they were strangers, jailers. I would not be tamed, I insisted on leaving. It only lasted a few months. I made them send me back to my grandparents in the shantytown. And for a while I lived with them again. The money continued to come in from Valencia, but it was my mother who got it. Sometimes grand toys arrived at our *chabola*, and they often disappeared. Now I had to go to school. It may have been my Valencian grandparents who insisted. I was always bright, I was at the top of the class, but I was always in trouble."

His mother had already taken up with the gypsy, and they quarreled with the grandparents and took him away. Perhaps it was about the money from Valencia; Sergio believes the gypsy took it all. Still, since they had no place of their own, they left him with the gypsy's mother and his younger brother of sixteen. No more school for Sergio, who was eight, and since this was not the shantytown he knew, he was often at home under the thumb of the gypsy's brother. He began to molest Sergio. He made Sergio masturbate him, and when he got tired of that, to fellate him. It nauseated Sergio. He threatened to tell the others, but the gypsy's brother beat him and said no one would believe him. Sergio decided that was likely and did not tell on him.

He spent only a few months there. It was the gypsy's talents that got him out. He could sing and dance and he worked up a flamenco act with Sergio's mother that brought them bookings in the city. They set up an apartment and brought Sergio to live with them.

("He has never married her," Sergio said. "You do not catch a gypsy signing any documents or tying himself down.") It was somewhat better for Sergio, but he does not remember any happiness. The gypsy did not mistreat him; he simply ignored him. It was his mother who harassed him and beat him. She was to send him to reform schools twice because she considered him unmanageable.

I asked Sergio how old she was when she brought him to live in Barcelona with her and the gypsy. He had to figure it out—twenty-four. For him she was never a young girl. She took him to a hospital one day when she found him unconscious in the apartment. He had drunk all the liquor he could find, some three half-bottles of cognac and liqueurs. When he was well, he was placed in an *asilo*, a reform school for boys run by priests. Every moment of the day was controlled by a strict schedule and even more stringent rules. There were punishments for every infraction. At the dispensary he managed to steal a bottle of pills. He took them all. He does not know what they were, but when he became ill, he confessed what he had done. His stomach was pumped and he recovered quickly. His first day out of the infirmary, an older boy slapped him hard and said, "You idiot, don't you ever do that again!"

"I fell in love with him," Sergio said. "I hung about him all the time, for I wanted to get close to him. I did not succeed. I loved him because he was the first person to care for me. I knew what that slap meant. Now, Miguel can say to me when I am in the middle of an argument with him, 'Let us leave this for another time.' Without raising his voice. He is a man of enormous coldness. Whereas I cannot control myself. I prefer being that way, though I fear it too."

When his mother took him out of the *asilo*, he went to public school again. As before, he did well in his studies and was always in trouble. He was fourteen when his mother took him out of school and found him a job as a delivery boy. He got into trouble again—he was accused of stealing—and his mother once more placed him in a reform school. He was there a year and then his mother took him out again. He suspects these shows of motherly feelings: he thinks she had other motives. The gypsy had got into movie-making, and they wanted Sergio for one in which the gypsy was playing a role. When there were no bit parts for Sergio, he again worked as a delivery boy. The money he earned, and the stipend from Valencia, went to them.

He was sixteen when he had his first affair. "She was probably forty. Married to a businessman. He was often away from the city and he had a mistress. I delivered groceries to their home. She was kind and generous with me. She gave me money and bought me clothes. But after a while they moved to Madrid."

He knew that he did not love her, because soon after she was gone he had his first experience of sexual pleasure. His mother and the gypsy were doing well, and they took him with them on a vacation in the country. There was nothing for him to do there but take long walks away from town. One afternoon he came upon a shepherd who was masturbating while leaning against a tree. Sergio stopped and stared. The shepherd motioned him over and played with him. "He kissed me too," Sergio said. "I remember the whole thing as an idyllic incident."

Soon after they were back in the city, an actress in a movie in which he appeared in one scene took him home with her. It happened a few times. As with the other woman, it was an affair in which he was almost a non-participant. "I was a very inhibited person. Nothing happened to me. The next summer I got a seasonal job in a Costa Brava resort, and that was when I met Carlos and fell in love as an adult for the first time. I used to hitchhike into Barcelona to see my parents—God knows why, for they always mistreated me. Carlos gave me a ride. He said he was a chauffeur for a rich family and asked me if I wanted to see the place. I said yes, I was curious, and we had the house and swimming pool to ourselves. He gave me good food and champagne and he made love to me. I never got to Barcelona, and early the next morning he drove me to the resort."

Carlos did not show up again. At first Sergio thought he must be busy on his job. Then on his days off he would be on the lookout for him. He did not know where the house was nor even the town. Walking on the Ramblas on his day off, he ran into Carlos again. They drove out to the house, and this time Carlos confessed that he was no chauffeur: the house was his and he lived on an inherited income. When the summer job was over, he went to live with

Carlos. That was his first love, and Sergio believes that he has never been as happy as the year and a half he spent with Carlos.

"He never said an unkind word to me. It was he who did everything for me. He started me on my modeling career. I had a beautiful body then and through friends of his I got my first job, modeling a famous new brand of bathing suits. Since you were in Barcelona ten years ago, you must have seen me—the posters were everywhere. Carlos also introduced me to an agent who turned me into a professional. But first I must tell you what happened with Carlos. He was away in France—a trip he had to take with his family—and when he came back, he confessed he had been unfaithful to me. He was in tears. It had been a small indiscretion, but what did I know about such things? I was deeply hurt and I left him. It was a decision that I have regretted all my life. I loved him so much that six months after I went to live with him I let him stick it in me.

"I think about that foolish decision these days. I always hated infidelity. For weeks now I can think of nothing but the sight of Miguel making love to an older man right here in our bed. This man had come here with some others, and Miguel asked me in front of him if he could stay. I agreed because after his last business trip he talked me into saying it was all right if we slept with others so long as we were open about it. I never did. And there in bed I could not go through with it. Miguel kept calling out to me as he rolled over that old man, 'Do this, do that.' But I did nothing, I was in a trauma."

Sergio's agent had big plans for him. He sent him to a school where he was taught to walk and talk, even how to sit at the dinner table and eat. "Of course, my agent discounted the cost of all this from my fees—he did not lose a penny on me. But I can mix with the best of people and not shame Miguel. To tell the truth, my manners are better than his and his friends." Thus equipped, he became part of a modeling troupe cast by his agent, which toured the Mediterranean resorts with a society orchestra. "It was all very elegant. While the orchestra played, we would walk around places like the Casino in Monte Carlo for the patrons to observe us. I often displayed gold-brocaded *smokings*.

"I did this for a long time. I got to earn seven thousand pesetas for each show, eventually two thousand for a still shot. I met many people and slept with celebrities—a minor movie star, diplomats, even the brother of a Spanish cabinet minister. Women as well as men. They gave me gifts. I was never a hustler. I remember one man who offered me two thousand pesetas when he dropped me off at the hotel. He said he was leaving in the morning and wanted to give me a gift, but I refused it. He insisted, and I said that it sounded as if he were trying to pay me. I said that if that was the case, my price was ten thousand pesetas. He paid it. But that kind of coarseness was an exception; I met only the finest people. And yet I was unhappy, I was frightened by what was happening to me, and I gave it all up and came back to Barcelona."

In Barcelona he vegetated for a while. He did not know what he wanted to do. One night he happened on a gay bar, and he was pleased that everyone without exception was interested in him. He walked out alone; he was still very inhibited about homosexuality, even nervously afraid of it. But he returned a few nights later and the owner came over to talk to him. He wanted to come to some arrangement to ensure Sergio's presence every night. Sergio said he should like to work behind the bar, and the owner eagerly gave him the job.

"I decided I was gay and now I went all the way. Sometimes I made three dates a day—sex, sex, sex. I slept with every man I fancied, sometimes in groups, sometimes with women as part of the group. There was nothing I did not do or would not try. I reveled in it so much that I did not take a night off from the bar, for I did not want to miss anyone new and there was no question that whoever it was he would choose me over all the others."

It was there that he met the next man with whom he fell in love, and eventually Miguel de Iriarte when he was in Barcelona on a business trip. But the other man came first, for it was typical of Miguel that he should control his impulses on first meeting Sergio. He told Sergio that they would get together another night because he had a date already set. On his next trip to Barcelona, Miguel came by the bar and asked him casually if he was free. Out of pride Sergio said he was busy. Perhaps also because he was already involved with the other man.

"Oh, this man was an idiot. I noticed him long before I talked to him. He used to come to the bar and stare and stare at me like an oaf. He was ordinary, he was not even handsome, but I finally let him sleep with me once. I had nothing better to do that night. He was not good in bed, but there was something nice about him. I did not give him another thought, yet he came back and I went out with him once more and then another time. I got to love him. Love does not depend on looks. The idiot had some dumb job and I moved in with him and gave up the bar. I took a dumb job too, in food distribution, and we lived happily in our little apartment."

Later in our interview, Sergio in the course of complaining about his social life with Miguel confessed that he prefers simple people. Their conversation is infinitely more interesting to him: it is more real. This is what attracted him about the man for whom he has no other name than "the idiot." Only with him has he been on the giving end of a relationship. He took him on a honeymoon when his Valencian grandfather died and left him some money plus another large amount, two million pesetas, to be paid when he married. "I took the idiot to Austria and we were having a marvelous time, but he had to return hurriedly because of his family. I should have known they would always make trouble."

Sergio lingered a bit in Vienna, and when he returned to Barcelona, he bought an apartment with what was left of his grandfather's money. "In no time the idiot's family moved in with us. The parents and three brothers. The mother tried to dominate us all and even handle my money. The brothers were three *locas*, flaming queens you could pick out a block away, but the mother acted as if she noticed nothing. You should have seen the men they brought to the apartment while all the while she was trying to arrange marriages for them. It was impossible—at one time I had to rent an apartment to have a place where I could make love to the idiot."

Sergio gave him up: it was impractical to go on with him. He then arranged to marry a lesbian acquaintance in order to collect the two million pesetas—some thirty-five thousand dollars, a considerable amount of money in Spain—that he could not inherit until he married. They lived together a couple of months for appearances' sake. He bought himself another apartment. He was twenty-three, he had a little money, he was free. He cast about for something to do, but he was in no hurry. Sometimes he thought of Carlos, but he did not look him up. In the street in Madrid, where he had gone to visit a friend, he ran into Miguel de Iriarte. Miguel said, "I think we should not put off going to bed any longer. The next time we meet I might be too old."

Now that his life's story got to Miguel, Sergio became anxious again. "We have been together since that night and now it is all over," he said. "I might as well take this off." He pulled up over his head a pendant on a heavy silver chain. The pendant was in the form of a sunburst about two inches in diameter, thickly studded with jade and carnelian. Miguel had bought two identical ones when Sergio moved into his Madrid apartment, and each wore his always, in place, Sergio said, of wedding bands. "He took his off last night and flung it on the floor. It was a symbol and he smashed it. That is why I hit him. Wait, I will show you." He left the study, and as he returned the phone rang. He picked it up and with the other hand dangled Miguel's pendant at arm's length, but at a distance there seemed nothing wrong with it.

This time Sergio made no attempt to keep his phone conversation private. He told the person at the other end that nothing new had happened, that "he" had not yet returned. "He will not forgive me," he said two or three times, and he promised that he would keep her informed. When he got off, he told me that it was the wife of one of Miguel's literary friends. "She is my only friend. He took me away from Barcelona and I live in his world. The people we see are really all his friends. One or two listen attentively when I speak, but it is only out of good manners—they are his friends not mine."

He pointed out where the enamel on which the stones were embedded had cracked on Miguel's pendant. One of the stones had also cracked and fallen out. "Even after he did this and I hit him, I kept begging his pardon. When his face swelled, I said, 'I know this will mean nothing to you, but I am sorry I hit you, I am sorry.' He said, 'It makes no difference now, we are through.' He can say that without raising his voice. He knows how to hurt me without hitting me, and he has always made me feel inferior. I do not think he will return today. He probably hopes that I will have moved out before he returns, but I cannot do that, I cannot."

The phone rang again and Sergio said yes into it two or three times. He appeared to be holding his breath. He hung up slowly. "That was he," he said, and shook his head to show me that the trite reassurances I had been proffering all morning had not come true.

"He only called to leave a message for you, that you are not to leave. He will be a little late, but he wants to see you. He did not tell me how he was. Nothing. He would have been kinder to the house-keeper.

"I do not know why people are always telling me that it is simply his aristocratic manner when he is rude and unfeeling. What is so aristocratic about his family, anyway? There was no money there for generations. If it had not been for his grandfather who got interested in business, they would have spent all that was left by now. He wants to dominate me with that manner of his. He sits and reads a book and wants me to do the same. Instead, I watch television. To show him, I wrote some poetry. He tells me it is good, and I know it is. There is nothing special in that."

The last time Miguel accepted an invitation from people who were friends of Sergio's was three years earlier. "It was for a Sunday luncheon, and they put themselves out to be friendly. They even served French champagne with the dessert. Miguel hardly said a word, and the moment he finished eating he said, 'I must sleep the siesta.' He went inside to a bedroom and slept from five until nine. I kept saying to my friends, I am going to wake Miguel, but they said, no, no, let him sleep, let him feel at home. They put a kind face on it.

"Whereas I sit and listen to his intellectual friends when I prefer the conversation of ordinary working people. They are not false. That is why the other day when they were gathered here and talking politics and democracy and going from one to the other, each saying where he stood and what he wanted—I said to them that I was of the Right. Absurd, isn't it, that they should all have said that they were of the Left? One of them was a marquis, the others all sons of millionaires with summer homes all over Spain, and they say they are of the Left. However they talk, they are of the Right. I am of the Right and I am not ashamed of it. I have no guilty conscience.

"I am of the Right because I love good things, beautiful things, expensive things. I like things that last. I do not throw away money. I do not spend thousands of pesetas of an evening eating and drinking at all the chic places, when you could have better at home and for a fraction of the cost. I would spend that money on a beautiful object that I can hold in my hands and look at. I am also of the Right because I know that all these people, these so-called left-wingers who complain so much now, would act the same if *they* were in power. The way Miguel acts with me. Oh, of course, there were abuses under Franco, but I do not believe he was so bad."

It was five hours since Miguel had left for the bank. "This has been good for me," Sergio said. "I have vomited all over you, but it was good for me." He picked up Miguel's pendant and said, "I had better return this—I do not want him to think I have been showing it to you." From the door of the study he added, "I do not know if I have given you a true picture. Perhaps you ought to speak to Miguel and get his story. Mine may be too one-sided."

I wondered how much he counted on me to use whatever influence I had with Miguel. He had left the study door open and I heard the front doorbell ring. Sergio, the housekeeper and I all showed up in the foyer together. It was Miguel. "How are you feeling, Don Miguel?" the housekeeper asked.

"Fine," he said automatically, but his grateful look made me realize that she had stayed two hours past her regular time to see him. "I have been to the doctors, they took X rays, and although there is a break in the bone of the bridge of the nose, it will heal by itself and nothing need be done." Miguel addressed himself to her. To me he said, "I am glad you stayed." To Sergio, nothing. "Now, for a whiskey."

The tray with glasses, ice, water, and Miguel's brand of Scotch was on the coffee table. The dining table was laid out, and Miguel brought his drink to it. The housekeeper was disappointed that he would not eat, and when she finished serving Sergio and me, she told Miguel that she was leaving his meal warming in the kitchen, and then left.

"Everything is fine," Miguel said to me. "I am the President's darling. I did not have to speak to the press. He took one look at me and sent me off to the doctors. I'm fine now, I'm full of pain-killers. But of course, as luck would have it, the first corner the taxi stopped at on my way to the clinic my sister saw me from the sidewalk. We seldom run into each other, and now all the relatives will be calling. They are certain I am suicidal—there was the car accident during the winter when I blacked out, you know."

I was startled. I did not know.

"Oh well, that is a whole other story," he said. He smiled, and I knew that it must have involved some indiscretion of his, and was not Sergio's fault. "We shall talk of it another time," he added in English.

Sergio went out of the room, and in the same tone Miguel asked me, "How did the interview go?"

"All right," I said.

"Did he lie much?" he asked.

"I don't know, but he omitted some things, such as his activities last night while we were at the reading," I replied. "Still, he is very sorry and he said I should get your side of the story."

Miguel was surprised. "That is extraordinary for Sergio. A step forward."

Sergio returned and before he sat down asked Miguel if he was ready to eat something now. Miguel could not get himself to look at him yet, but he said, "No, but you could get me another whiskey."

Sergio took his glass eagerly, like someone who had been forgiven, and left to fix the drink.

"Don't look worried," Miguel said to me. "Everything is going to be fine, just fine." He laughed bitterly.

8

The Lost
Falange

Manuel Cantarero del Castillo—what a resoundingly Spanish name! All those open oratorical vowels strung firmly on a series of harsh consonants, like a rope of pearls, ring with tradition and promise an aristocratic lineage and a proud, upper-class mien. It is a pleasure to discover that the name belongs to an energetic, voluble man of middle height fast accumulating the fat of middle age but retaining the bright, eager eyes of youth. And it takes but one look to gather that he is irredeemably middle class. You need not study him: there is no reserve in him, no mystery or suggestion of private suffering, all the qualities that force one to linger over a Velázquez portrait, which is also the image that Cantarero's name calls up. This appearance of middle-class ordinariness turns out, like everything else about him, to be perfectly right. Yet he grew up in the youth organizations of the Falange, the fascist party from which the Franco regime borrowed its ideology, and without ever disavowing or repenting his past, he became perhaps Spain's most prominent social democrat towards the end of the Franco years. All of it makes sense, but it takes a bit of explaining. The explanation should reveal the peculiar habiliments of Spanish fascism: social democrats have turned fascist in the past, but only in Spain has the process been reversed.

Cantarero was ten when the Civil War broke out. He lived in Málaga. His father was an officer in the merchant marine and a left-wing Republican; his mother a conservative Catholic, the only daughter of a retired Army colonel. A few years earlier, when the rise of the Republic exacerbated all political differences, they had separated. Under the Republic, divorce was legal, but this was a solution to which Cantarero's mother would never agree. She did consent to share the rearing of their son, a remarkable compromise for a woman totally committed to traditional Spanish orthodoxy. Manuel spent three days with his mother and grandfather, and three days with his father; but this was not a modern, liberated up-bringing—it was a tug of war.

At each home he was scrutinized for undesirable behavior and ideas picked up at the other, and treated to a kind of ideological fumigation. His father, however, allowed him to spend his summers in the country in a small villa his grandfather owned in the mountains, and he was there when the Army revolted in July, 1936. He was not to see his father again. His father remained in Málaga until a few days before it fell in February, 1937, and continued to serve the Republic in Valencia to the very end. He went into exile, first to France, then to Mexico. Each week—punctually, says Manuel—he wrote his son a letter in which he still tried to win him over to his point of view. When he died suddenly of a heart attack in 1962, they found in his pocket an airline ticket and a visa to travel to Spain. Manuel never tried to choose between his parents' ideologies but rather, in his words, to surmount them. This was, of course, what more than a decade earlier José Antonio Primo de Rivera had tried to do when he founded the Falange in 1933, to include yet rise above the objectives of both the Right and Left, the classic, not to be realized goal of fascism.

The two Spains confronted themselves not only in Manuel's family but also in the place where he lived. Indeed, the province of Málaga in those days provided the cruelest crucible in all of Spain. Here were the greatest extremes of wealth and poverty, power and subjection, Catholic orthodoxy and anarchist aspirations. The proletarian peasantry reacted violently to the Army's uprising. The stories of their revenge are endless, particularly those told by Franco's adherents, but one of the least violent is to me the most instructive. Gerald Brenan, the English writer who among foreigners is unexcelled in his writings on modern Spain, was there, and he came upon anarchists burning stocks of the gourmet shops in the middle of Málaga's finest shopping street. He thought the food could be put to better use and said so. An anarchist replied, "We are not thieves."

A few days before I met Cantarero, I had spent an afternoon with Javier Muguerza, a professor of philosophy whose family had also spent summers on lands they owned in the mountain towns of Málaga. He was a month-old infant when the uprising came, and he lost his father during the first week of the uprising when anarchists killed his paternal grandfather and two uncles as well. Muguerza was brought up on stories of such atrocities, and although further on I shall have more to say about his political development, I mention him now because I used his case to ask Cantarero if he too had been influenced by such stories. He knew the Muguerza case; their families had been summer neighbors.

"Of course, the anarcho-syndicalists committed many errors and crimes," he said, "but the bourgeoisie of Málaga had been especially arrogant and unfeeling. On the other side of the river lived thousands of people in the most terrible conditions, subject to hunger and infection every day of their lives." And he went on to tell me that when the city fell, the Nationalists revenged themselves unmercifully. I knew this: there was no other area of Spain, except Seville, where the revanche was worse than in Málaga.

Thus, even as a boy, Manuel knew that the Nationalists were at least as culpable as the Reds. For example, the middle-aged woman and her teen-aged daughter who lived in as servants in their Málaga apartment. They had worked for his mother's family all their lives, and because some redecoration was being done on the apartment that summer they had stayed in the city to take care of it. They were, thus, on their own after the uprising until the family returned early the following year when the city fell to the Nationalists. They took care of the apartment; they kept it from being sacked by anarchists during the first weeks, and when Manuel's mother and grandfather returned to it, they found it intact. But the women had disappeared.

Eventually the grandfather learned the whole story. The young daughter was engaged to a young man who was an anarchist. He gave her a present of a pretty shawl which had probably been stolen from a rich home, but she never wore it, for mother and daughter never left the apartment except to shop. They knew their job was to hold out until their masters returned, but during the final siege of the city, food was not to be found except for a great deal of money. There was no food in the house when the city fell, but they knew it was a matter of days before Manuel's family would be back: they even had a message from them. Together they went out to a pawnshop to sell the shawl to buy food. They were immediately arrested.

"Two days later we were home. No one knew where the servants were. My grandfather began looking for them. Since he was an Army man, he had no problem about approaching the authorities. He went to the police two or three times. On his last visit, someone there remembered the names he gave them from a list of people arrested. They showed him the pile of bodies executed that day, and he recognized them although both their heads had been shaved. Just a few hours earlier they had been alive. All for a shawl."

In those early days of the Franco regime, the Falange supplied the mass ideology for the government's reason for being. Of all the forces that the uprising gathered about itself, only the Falange, with its talk of social justice, had a chance of reaching the people. Like all the children, Manuel was inscribed in the Falangist youth organization, but unlike most, he was an eager *Flecha*, an Arrow, as its members were called. (Such was not the fate of Javier Muguerza who was ten years younger and whose Madrid family was more socially finicky.) The revolutionary ideology of the Falange enthralled Manuel. He likes to quote one of the old slogans they used to shout: *Menos coche oficial y más justicia social*—Less official cars and more social justice. And a stanza from the organization's old anthem:

> *No más reyes de estirpe extranjera*
> *ni más hombres sin pan que comer.*
> *El trabajo será para todos*
> *un derecho más bien que un deber . . .*

> No more kings of foreign stock
> nor more men without bread to eat.
> Work shall be for all
> a right rather than a duty . . .

The Falangist youth organization provided idealistic youth with a program which made them feel they were helping their country and an ideology that appealed to the natural rebelliousness of young people. To them was addressed the radical program of the prewar Falangist leaders: separation of Church and state; a single, obligatory, free educational system; nationalization of the banks and all public services; agrarian reform. In the introduction to a collection of his speeches and writings, Cantarero puts it this way, "They had to enliven the *street*, the masses, and to this end the youth were encouraged in the only manner that young people can be in a gravely unjust society: by proposing to them a radical, revolutionary transformation and the construction of society on completely new bases."

His was the generation that ate cornbread. "Risen from mourning, pain, and hunger, living within a reality so recently visited by tragedy, my generation had to be one given to faith and hope. And so it was, one with a moral charge difficult to better. The Revolution towards which we were incited seemed to us like the exigency and justification for all the suffering and sacrifice we had seen and also, in large part, shared . . . And in good faith, this revolutionary project set us afire and involved us all in the most enthusiastic manner! For a long decade this generation of mine grew up with the most absolute personal commitment and with the most illusory *revolutionary impatience*."

In person he says this in more homely images. "Do you know that until I was twenty I did not know how to dance? Imagine, a Spanish youth who did not know how to dance! But I spent all my weekends in the country planting trees all over. Young Falangists like me planted hundreds of thousands of trees throughout Spain. Can you understand such dedication?"

I nodded. I had heard from Carlos Paris, a professor at the Autonomous University of Madrid, about his own experiences. He was the same age as Cantarero but came of a better placed family in Valladolid; yet he too was inspired by the social ideals of José Antonio and felt that his generation would make of Spain an example for the whole world. He too planted trees, and while at the university, volunteered for one of the "socialist" programs of the

Falange called the National Work Service, and spent one summer working the mines. Even when he went to Italy for post-graduate work, he and other Spanish students kept themselves apart, immersed always in their studies. "We had a vague notion, hard to describe, that as representatives of the new Spain we had a great contribution to make. And yet we were not Franquistas—I never liked Franco."

Neither did Cantarero. In 1942, he attended an enormous gathering of the Falangist youth at the Escorial. It was the most moving experience of his youth, but at the end of it, Franco addressed them, and he was disappointed. Perhaps it was Franco's thin little voice, his dry, uninspiring delivery, but there was nothing of the vision of José Antonio in what he said. Cantarero agreed that his own view of the founder of the Falange might be as positive as it is because Cantarero's knowledge of him is, in a sense, out of historical context. José Antonio's death in 1936 and the absence in the post-Civil War period of any other permitted alternative ideologies magnified José Antonio's virtues and gave the kind of weight to his social ideals and personality that during his life were at most of secondary importance.

The social reforms in José Antonio's program can be found in Mussolini's and Hitler's too. His Syndicalist State was Mussolini's Corporate one. In a country in which the distinct national cultures of the Basques, Catalans, and Galicians required, at least, autonomy for these peoples to be free, José Antonio would submerge the entire peninsula in the Hispanicism of Castile, and talked of imperial rule. He had contempt for democracy, and reluctantly or not, he allowed his followers to settle political arguments by murder. The Church and the Army were institutions he was not only loyal to but ones that he wanted to restore to their old power as during Spain's most reactionary days. Hitler looked back to Wagnerian nonsense, Mussolini to Imperial Rome, and José Antonio projected a vision of Spain that in its time was already an anachronism—the mad Spain of the Counter-Reformation.

Yet there seems to me no doubt that José Antonio was an extraordinarily attractive person. Cantarero likes to quote from the letter written in 1936 by Unamuno to a friend while José Antonio was in jail. Unamuno is worried about what may be happening to him, and adds, "I have followed him with attention and can assure you that his is a privileged mind. Perhaps the most promising one of contemporary Europe. His head functions perfectly." José Antonio more than reciprocated Unamuno's admiration: he considered himself a follower of his, particularly because of Unamuno's tormented reflections on Hispanicism and despite Unamuno's having gone into exile in the twenties during José Antonio's father's benevolent dictatorship.

José Antonio leaned even more on Ortega y Gasset for many of his ideas, to the point that Marxists have often said that Ortega y Gasset bears some responsibility for Spanish fascism. In the draft of a letter José Antonio wrote in jail in August, 1936, he recommends a cessation of hostilities, and goes on to envision a government that could rule Spain equitably and to outline a cabinet that would include Ortega y Gasset as Minister of Education. He admired intellectuals and cultural figures. He was a personal friend of García Lorca, and Lorca in Granada quite naturally sought refuge during the uprising in the home of the Falangist poet Luis Rosales. Lorca was taken from there, after having been denounced not by the Falangists as was first believed but by a member of the right-wing Catholic party, CEDA, and executed by the military.

Indeed, José Antonio's admiration and love of culture and its creators were a weakness—or, in any case, an anomaly—for a fascist leader. In the best of his speeches his language is impeccable and his formulations literary. He could take time from the organizing of his movement to write an article entitled "Homage and Reproach to Ortega y Gasset." Cantarero points out that neither in his writings nor in his projections of a syndicalist state does José Antonio ever show any desire to manipulate, control, or stifle artists, as have other totalitarian leaders. This stance became a legacy to what Cantarero calls the radical or left-wing Falangists.

The witty sociologist Amando de Miguel, in his book *La sociología del Franquismo*, which is a funny exposition of the awful rhetoric of the Francoists, gives the Falangists little quarter, but he does say,"The most positive thing about the Falange has undoubtedly been what we could call liberal Falangism's orientation toward intellectual life, a characteristic very contrary to that adopted by Don Miguel Primo de Rivera [José Antonio's father] and by fascist regimes." De Miguel goes on to quote one of the surprising formulations adopted at the 1953 Congress of the Falange:

> The Falange has supported and supports the necessity of incorporating intelligence in political work.
>
> The Falange considers that this incorporation and respect for intelligence constitute the essence of Spanish intellectual tradition, the supreme assumption of Western culture, and the quintessence of thought and Catholic political tradition.
>
> Culture, in regard to the creation of values, only is possible within an ambience of liberty and of trust in intelligence.

Amando de Miguel does not say it, but it is obvious that José Antonio did not pass on his gift for elegant language to the writer of that resolution. Still, the thought is there. Perhaps that is why there were no more National Congresses of the Falange. The process of separating the regime from the social rhetoric of the Falange, begun when the Axis appeared incapable of winning the war, was almost completed. Compassionate and talented Falangists like Dionisio Ridruejo and Pedro Laín Entralgo were still in government, but in the next few years they were to move further left, until they emerged as prominent members of the opposition to the regime.

I asked Cantarero why he had not, like them, broken irrevocably with the Falange. "Because I am unwilling to repent," he said. "Do you know that Laín has gone so far as to make an act of contrition in public and ask to be forgiven for his past?" These men were ten years older than he and were already leading spokesmen of the Falange during the Civil War and the years following; whereas Cantarero entered the Falange as a boy after the war and evolved guiltlessly in the ambience of its social ideals. "Indeed, men like them were the ones I looked up to as a boy—the problem is an emotional one, too, with me. Besides, I have tried to carry with me all those old comrades of mine in the Falange's youth organizations—I have to show them that those old ideals that inspired us are to be found in socialism."

Those old ideals—the lost Falange, Cantarero often calls

them—were never put into effect by the victors in the war. By the war's end, José Antonio and some of his most radical colleagues were dead (indeed, many believe that Franco allowed José Antonio to be executed by never coming to agreement with the Republic about an exchange of prisoners because he wanted José Antonio out of the way) and by then Franco, always supremely practical about not sharing power, had diluted the Falange. In 1937, he issued the Decree of Unification, presumably making the Falange the sole political arm of the state but, in effect, bringing into it all the old parties of the Right. To the old name of *Falange Español y Juntas de Ofensiva Nacional Sindicalista* was added the word *Tradicionalista*, and to the new constitution of the party a statute which is one of the most grandiloquent statements of Franco's rule. It was to set the tone of all statements about Franco in the future: "The national leader of FET and JONS, supreme Caudillo of the Movement, personifies all the values and all the honors of the same as author of the historic era in which Spain acquires the possibilities of realizing its destiny and with it the yearnings of the Movement; the leader assumes in all its plenitude the most absolute authority. The leader answers to God and to History."

This usurpation and dilution of the Falange continued throughout the years as Franco maneuvered, usually in response to changes in the outside world, to give a different interpretation to his rule. The very name Falange became an embarrassment and "the Movement" was used more and more to refer to the political base of his rule. In 1956, when the phrase "organic democracy" had already begun to gain unashamed currency, the new law changed the name officially to the Movement. Amando de Miguel has great fun in his book tracing the changing names and definitions by different political leaders. Defining the Movement became a kind of ploy, the meaning more willful and vague each year; de Miguel climaxes this passage in his book with a wonderful quotation from one important political leader who in 1972 said that the Movement played the same role in Spain that the "American Way of Life" plays in the United States. I know that in 1965 for an ordinary uneducated peasant like a cousin I discovered in Galicia, the Movement had lost even its national identity. I told my cousin that until we met I had not known of his existence, and he said, "I knew about you, that you lived in

Tampa in America, and when there was war in Europe I used to wonder if the Movement had taken you there to fight."

From the moment of his death José Antonio was deified. He was called the Absent One, and on an outside wall of every church in Spain his name was inscribed in large letters along with the yoke and arrows of the Falange above the word *Presente*. In recent years these inscriptions have become fainter through neglect. The many cabinets that Franco juggled in the years he ruled always contained Falangists—whether they were *true* Falangists is a matter of controversy—but none of José Antonio's social reforms ever achieved the status of a national project. At the twentieth anniversary of his death in 1956, an old Falangist who was then in the cabinet addressed an eloquent homage to him in which he was bold enough to ask the dead leader, "Are you happy with us?" and to reply, "I think not."

The cabinet minister went on to list the things they had failed to do, and summed up, "You cannot be happy with this mediocre and sensual life of ours." But there was an upbeat ending to his eulogy: he promised José Antonio that his followers would change this situation, visualizing their efforts in poetic images, none of them arising out of any practical program. He had no power, of course; he was only a cabinet minister. Later, he was to say that although as Minister of Housing he had a plan for building hundreds of thousands of workers' homes, he had no budget and no chance of directing any monies to his ministry.

Nevertheless, events such as this speech, which were not publicized by the official press, gave young men like Cantarero heart. He was working on a Moroccan newspaper and read that particular speech on the France-Presse teletype, and the rush of feeling he experienced was the sort of thing that helped create in him and others a self-tranquilizing frame of mind, the false assurance that there was an "impending revolution." He had not gone to college but to the merchant marine school in Cádiz, again reconciling his father's life (his father had been an officer in the merchant marine) and the practical work needed to build the new Spain. He shipped out to learn the machinist's trade, and he owes to this his first close contact with workers and with the forbidden literature. He remembers the shock of reading Rousseau and finding out that it was not what he had been told. He read Marx, too—"He is key to understanding the need for socialism," he says—but his new knowledge did not alienate him from the Falange but deepened his understanding of its social program. He decided he needed to study more, and left the merchant marine for the University of Madrid.

It is interesting to compare his life at this point with that of Javier Muguerza, whose family were summer neighbors of Cantarero's when he was a boy. Muguerza was a new-born infant when the Civil War broke out, ten years younger than Cantarero. (The difference of a decade in ages has its significance: had Cantarero been ten years older, like Ridruejo and Laín Entralgo, he might not have stayed in the Falange so long or tried to base his present socialist politics on that past; if ten years younger, like Muguerza, he might have been totally untouched.) The only adult male in the Muguerza family to survive the visit of the Anarchist militia was an uncle who hid and then fled. The family was to join him in Madrid after the war. While their summer place was in the hands of the Republicans, the women and children had a difficult time surviving. "Peasants who lived on my grandfather's lands brought us food," Muguerza said impatiently. "I was brought up on all those hard luck stories."

Muguerza knew I was joking when I said that he was a traitor to his family, but he replied seriously, nevertheless. "Of course, there were horrors committed by the Republicans, but that was not what I experienced. I lived the reality of the victors' Spain, and that was a concentration camp. Anyway, it is easier to forgive ignorant and hungry people their violent acts than to forgive those who have presumably taken power to establish a civilized Christian order."

For him the hungry years mean the scene repeated again and again, when he was four, across the road from their fine villa on the outskirts of Madrid. There was much empty land there, and the garbage collectors had taken to dumping their loads without permission or even the knowledge of public officials within sight of their home. His family was outraged, and they were able after a while to get that practice stopped. But for some months, Muguerza remembers watching entire families combing the hill of refuse for food from the earliest hours of the morning until nightfall.

He was never enrolled in the Falangist youth organization. His family did not want him mixing with common children. He was sent to the German school in Madrid when he was five; his family thought the Germans were on their way to rule the world. Except for his mother, he has not seen his relatives for years. He laughs and says that at five he committed his first rebellious act: he scratched his armpit while giving the required Nazi salute to Hitler's portrait in school. Three years later, when the Germans had lost the war and Nazis in Madrid were scurrying for cover, he ran across one of his Nazi teachers in the street and gleefully gave him the salute and called, "*Sieg Heil!*" The teacher said, "No, no!" and ran.

By that time his family, keen about the political weather, had already transferred him to a Church school. The school sponsored pious outings on Sundays to country towns within driving distance of Madrid. "Imagine, to those hungry people we children passed out not food, which they desperately needed, but tracts. I refused to go again after one Sunday when we came upon the scene of an entire block of people routed out of their homes and being beaten right there in the street. The Falange was looking for a Red and this was their way of finding him."

The Falange never had a chance with Muguerza. When he was nine or ten, at a time when Cantarero was training for the merchant marine and fervent about the revolution the Falange would create, Muguerza was summering again with his family in the mountain town of Coín southwest of Málaga. It was the period when the exiles, without the backing of the Allies, had sent guerrillas across the border as far south as these mountains. One day an older cousin took Muguerza to the town square. The cousin had heard that some guerrillas had been caught. Townspeople stood around silently watching. He remembers the Civil Guards and the Falangists standing guard over a wounded man. The face of another guerrilla they displayed was a mass of caked blood. He was dead. This show was meant as a warning. To Muguerza those two men in the square were a confirmation of what had only been a rumor.

Such events alone might have been sufficient to keep Muguerza from absorbing uncritically the ideology of the Falange or the political opportunism of the regime, but there were also the differences between his paternal and maternal families, which were perhaps minimal once Franco won but which had their influence on him. His paternal grandfather, like Cantarero's maternal one, was a retired Army man, and his summary execution had not been an entirely gratuitous act of the anarchists, for he had had knowledge of the coming uprising and had supported it. When Muguerza learned this as a boy, he came across another astonishing fact—one of his father's brothers, also killed by the anarchists, had been a socialist sympathizer and a friend of Negrín, who was soon to become the Prime Minister of the Republic. To this day he remarks how terrible it must have been for his uncle to be killed by people with whose politics he agreed.

But the paternal uncle who survived and with whom they were close in Madrid was the kind of man who burned the works of Voltaire to keep warm. They meant that little to him. There were many people like him in that first decade of the Franco regime, but most often they burned the books to be safe. Not in Muguerza's mother's family. There were classics there of the kind that Cantarero was not to find until he shipped out in the merchant marine, and Muguerza was allowed to read them. It was his reading and his scholarly bent that first got him into trouble in high school.

His mother's family did not, of course, mean to turn him into a critic of the regime. They sent him to the German school and later to the Church school, and they did not let him forget the terrors of Republican rule. But his mother stood by him when he was dismissed from high school because the officials learned he had started a study circle to read a new book by José Luis Lopez Aranguren. "It was a rather pious work, for you must remember that Aranguren started as a Catholic philosopher," Muguerza explained, and laughed: the ironies of life under Franco keep him in good humor. (Aranguren was later to be a major influence when he studied philosophy under him at the University of Madrid, and Aranguren was expelled from the University in 1965 when with two other professors he led a march of some three thousand students into the heart of Madrid. I met Muguerza at Aranguren's home.) "And in time that Army grandfather of mine was helpful even in death," he added.

Muguerza was arrested in 1956, two years before Cantarero was radicalized and eight before Cantarero finally resigned his last position in the Falange. Muguerza was at the University then, but too new a student to be in the leadership of what was called "the

147

nephews' rebellion." Three of the student leaders were nephews of García Lorca, Pedro Salinas, and the right-wing martyr whose assassination by Republicans is credited with sparking the military uprising in 1936, Calvo Sotelo. Since they were accused of subversion, they were to be tried by a military court. Muguerza spent eleven months in jail waiting for his case to come up. The judge turned out to be a colonel who had served under his grandfather, and he was so well disposed towards Muguerza, after he learned who he was, that he addressed him with the familiar *tú* and took a fatherly tone with him.

The colonel looked at the charges and saw that Muguerza was known to have led a study circle on Hegel. "How do you pronounce that?" he asked Muguerza, and when Muguerza replied, he exclaimed, "Ah yes, Egel—the one who was always with Marx!" Muguerza could be sentenced to a minimum of twelve years and a maximum of death, but the judge indicated to his lawyer that he was going to let him off. He must be a good boy—he was a Muguerza. In any case, before the trial was done, Pope Pius died and Muguerza was released under the amnesty that followed. For Muguerza, all the forces that propped the Franco regime—the Army, Falange, *Opus Dei*—were farcical when they were not sinister. To derive one's social conscience from any of them would appear laughable to him.

Not, of course, to Cantarero. After studying law and journalism in Madrid and working on the Moroccan newspaper, he became head of the cultural activities of the Falangist youth organization and editor of its weekly *Juventud*. In these positions he began to give exposure to the work of writers like García Lorca, Miguel Hernandez, Rafael Albertí, Pedro Salinas, thus trying to bridge the cultural gap that the censorship until then had maintained. Spaniards had been cut off entirely from these literary men of the twenties, and Cantarero was trying to perform the service for young people that his reading while in the merchant marine had done for him. He was an extraordinarily busy man. He completed his law and journalism degrees and continued studies in sociology while directing the cultural activities of the Falange youth organization and editing its newspaper.

In a 1970 collection of his speeches, lectures, articles, interviews, some of which go back as far as 1958, there is evidence of his liberalism and critical stance with the old-guard Francoists. They are cautious statements, to be sure, but it was a time when to speak of reconciliation or to pay homage to exiles required boldness and some courage. He must have felt that his work was making a contribution to the socialist future he already believed in, for in the early sixties he also accepted the appointment as national secretary of the SEU, the official student organization which at first provided an outlet for unorthodox cultural activities. But when he became its head, its function was an oppressive one, and he resigned in 1964 when student agitation against the SEU became serious. "I agreed with the students," he said, "and disagreed with the educational policies of the government."

From then on his writings and conferences and speeches are all devoted to socialism as the solution to Spain's problems and the means by which the two Spains can be reconciled. His was not, of course, the socialism of the illegal opposition parties but that of social democracy, rooted always in his experience in the Falange. He did not break any of his old ties; he was even reelected in 1970 national president of one of those associations the government favored—Old Members of the Youth Front. None of these jobs were remunerative (not one of his critics accuse him of being *enchufado*, plugged in) and he made his living practicing law. He worked a short while for a national travel agency that also owns luxury hotels, but he did not like that. He was not interested in making money or in business; politics was his passion.

An often anguished passion. The worst of it was bearing towards the end of the fifties the disillusion that the official Falange was going to keep the revolution "impending" forever, that his old comrades' hopes were illusory. There was also his uneasy relation to the ideas and concepts he found in Marx. He loved Marx, but it was hurtful for a social democrat to read him or the modern European Marxists: the term social democrat appears always in the pejorative. Just as José Antonio was harsher with the old Spanish Right and the latifundists than with the Left, so were the Marxists more contemptuous of the social democrats than of the capitalists. On one of the occasions that I saw Cantarero in 1976, the current issue of a new liberal magazine was devoted to the proliferating parties of the Left. The magazine gave the officers of each, described its approach to issues, outlined its long-term political program, speculated about possible coalitions among them; but *La Reforma Social Española*, the party Cantarero had founded, was neither listed nor assessed, and Cantarero's name did not appear in the issue. They simply did not consider him and his party left-wing. A judgment Muguerza might well concur with.

This hurts Cantarero in a personal way. In an interview that he gave in 1972, he allows himself to express a certain pique when explaining why reformism has not been popular in Spain. "Reformism exorcises the danger of chaotic revolutionism and it is never the Trojan horse of extremists of any kind. But, you are right, reformism is not brilliant, it is not *esthetic*. In Spain there has been a tendency, now on the decline, to think of politics much more as esthetics than as an attempt at the practical manipulation of reality in a positive determined sense. Spanish rationalism has been a rationalism of *pure reason* and not a rationalism of *common sense*, which is what is valid in politics. There has been no effort to fit political formulations to the exigencies of reality in its rambling process of change, but to adapt that reality to an a priori scheme of ideas totally conceived outside its conditions."

Yet very often Cantarero has been the most impractical of politicians. He has persisted in maintaining his identification with the Falange during years when it has not only lost all relation to power but has been contemptuously rejected in all quarters. The old politicians scrambling for new positions in what everyone has known, long before Franco died, must be the inevitable democratic future, have been expounding as openly as they could that they were never Falangists, that the Movement was simply the channel in which all Spaniards were obliged to make their contribution. The rhetoric was vague; the putdown of the Falange clear. In the days immediately following the Civil War, some rank-and-file left-wingers joined the Falange, some to escape punishment, but most in order to participate in its social program. But that had also for three decades ceased to be the case with the Left. Yet in 1973, Cantarero was capable of publishing a book, long and closely argued, entitled, *The Falange and Socialism*; it tries to persuade the reader, often convincingly, that the true Falange was always on the side of the angels.

And in 1976, when the hugely expanded lower middle class and moderates, who were the natural base for Cantarero's social democratic party, were enthusiastic about the young king and hopeful that he would, indeed, manage a democratic transition, Cantarero was anti-monarchical. I asked him if he was muting this aspect of his program. Wasn't it, after all, an unimportant issue? "No, no, it is very important ideologically," he insisted. "How can we talk of democracy and make the head of state an office that is gained by inheritance? I do not avoid the issue. It comes up at every meeting where I appear and I say so."

But neither did he gain the support of intransigent Republicans. He responded on the two occasions when Juan Carlos asked to see him, once when he was still prince and once after his coronation. At the first audience, Cantarero began, "You know that we . . ." and the prince said, "I know, I know the songs you people sang." And at the second he warned the chief of protocol that he would not address the king as " 'Your Majesty' or any of that," and that, too, was acceptable to Juan Carlos. But in March, 1976, his republicanism became almost purely a matter of form when his party addressed a message of support to the king.

The message is typical of Cantarero in that it uses the occasion to preach. It states that if they have changed from a "merely passive acceptance" of the king's sovereignty to an "active" one, it is not because of "an ideological identification." Rather, because they are now certain the king means to establish a monarchy which, like those of advanced European countries, "would permit real options" for social democracy to come to power through elections. On the whole, the message of support could not have pleased Juan Carlos very much.

No more than it pleased the opposition in 1975 that Cantarero applied for legal recognition for his *Reforma Social Española* under the Franco regime's new law permitting political associations, and obtained it. The law was a maneuver of the old guard by which they hoped to defuse the widespread demand for political democracy, basic to which was the legalization of political parties. It was not just the Left which rejected this new law but also conservatives and liberals desirous of entering the European Common Market. Under the law, the associations that applied for recognition had to be approved by the Movement, and the freedom to be given them to organize and hold meetings was a highly limited one, since there were no plans to hold any elections in which they could participate. They were only associations, after all, not political parties.

Cantarero pointed out to me the passage in their application in which they promised to uphold the principles of the Movement and the Fundamental Law of the State. He thought it was a pragmatic compromise. Others did not; they thought that those who complied with the law were helping the Franco regime cloak itself with respectability. Indeed, by the fall of 1975, the demand for free political parties had reached a new stage, since most parties of the Left were being promised legality; but the Left's demand now included a refusal to accept legality if it was not also extended to the Communist Party. To be operating legally as an approved political association in 1975 was so great a practical political error that it could be argued that such pragmatism was indistinguishable from opportunism.

These new political issues make Cantarero restive. He shifted around in his chair when I asked him about them. On the one hand, he had been an old spokesman for national reconciliation; on the other, he had slowly evolved a political ideology that rejected extremists and blamed them for provoking the Right into the 1936 uprising. This was a conclusion that he stated firmly in a book he had just published in 1975 called *The Tragedy of Spanish Socialism*. He was, after all, a social democrat in whom anti-communism dies hard. "I do not know, we shall have to wait on what happens in France and Italy before one can decide about the Communists," he said. "After all, if you believe what they are saying now—that they are for multi-party democracy, free trade unions, etc.—they are, in effect, dismantling the Third International. Can that be? I do not trust them."

A week earlier, I had asked Javier Muguerza, if he was a member of any of the opposition parties. He was not. I asked him if there was one that he supported above the others, for he, too, wanted to see socialists unite and end the quarrels of the past. It was this hopefulness that had kept him in Spain, for he had had to fight for years the Ministry of Education and the Falangist and *Opus Dei* professors in the universities in order to get a teaching post (a long odyssey, dismaying and funny by turns, that is not appropriate at this point) and had, consequently, often been tempted to exile himself. He delayed his reply to me on his stand on the political parties with an exemplary tale on the necessity of staying in Spain and persisting there.

At the time that Muguerza's old mentor Aranguren was expelled from the University of Madrid a decade earlier, another professor there, in the science department, was so outraged that he wrote an insulting letter to the Minister of Education resigning his position. He got a job in a Midwestern university in the United States and went into exile. Every morning now, after making himself a Spanish breakfast, the ingredients for which are difficult to find in the Midwest, he reads Spanish newspapers which are at least one week old by the time he receives them. He then writes disrespectful letters to Spanish officials concerning actions he has read about in the papers, and only then goes off to his classes. His only friends are other Spaniards with whom he can share his anger, and his only outings are to Spanish restaurants, also hard to come by. "He is going mad," Muguerza said. "It is the only alternative."

"Therefore, I am for all parties that are going to make the socialist revolution," Muguerza said. He smiled at the grandiloquence and vagueness of that statement. "I tell you which party I support: I support whichever party is denied legality."

Many Spaniards were "wasted" by the Franco years, to use wasted in the American vernacular; or "burned," to use *quemados* in the Spanish. There were those, as many say is true of the anti-Franco intellectuals of the fifties and early sixties who prematurely hailed the coming of a new day, whose energies were used up and their hopefulness gone too far astray to have something to say to the new generation. And, in a different, pejorative sense, there were spokesmen who are discredited by their past. At the time I was talking to Cantarero, the foreign minister, José María de Areilza, in the king's first cabinet, was cited by the foreign press as the liberal who along with Fraga Iribarne, an even more powerful minister, was working hard to turn Spain into a democracy. But in Spain everyone knew the changing roles Areilza had played in the Franco regime, including his early days as a liberal Falangist when he inveighed against international capital, contrasting it with the work ethics and morality of business managers, as speculators and dealers in "anonymous money—without a nation and Jewish." And about Fraga Iribarne, who had served Franco well as Minister of Tourism in the government of the "bright technicians" in the early sixties, there was no doubt of his insincerity. Theirs may be Cantarero's fate.

Amando de Miguel, whose book on the changing rhetoric of the Franco regime I have cited, exhibits all the impatience, irritableness, and longing to be done with such men that Spaniards raised under the dictatorship feel. Who cares about all the fine distinctions that, say, Cantarero makes throughout his long book on the Falange about the manner in which true Falangists kept its social ideals and how they were frustrated in implementing them? De Miguel says, "The modern face of the Falange was, finally, a literary, grimacing style with which to cloak the shame of a poor, battered society with an essentially conservative politics. Perhaps this society stands out more as a conglomerate of forces with even more nationalist and conservative tones, but *liberal Falangism* does not cease to be a superficial patina of wordly avant-gardism."

In early 1976, when I first met Cantarero, the newspapers had carried an item about a group of liberal politicians, among whom were prominent monarchists and members of the *Opus Dei*, meeting to explore the possibility of forming a new liberal party. It was not an unusual piece of news. The promise of free political parties was in the air, though they were all still illegal, and every few days a new one was announced without any reaction from the tolerant government. What was surprising to me about this news item was that Cantarero appeared in the group. I asked one member of the *Opus Dei* and one monarchist about this, and the former replied, "One lesson I recommend to Americans about Spanish politics: when you read liberal, you must translate that as conservative, and social democrat as liberal." The monarchist said, "The socialism of social democrats is so far in the future that it is no problem to contemplate a coalition with them now."

Later that year, I told Cantarero that his book on the Falange convinced me that its best ideals had provided young people in the closed world of the post-Civil War period with an outlet for their finest sentiments. It had been, as Cantarero puts it, a seedbed for socialist ideas. Since their principal enemy in Spain was the Franco regime, had they ever fought against it? Cantarero said there were many, many cases of discrimination of all sorts against Falangists. I insisted: could he tell me of any actions by true Falangists against the Franco government? Cantarero replied that once at a meeting of the Falangist youth that Franco addressed, one young man called out, "Franco, traitor to the Falange!" He went to prison for several years. I asked no more; I felt like a lawyer who after a deadly question to the defendant rests his case.

I did not want to feel that way: only a Spaniard who had lived those years should allow himself to undercut the worth of the political road Cantarero had followed. I remembered him talking of the good slogans and songs and of the fervor he felt for social justice and his learning on his own to put aside the elitist, authoritarian means by which the Falange had hoped to rule. "It was difficult to learn the value of democracy, to comprehend that evolution may be slower but that it is also more humane, more efficacious, and effects change more profoundly," he had said to me, and I preferred to think of him that way.

We first met on a wet, rainy day. He had agreed on the phone to see me at his office, and when I got there he walked stiffly and winced when I shook his hand. He explained that in the interval of three hours since we had talked he had slipped on the sidewalk and cracked two ribs. I excused him from our appointment. "No, no," he said, leading me into his small, modest office, "it does not hurt to talk." He is committed to talk, and perhaps now, in a more liberal and less dangerous atmosphere, Cantarero and others like him who have no talent for heroism can at last be useful.

9

The Anti-Semite

I wanted to meet Don Anselmo because he was seventy-six—he did not take part in the Civil War, he spent several years of his young manhood in New York City, and he owed his middle-class status to a father who began life as a peasant laborer in Andalusia but rose to become a prominent businessman in Seville. All this promised a different point of view about life under Franco. I had only incidentally learned these few facts about Don Anselmo from the young son of his middle age, Esteban, with whom I had spent many hours in Sevillian cafés discussing the new socialist politics of Andalusia. Esteban was not sure that his father would see me. Don Anselmo did not know that Esteban was a member of the Socialist Alliance of Andalusia, but since Esteban still lived at home, they had had many ideological arguments: Don Anselmo might well be wary of me. Also, the old man lived a very private life; he even ran his small agency business from a study in their apartment. Nevertheless, I called him. Don Anselmo was as courteous as his name sounds; he tried out an English sentence with me, and invited me to spend an afternoon with him. Only after I had made the date did Esteban say to me, "I am anti-Zionist but not anti-Semitic—like my father."

He said it casually, almost as an aside, towards the end of a long day during which, among other things, Esteban and I had marched with fifty thousand people in the first legal demonstration in Seville for amnesty for political prisoners. I remember thinking, Well, most middle-class Spaniards are anti-Semitic, and replied, "That is not what we shall be talking about." Esteban smiled and said no more. I did not suspect then that I would be unable to distract Don Anselmo from his subject. Indeed, his anti-Semitism turned out to be the most interesting thing about him. His was a classical case predating the fevers of Nazism—he would have been horrified to have been ideologically connected with the crimes of the holocaust—and it was almost a pleasure to find someone who openly, shamelessly, expressed the ancient prejudices that literate Spaniards, even of the most liberal political persuasion, feel and are careful, with foreigners, not to reveal.

"What is wrong with Spain?" Don Anselmo will ask rhetorically. "There was no Expulsion of the Jews—a mere one hundred thousand left. But two, three, four million remained and they are in our blood!"

Historians say that the number who left was higher and the total of Spanish Jews then considerably less, but Don Anselmo has picked up his history helter-skelter always to feed his inflamed imagination. I had provoked that statement from him when I told him that the modern novelist Juan Goytisolo felt very strongly that the troubles of Spain all dated from the expulsion of the Arabs and Jews, from the breakup of what had been an extraordinary civilization in which Christians, Arabs, and Jews coexisted. I also used the paradigmatic image, taken from Samuel Eliot Morison's history of the southern voyages, of Columbus sailing west out of the Bay of Cádiz at the same time that another ship headed east with Jews. The metaphor for Spain's historical miscarriage sailed right by Don Anselmo unperceived. "No, that could not be," he replied. "The Expulsion came much earlier—by then the Inquisition had long been in effect."

The Inquisition was, of course, another means, once the Jews had been forcibly converted, of continuing the Expulsion, but this was a history, less of religion or race than of the pursuit of power, and I did not want to take it up with Don Anselmo, nor here. In any case, Don Anselmo was not interested in what might have been. He prided himself in being, as in all things, a practical man. The deed was done; now, let us look at its effects—that was his stance. Yet it was not common sense that impelled him but the need to be locked into his subject. It was his round of despair, for it was also apparent that he was not looking for a solution in the present day—in this the horrifying example of Nazism may have affected him. Don Anselmo was a Don Quixote who never would leave home. How did he get that way?

A few months earlier, in Madrid, I had spent an afternoon in the lower middle-class apartment of a Spaniard who, perhaps because he was twenty years younger than Don Anselmo, did saddle his Rocinante and go out to do battle. He was Mariano Sanchez Cobisa, leader of the extreme right-wing, street-action group called the Guerrillas of Christ the King, and as he put it, "an admirer of all fascisms." He did not have Jews on his mind. He was more worried about Masons. He was a chemical engineer, lived in tacky austerity in an old-fashioned apartment below Puerta del Sol, and was as obsessed as Don Anselmo. He had fought for the Nationalists in the Civil War, for Hitler with the Blue Division on the Russian front, less orthodoxly within Spain since then to keep the Movement pure, and in recent years led his Guerrillas into the streets regularly to administer beatings to those, as he said, who would not listen to reason.

With him I had to bring up the subject of the Jews, since he never mentioned them. I asked him what he had thought of Franco's allowing Jews to enter Spain after the occupation of France by the Nazis, and without hesitation he said that had been a good act. He did not believe in persecuting people for what they are, as a nation or race, but for what they do. In Germany Hitler had thought it necessary to single out Jews, but that may have been a mistake of his. For Spaniards such actions would have been wrong. He admired Hitler, but he would have fought any attempt to force German fascism on Spain.

"I know that Hitler had special treatment for the Jews. I saw it when I was in Berlin on my way back from the Russian front. They had to wear a distinguishing symbol, and in the Metro they had to sit in special seats under a placard. But those stories about concentration camps and extermination are not true."

I said, "You do not believe that six million Jews were exterminated?"

"Oh no, if Hitler had done that, I should not admire him,"

Sanchez Cobisa replied. "His fascism was correct for the German people, though it would not have been for us, and I saw that they all backed him. I shall tell you why Hitler did not kill Jews. If Jews were being killed in Germany, the people would have known it, for it could not have been hidden. And they would not have allowed it. The German people are a very civilized, fine people."

"There are witnesses, documents, photographs," I said. "You do not believe them?"

He shook his head. I tried to hold his gaze. "You do not believe the Nazis exterminated six million Jews?" His eyes shifted and went blank.

"It is a lie," he said.

"Now, about the Masons, you seem to think they make up a dangerous secret society," I said. He nodded eagerly, glad to get off the subject of the Jews. "It is difficult for an American to believe this because in our country they are organized into fraternal lodges devoted mainly to having a good time."

"Yes, yes, it is a secret society," he said. "They inspire all kinds of subversive actions. It explains how the sons of old families have been turned into Communists."

Thinking about him later, I speculated about why people like Sanchez Cobisa had not selected Jews as their scapegoat. Had the Nazis preempted the issue and given it a bad name? Had their own Inquisition done that? There is an enormous scholarship on the Inquisition that would seem to make it possible to trace the descendants of all *conversos:* too constricting for the kind of scare fascists must raise. In any case, the number of practicing Jews in Spain is negligible. Masons are handier. Defining them, tracking them down, gives you more free play. Jews are not a fruitful issue.

The Jewish community in Spain is pitifully small. On Gran Vía, in Madrid, there are two or three shops catering to tourists which use the menorah or the Star of David as a colophon. That such distinguishing marks are displayed is a sign of toleration (inadmissible during most of Franco's reign); they also appear on the front of the city's new synagogue, the only one for the entire city. I went there for Friday night service, and found the synagogue, hidden away at the end of a short street, almost filled with two hundred to three hundred people. The prayer books were a donation from New York

Sephardic Jews, and the synagogue was built with funds from the American Jewish Committee. It was an Orthodox congregation with all the women sitting up in the balcony, not participating in the service in any way, allowed only to look down on the men conducting the serious affairs of worship. But there was a spirit of gladness in the place, stronger than I have seen in the few synagogues I have visited in the United States, and it was due, undoubtedly, to their being able to express their Jewishness openly this one day of the week.

The Jews I spoke to all said that the congregation was almost entirely of Moroccan origin come to Madrid shortly after the Six-Day War. None knew a Spanish-born Jew. Yet whether one is a descendant of the ancient Jewish families interests Spaniards not a little. The sophisticated will volunteer that one or the other of his parents' families or both must have once been Jewish, but they will be very irritated if someone else says it of him. There were, it is true, ghettos all over Spain, and this underground current of concern as to whether one's friends are descended from them is a corruption of the scholarship on the subject. In 1964, I used to ask jokingly, "Is everyone in Mallorca Jewish?" With intellectuals it seems to be no more than mildly nasty gossip, and to my knowledge such questionable ancestry does not subject you to the slightest ostracism. But the prejudice is sufficiently there to keep them from objecting to—or even noticing—when, say, a prominent writer publishes an essay gratuitously and grossly anti-Semitic, as happened in one case I know in 1976. But this latter case was unusual, and no one erects an ideology or even a series of opinions on which anti-Semitism plays any consistent part.

Don Anselmo then is an oddity. He lives quietly in Seville out of tune with his son's life and with everything else going on in Spain, but scratch any Spaniard, as a Jew might say, and you will find a bit of Don Anselmo in him. After several hours of talk, during which I never quarreled or argued with him, he noticed the tolerant smile with which I must have been responding to his characterization of Jews, and said, "Now, you might well say that this is a mania with me. I do not deny it. It is a mania, but I also say that penicillin would not have been discovered if it had not been a mania with someone." He returns to the subject time and again, he is often impassioned in his assertations, but there is about him an air of disinterest that research scientists might well emulate.

For example, he knew from me that my father was a Galician from the province of La Coruña, but this did not deter him from unfolding his own theory about Galicians being descendants of the Biblical people of Galilee. "Not only the Galicians are their descendants," he said, "but also the Welsh, the Galizianos of eastern Austria, and the Gauls. Now, Galilee was but a small province of Palestine and it is true also that it was not supposed to be Hebrew in its general population. But given the smallness of that whole area, there must have been a great deal of seepage along those borders— they were a nomadic people—and consequently you can count on the Galileans being infiltrated by Jews. Why would they, too, have been dispersed if they were not?

"It is to this that you can trace the bad characteristics of Spanish Galicians, who have, of course, many fine ones, too. I have always said that the French—today's Gauls—and the Galicians have two things in common—love of sex and money. They are so passionate about sex that they will kill for it—notice how Galician fiestas always end in fights about women?—and about money both are notoriously tight-fisted."

Don Anselmo had just ruined an old joke of mine: one that consisted of my objecting when some American Jewish friend teased another by accusing him of being a Galiziano—meaning hard-headed and canny—because, I would interrupt, my father was a Spanish Galiziano, about whom the same calumnies are repeated in Spain. It was always good for a laugh, to connect Galicia in Spain with Galicia in Poland. My flight of the imagination had just run aground in Seville, but I knew Don Anselmo meant nothing personal. He was as objective about his own family background. "Names, that is another way you can tell, though after my years in New York I pride myself on recognizing the physical characteristics of Jews at a glance. All names ending in ez, for one. It means son of, and mine, Marquez, means son of Marcos. It does not always follow and I hope it does not in my case. But take my father. That audacity of his, that mercantile ability—so clearly Jewish."

His father came up to Seville from the countryside around Granada before the end of the last century, and by the time Don

Anselmo was eighteen at the end of the first World War, he had a flourishing business as representative for Brazilian coffee growers and timber interests. At one time, he was the sole distributor of Brazilian coffee in Spain and Europe, and besides his offices in the *centro*, downtown, in Seville, he directed agents in the major ports of Europe. But none of this went to his head: he made no attempt to break into Andalusian society, and when Don Anselmo said he wanted to go to the university, which in those days meant going to Madrid, the old man replied, "So you want to be a *señorito?*" and refused.

Don Anselmo was the oldest of four sons, and his father meant him to take over the business. The armistice had just been signed in Europe, and he could now send his son to the United States to learn by doing. He expected Don Anselmo to pick up English and modern ways of doing business. Don Anselmo was a timid young man and he left with trepidation but obediently. He was on his own when he reached New York; his father had not paved his way. Don Anselmo answered advertisements and found jobs in business offices. He took English courses at Columbia University the first year; later, accounting courses at New York University. He often got fired and he never learned why.

He did not make many friends in New York. He lived in rooming houses and once rented a room with a Spanish family. But New York City life did not provide the opportunity to join a circle of young men at, say, the cafés in the evening. In Spain even the most retiring person could fall in with such a group, but not here. The jobs he found, most often in importing offices that could use a young man with a knowledge of Spanish, did not gain him any unusual business experience. Still, he had begun to find his place in the city and did not often write to his father nor tell him much of what he was doing. After a couple of years, his father began to question what he had learned thus far and to suggest that it might be time to return to Seville.

"I always replied that I was gathering valuable experience. Of course, I hoped to, but I knew that what I did was routine work," Don Anselmo said. "I was not ready to go back yet."

Don Anselmo's wife, who is some twenty-three years younger than he and looks even younger, was drinking coffee with us when he said that. She looked at him with raised eyebrows, as if to say he had been sowing his oats in New York. I suggested that having put the Atlantic between himself and his father, he was engaging in the kind of rebellion that young people seem to need to go through. "Oh no, we were not like that in those days," he said. "We respected our fathers, not like the youth of today who think nothing of rejecting all advice."

"Girls, then?" I said.

He shook his head and smiled to himself. "I was a timid fellow, as I said. Even in Sevilla I did not have a girlfriend." But when his wife momentarily left the living room, he launched on a story about a New York girl who worked in his office that he felt illustrated his innocence and the marvelousness of that city.

"She was a secretary and she had all the self-confidence of New York girls. I had only just begun working there in some menial capacity when she asked me if I knew how to skate. I said 'Yes,' and she said, 'So why don't you take me skating?' I was obliged to. We went out more than once, and I thought she was my girlfriend. One evening at the Times Square subway station, while waiting on the platform where both the uptown and downtown trains stop, I thought of a novel by Zamacois, a novel that had been very popular in Spain. It was a story about adultery, and the hero gains the woman by a bet which obliges her to come to his room. I said to my girl, 'If my train comes in first, you come uptown to my room; if yours, I take you home to Brooklyn.' Well, my train came in first and she went home with me. It was very daring, for at that time I was renting a room with a Spanish family."

His wife was back in the room, and she said, "And yet you complain about the young people today!"

Don Anselmo saw no humor or relevance in this. "I am answering this gentleman's question about the differences that existed in social relations among young people in Spain and the United States."

Don Anselmo pointed out to his wife that he wanted more coffee, and when she dutifully poured it for him, her compliance allowed him to regain his composure. "From then on, when I arrived at the office in the morning, she would signal to me and I would go to the stationery room which was at the end of the hall to the back. There she would give me a good-morning kiss each day. One day she was absent from work, and when I asked her the next day if she had been ill, she told me she had taken the day off to get married. 'To whom?' I asked, and she said, 'That fellow I introduced you to downstairs last week.' I was amazed!

"He was a tall, strapping fellow, just the opposite of me. He was studying law, and incredibly enough, they went on living as before—he as a student and she as a secretary! She had gone out with me because he was so often busy studying in the evening. Later, I realized she was Jewish. At the time I thought she was Polish because she had one of those funny names, but of course I should have realized—the way she went out with me while engaged to be married, so enterprising, so clearly Jewish."

He had no other amorous adventure in New York. Yet it defined his view of the place and the nature of New York women. "When I arrived in 1919, women were still working on the trolleys collecting fares though the war was over. In the mornings you saw young women entering the office buildings to work in almost as great numbers as men. Yes, the women there were very different, very independent. They were unchaperoned, but there was no vulgarity. New York is the essence of vitality and progress, not the vulgar license that goes on here. Even in the movies now!"

He took as his example Bardem's *Furtivos*, which had gained prizes abroad, a very fine gloomy film about a peasant woman and her grown illegitimate son. Don Anselmo did not like the gross, lower-class nature of its characters and the senseless violent killing of the woman by her son at the movie's end. That sort of thing was simply shocking, he thought, but it turned out that he had missed the most important element of the plot. The mother and son had had an incestuous relationship, and he had killed her in revenge for her own murder of a woman with whom he had found love. Don Anselmo's wife tried to explain this to him (I said I had not seen the film), but he would have none of it. For him that would have been more shocking: better senseless killing than incest. "At no place did they tell you any of that," he insisted, preferring his innocence to what should have been for him even more conclusive evidence of present-day vulgarity.

When I told Esteban, Don Anselmo's son, the anecdote of his father's affair with the girl in his office, he screwed up his eyes with delight. "I had wondered about the old man. I have had inklings that he played around," he said. Physically, Esteban is a young Don Anselmo, thin, nervous, talkative, and I teased him with my opinion that temperamentally they were much the same. But whereas Don Anselmo is an observer, Esteban is an activist—in sex and politics. Even in talk: he turns every conversation into an argument. His arguments with his father went nowhere, however; it was his mother whom he thought he affected.

Esteban believed that his mother's defense of *Furtivos* was due to his own influence on her. "She is a very interesting woman, a hysteric actually. She married him when she was twenty-three and he forty-six. There must have been something to him. He is a passionate man but also a very cold one. He saddled her with all responsibilities, from the most minor one to the education of the children. He never lifts a finger. He goes out occasionally to see a customer, and their business is done in a moment, but he drags it out into a two-hour visit and then comes home and is aloof and cold.

"There is no getting through to him, but I see changes in her. The other day she said to me that she was going away to stay with friends at the beach for a few days. 'I am going alone, like a Swede, she said,' and laughed. Imagine! That she should even admit to the knowledge of what Swedish women on vacation do at the beaches. With her upbringing! It is only from me that she hears of real life. She said to me recently, 'Why can't you lead a normal life?' I said, 'A normal life, what is a normal life?' She said no more. She could tell what she might have let herself in for if she had replied, because hers has certainly not been a normal life. I wish she had tried to answer me, what a chance that would have been for me."

Esteban had me to tell him about his father's youth, but Don Anselmo has no one from whom to learn that Esteban rents a tiny studio from a friend for a nominal sum, where he takes his girls. The place gets too hot in summer, however, and during the time I was in Seville, the blazing heat caused him to make innumerable other arrangements. At twenty-five, he writes feature stories for a daily newspaper, runs a kind of disc jockey program on a local station, files stories as a stringer for a Madrid left-wing magazine, and meets continually with one leader or the other of the Socialist Alliance of Andalusia to discuss organizing tactics. He has given up painting and playing with a rock group, two activities that took much of his time in his late teens. His parents see him only during the morning and midday hours when he shows up at home to sleep.

Esteban lost his virginity when he was sixteen. That was the way he put it, and we both laughed because the old phrase was hardly apt. We were looking at a small formal park in the old section of Seville, and he said, "When I was fourteen, our crowd would be here until all hours of the night. We used to throw rocks at the bulbs in the lamps to create a dark privacy for our doings." He was not in love at the moment; a year earlier he had finally broken with a girl who had persuaded him to share her with another young man with whom she was temporarily infatuated. "Those months broke something in me," he said. Our first evening together a beautiful upper-class girl named Lila had driven us around in her car. "But Lila?" I said to him now. He replied, "No, no, we are only friends." Occasionally they slept together for the fun of it, without possessiveness or jealousy, the kind of ideal relationship that intelligent young people, he said, were now achieving. A week later, he confessed that Lila had just learned that he had spent a night with another girl and she had thrown a jealous fit and given him an ultimatum.

Don Anselmo no more suspects any of this than the incestuous relationship that escaped him in *Furtivos*. His years in New York were those of an outsider, and conditioned him to live as an observer trying to figure out what makes the world run the way it does. The Jews as a sociological concept were a godsend to him. How else explain how he went from job to job never rising to a position that taught him more than the clerkly forms of the business? In nothing he did was he a mover; even with the girl at the office, she had taken the initiative. Of him it could be said that he lost his virginity and then never went on to be the seducer.

He did not actively oppose his father's calls to return home; he simply turned a deaf ear. His father took to having business friends who were traveling to New York look him up to speak for him. He finally wrote the bank where Don Anselmo was now working telling them that he wanted his son to come home, and the president called Don Anselmo into his office and questioned him. Don Anselmo thought he explained the situation well to the bank president and that his father's letter would not prejudice him. At the end of the week he was fired. He was ready to give up, but when he returned home that evening there was a reply from an importing house whose job advertisement he had answered. He took the new job, but one day when an older woman there went out during her lunch hour to make a booking on a French liner for a vacation she had planned for years, Don Anselmo to his own surprise asked her to make a reservation for him, too. He was now twenty-seven.

"When I got back to Sevilla, I saw that my father and his business were neither of them what they had once been. That big suite of offices in the *centro* was gone. It had been bustling with business when I left—there were at least twenty people working at desks, and messengers to do their bidding. Now there was just an office on the ground floor of our home, with only one assistant, one secretary, and one messenger. The end of the World War had caused the business to dwindle away. There used to be a lot of commerce with Spain because we were neutral, and when the war ended, Europe did not have to come to Spain for its supplies."

Don Anselmo's father was not the same confident man he had been. "His mind did not have the capacity of concentration it once had, and I could not get a clear response from him whether I was to work for him. I was his oldest son and he had once expected me to take over, but now his assistant, who was a perfect Jew, was really in charge. And the truth was I had learned very little about business and was still very timid." And in Seville one did not obtain a job by answering advertisements. Don Anselmo lived again with his parents and went out each day to see friends and approach them obliquely about jobs.

It all compared very badly with the lively, progressive way of doing things in New York. Don Anselmo gave me an example: how he got a job teaching English at the science department of the University of Seville. "Not as a tenured professor, of course, but as an adjunct to teach a course once a week, to enable science students to read some of the technical books unavailable in Spanish. Yet one had to go through the traditional *oposiciones*, a competitive oral examination before four judges. One of them was the famous poet Jorge Guillen. It was a simple affair—to translate a passage from an English classic—and I doubt anyone was going to appear there better qualified than I. But before the examination took place, my family talked to friends who were friends of the judges so they would be well disposed towards me. I got the job and kept it for years. That is Spain."

The job used up only one of his evenings, and he still went out each day to meet friends at cafés with an ear cocked for another position. "That was how I heard about the marvelous enterprise that Fischer was undertaking, the kind of thing that should have been done centuries earlier but that the big land-owning families never paid attention to. I got a job with him, and while it lasted it was very exciting. Fischer was a Jew, of course, a son of a lieutenant of Kossuth's, and he came here from Egypt with a friend who was his partner and also a Jew, no doubt, or they would not have been so close. Fischer conceived of a great land reclamation project that has not been carried out to this day. Only a Jew could have arrived at such a grand conception—to build a series of dams along Isla Mayor [a swampy area of land between the Guadalquivir River and a subsidiary river] and thus turn that useless land into fertile fields to cultivate cereals and vegetables!"

Don Anselmo was in charge of personnel; he kept the work records with the assistance of secretaries for almost one thousand field workers and for the office workers. His was only an inside job, but for two years he was in touch with greatness. "It was an enormous and intricate enterprise. Complicated because the Guadalquivir River is subject to the tides and salt water comes up as far as Sevilla and leaves deposits in the soil. I think they meant first to flood Isla Mayor with fresh water and grow rice to desalinate the ground. Some farmers in the area fought the project and got it stopped, but Fischer had friends in Madrid and the order to stop work was reversed. Still, they lost time and Isla Mayor was not completely dammed the first year. Tremendous rains came—the worst in years and years—and the dams broke. A terrible tragedy."

"What a grand idea it was!" Don Anselmo said, and managed a kind of irritable sigh. "A Spaniard can think of growing enough food to eat but never to create a surplus and to export. We need Jews to teach us that. Fischer raised enough money to start anew the second year, but it was a long-range project, it required more than a year to pay for itself. And the third year was 1929—they could no longer borrow enough capital to keep going. The offices were closed and

Fischer moved to another country, as Jews do. I do not know what became of him."

When the offices were closed, all the files were burned. Don Anselmo managed to take with him the plans for reclaiming Isla Mayor. "Fischer himself had written on them 'Strictly Confidential.' I thought that someday they could be put to use again, this time successfully, that it would not always be in Andalucía as with the old aristocracy which keeps the land untilled. But in moving around I lost all those papers, and to this day Andalucía has no such project. The vision—the grand concept—is lacking."

Don Anselmo is both right and wrong about this. In the last ten years of Franco's regime, the old ways of working the land in Andalusia have changed. Not as a result of government planning, though under the technocrats of the *Opus Dei* studies were done, recommendations made, and even some action taken that broke up some *latifundios*. Some of the old *latifundios* were incorporated or bought out by banking interests, and the planting and tillage extended greatly with modern machinery. At the same time, the landless farm workers emigrated to the cities and Europe for jobs and made the traditional crops, like the olives, uneconomical to harvest. One has only to drive from Córdoba to Cádiz to see this change everywhere.

Don Anselmo is also both right and wrong about the Jews. In his fears of them he is a paradigm of the anti-Semitism of the peasantry of the fourteenth and fifteenth centuries who supported the Expulsion and the Inquisition because they saw the Jews as the carriers of capitalism, a role which the Jews were forced to play, as Isaac Deutscher says in another context. In his admiration of the Jews, however, Don Anselmo embodies the frustrations of urban Spaniards who feel, in as confused a way as the peasants, that the traditional aristocracy and Church, with their closely allied political and economic interests, have cut off Spain from modern times for five centuries. The forces that won out in the political struggle euphemistically called the Reconquest have been bad—the Jews, therefore, are good. It is in this spirit that Don Anselmo, with unconscious admiration, looks among Spaniards for descendants of the Spanish Jews of the fifteenth century trapped in the peninsula.

But when he thinks of his own diminished life and blames his bad luck and his timidity, the enterprising activity which he never achieved becomes pejoratively a characteristic of the Jews. As do any number of other things—a materialistic view of life or force of intellect or audacity in business. Even single-mindedness and feuding. "How can you explain the internecine fight that our Civil War became? It is the Jewish element in us—have you ever seen two Jews who got along with each other?"

Franco's Jewishness has been both good and bad. "Franco is, of course, a Jewish name," he explained. "And Bahamonde, his other surname, even more so. Vagabond is what it means—the wandering Jew. And there is the physical evidence. I saw it unmistakably years later in a photograph that appeared in *Newsweek*, a ferociously anti-Franco publication, obviously Jewish, so that it would not have any interest in promoting this view of him. It was a photograph in which Franco held up his grandchild, and the angle at which the camera caught him revealed for the first time his physical inheritance.

"I had known it long before, from his name and from his forwardness, his vision, his ambition to be always number one. Remember that he had been the youngest general any army in Europe had ever had, that he started here the first serious military academy, that he was probably the youngest Chief of State our nation ever had. Yet he had been only one of several generals who rose against the Republic, he was cautious until he knew they could win, he managed to have himself named El Caudillo at the very start. He was a Galician, besides. And then, like a Jew, he hung on too long, would not give up his prerogatives or his position."

After his involvement in Fischer's Isla Mayor project, Don Anselmo's life becomes singularly uneventful, in inverse proportion to Spain's, at least in his telling of it. He was thirty when the offices were closed down and he brought home the plans of the reclamation project. He still lived with his parents. He went out again less hopefully to the cafés. By default he began to work in what was left of his father's agency business. There were no more epiphanies. Even his marriage in 1946, after both parents died, seemed but a continuation of his previous life. He settled down to his present nervous frustration: it would seem that the failure of the land reclamation project in 1929 was his last chance to be "Jewish."

"You would think that after my years in New York City, I should be a Republican. Well, my sympathies were with it, but when it came in 1931, it was chaos, chaos, chaos. The uprising was necessary. We could not have gone on that way." He became, as were most of Spain's middle class, an unbudgable supporter of Franco's rule but an indifferent onlooker at all its activities. He joined no organizations and marched in no parades. None of it had any impact on him.

The taking of Seville by the Nationalists was a clever ruse of General Quiepo de Llano, the ranting demagogue who first used radio as an instrument of war. The revanche in Seville was especially brutal. The stories of the depredations of the Moors quartered in the beautiful María Luisa Park are endlessly shocking. But Don Anselmo seemed almost unaware of any of this. He was surprised that I should ask. "Oh, there were injustices committed in the first days of confusion on both sides, as happens in war. After that there has been no trouble . . . But there is no help for this country. The cause of any ills is in the Spanish people—those three or four million Jews in our blood. It shows in everything—the exiled Reds with their calumnies of what happened. Why have they not returned? I ask them. They have not returned because they are cowards. There has been nothing to fear here if you have not committed any crimes."

This characterization of the exiles is an old hypocritical response of Franco newspapers and spokesmen, but Don Anselmo can say it with conviction because his attention has been elsewhere. For example, one of his younger brothers was a militant founder of the Falange in Seville, but Don Anselmo did not learn it until after the Civil War broke out. The brother had even been involved in the conspiracy for the uprising and had been one of the handful of men within the city who helped Quiepo de Llano capture it. He went on to fight at the front, was wounded, and could have had a good post behind the lines, but he insisted on being sent back to the shock troops and was thus killed in action. Only a few years ago, Don Anselmo finally deduced that it was to this brother that he owed the loss of his job at the university during the Republic.

He had been used to teaching his classes and going by the departmental office only to collect his salary, he said, neglecting to pay flattering attention to the Dean. He thought it was this that lost him his job. Without warning, he saw a bulletin-board announcement of a new professor of English for the next term. The old family friends tried to help him again. One went to Jorge Guillen once more, and Guillen said, "I shall do what I can, but you know he is a fascist." Don Anselmo was astounded when this got back to him, but a couple of years ago, talking to one of his remaining brothers, he came to the conclusion that since the Socialists used to raid the Falange headquarters, they must have found his brother's name on a list and mistaken it for his. "My brother agreed," Don Anselmo said. "He told me that our brother even used to raise money for the Falange by selling stamps the way the Workers Commissions do now."

Don Anselmo got his job back teaching English after the war when the university reopened. It was there he met his wife; she was one of his students. The Civil War was for him a time when the supply of Yugoslavian hardwoods was cut off, and the agency then began to deal in good pine from Galicia. It still does. He has a few customers with whom he conducts business in the old gentlemanly ways. The consummation of an order gets blanketed during the long visit by coffee and drinks and much conversation. It makes a business transaction less coarse. He owns a house in the country near Granada, and it is no problem to create long stretches of time to spend there. But he will stubbornly refuse to leave for it when the family is anxious to go, as was happening the day I spent with him, because he has an important business meeting that cannot be updated or delayed. (Esteban believes his father could settle the whole thing with a phonecall.) They now will sometimes leave ahead of him, and for this reason his wife can contemplate going off to the beach alone like a Swede.

Esteban said that small though the business is it brings his father in some money. They could get along without it, but it gives the old man something to do. Otherwise, he would have only his obsession to occupy him. "What does he do the rest of the time?" I asked. Esteban replied, "He has his history books in which he looks for evidence of Jewish activities."

I asked Don Anselmo which of the modern historians he read and most liked. He said Américo de Castro. De Castro is, indeed, one of the great ones; he died in exile after a long and honorable stay at

Princeton University. Don Anselmo was surprised to hear this. He thought de Castro had stayed in Spain. "He is a brilliant man," he said, excusing him. "He is probably a Jew. They made their way into all professions, you know. Medicine, law, government—even the religious orders."

I nodded.

He leaned forward as if to let me in on a secret. "You know about Santa Teresa, our greatest saint? Her whole family was Jewish." He went through the whole rosary; the author of *La Celestina*; Luis Vives, the medieval Catholic philosopher; Loyola, the founder of the Jesuit Society; Columbus. Of Spain's *Siglo de Oro*, only Cervantes seemed to be exempt. I had nodded and nodded as he listed them. I do not know what led me to add a bead he had somehow overlooked, perhaps the little bit of Don Anselmo in all of us. I said, "And of course, Saint John of the Cross."

For a moment he only stared. "Who told you?" he asked, half rising out of his seat with delight. "I have always suspected it but never, never have I read any evidence about him! And you say it is true, what a marvel! Saint John of the Cross, too! I knew it, I knew it!" I had made his day.

10

Andalusia:
Breaking Into Politics

The leader of the Socialist Alliance of Andalusia, Alejandro Rojas-Marcos, is a dissident member of an old and rich, and consequently powerful, Andalusian family. In the towns and cities of the south you often find a prominent street named after one or other Rojas-Marcos, a tribute never extended for some historic or cultural achievement of the particular Rojas-Marcos being honored, but solely because, as Alejandro says, the Rojas-Marcoses are rich. They are landowners and bankers, and were, for a while, the only industrialists in Andalusia. Alejandro belongs to the industrial branch of the family, and for some time after he finished his studies in 1964, he displayed unusual talent for business which gladdened his apprehensive family; but for years now (he was thirty-six when I met him) he has been notorious for his activities against the regime and his socialist politics. The rebel son of the rich is not unusual in Spain; the left-wing intelligentsia of Madrid abounds in the sons and daughters of Franco cabinet ministers and Nationalist heroes. Indeed, the Duchess of Medina-Sidonia, to whose family the kings of Spain of the last few centuries are nouveaux arrivés, was sent to jail for a year by the Franco government for her protest activities. They are a phenomenon common in Latin American countries too: the upper class supplies the political leaders of the Establishment and the opposition. But Alejandro Rojas-Marcos interested me, when we spent time together in Seville, more as an example of how Spaniards born under Franco and reared in that regime's controlled environment broke the confines set for them and on their own created a new life for themselves. In the Socialist Alliance which Alejandro heads, I met young men of the lower classes whose differing pilgrimages towards socialism with an Andalusian orientation contrasted interestingly with Alejandro's, but he had had to find a way not only out of Spain's arid isolation but also out of the especially rigid traditionalism and provinciality of Andalusia's upper class.

Alejandro was not a naturally rebellious child, and when he thinks about his youth today, he cannot remember any decisive turning point either. His father does: he blames it all on a summer Alejandro spent in England when he was fifteen. Alejandro had returned after a few uneventful months there, during which English workers had held major strikes, and scandalized his father when he said, without any notion that he was challenging anyone's views, that the English strikers had had no other recourse. Later, after his views and activities became a real cause for scandal in Seville, he heard his father say to his mother, who had encouraged Alejandro's summer trips, "It was that trip to England that is the cause of all this." Alejandro smiles when he tells the story; he likes the drama of it, but he does not quite believe it.

He was the oldest of the two boys and two girls in a family in which primogeniture is of major importance. He must have had a sense of this as a boy, for unlike the other children he looked to his parents for guidance. His brother had only to receive a suggestion from his father to decide for the opposite. Alejandro always took the advice in good faith and differed only when he learned on his own that it was wrong. "And yet we have all turned out the same," Alejandro said. "All of us are socialists and so are our wives and husbands—a family disaster!"

He was born in 1940, a year after the Civil War ended, and the first ten years of his childhood were the years of hunger for Spain. He had no experience of it. His was a perfectly circumscribed life: he went to a Jesuit school in Seville, which only children of the upper class attended, and in summer the household was transferred to a large home by the Cantabrian coast just outside Santander. Only in summer did he come in contact with children not of his class. He played with them on the shore, but he never questioned that later they never showed up at the Casino, to which only good families belonged. This life was an old family ritual. His father, too, had each year spent nine months in Seville, three in Santander, and he had married a girl of a rich Santander family. Thus Alejandro never felt a jarring note in going from one place to the other: he moved always within the family and it did not even seem a privilege to be rich.

Yet there was a factor in this family situation that helped Alejandro break away, and thus leap the fences of provincial upper-class life. (None of this applies to the great aristocratic families of Andalusia—the Medina-Sidonias, the Infantadas—with their palaces in Madrid and their periodic stays in European capitals; they spend little time on their feudal estates in Andalusia.) The bourgeois families of Santander to which Alejandro's mother belonged, like their neighbors in the industrial Basque country, were more socially venturesome than the Andalusians. Alejandro's mother believed, for example, that he should learn foreign languages and that the best way to consolidate his study of them, when he reached his teens, was to spend part of each summer in some foreign country. His father was not too keen about that—Andalusians of his class are generally too proud of their ways to believe they have anything to learn from foreigners, though a decade later economic development changed this somewhat—and that is why his comment on Alejandro's English stay was his way of blaming his wife for its bad results.

Not that Alejandro was sent off on his own to work or rough it. That was inconceivable. At fifteen his family found him a family in England with whom to live while he attended classes, and they had no reason to expect that it would work any differently than in Germany and France in previous years. Perhaps England had more of an effect because he spent six rather than just two summer months, and he did not live all of them with the family to whom he was sent. This last was not Alejandro's idea; some unforeseen difficulty came up and he had to move during the last two months. But England had made a difference—he did not inform his parents he was living alone; they would have sent for him.

"I had made friends, I was enjoying myself, that was all," he says. "I did not form any left-wing opinions, I did not read Marxist literature, I was not questioning anything I had known." Indeed, he remembers telling his young English friends about his studies at the

Jesuit school in Seville. "Quite ingenuously," Alejandro explains. "I was just describing my studies, perhaps with a little pride. They were outraged for my sake, and I thought that was curious."

It was 1955, and although the cold war had already brought Spain within the orbit of American friendship, the dictatorship and the censorship were still ferocious. Any Spaniard who was lucky enough to travel and had the slightest intellectual interests returned with some of the forbidden books. Not Alejandro. Probably because within his family ambience there was not enough for him to rebel against; his father and uncles did not identify totally with the Franco regime or its chameleon ideology, though they were, as a class, one of its stronger props. They had been there before Franco, always closely allied with the Church, and although Franco was, in a sense, their servant, Alejandro did not need to feel, in the persons of his father and uncles, any guilt for what the government in Madrid did.

There was never, of course, any question about Alejandro's father's politics. He had been a young officer in the Army when the uprising came and he sided with it as a matter of course. He was taken prisoner by the Republicans, three times condemned to death, and as many times taken out to be executed. On the last occasion, the firing squad had already taken aim when someone came up with a truck and it was decided that it was more convenient to take the condemned men elsewhere. The experience bound him forever to his side in the war, and since the Franco regime not only obliterated his enemies but returned people like him even more solidly to power than they had enjoyed in the best of days, he had no reason to want to change the way things were under Franco.

Still, the Rojas-Marcoses were not fascists. They were right-wing Catholics (at one time the adjective would have been redundant) and the Falange was distasteful to them. Depending at what remove one observes the years of Franco's rule, these differences among his supporters will seem pointless or significant. In Seville, I met an elderly man who had been a member of the POUM, the Trotskyist party that during the Civil War had been as persecuted by the Socialists and Communists as by the fascists, who inscribed for me the book he had published on the years he spent in jail with Maurín, the founder of the POUM, with the undifferentiating statement that his last forty years and Spain's too had been "an absolute evil."

There are many like him; one does not need to have lived away from Spain to lump all Franco's supporters together. But only the microscopic view is interesting: in Alejandro's father's case it explains the peculiar tolerance with which he viewed his son's first political activities at the University of Seville.

In actuality, Alejandro's actions were scarcely political. He was studying law and for the first time made friends outside his class—one might almost say caste, for there were no children of workers at the university then. Without any books or publications to impel them, they discussed independently what was happening in Seville and particularly at school. "They were all as ingenuous as I," Alejandro recalled. They were members of SEU, the official student organization all were forced to join, and they began to speak up there. "We questioned small matters, budgetary ones in the main. How money was being spent on student activities. It was obvious there was corruption. We raised enough trouble to cause the head of SEU to be removed and another appointed. The new man was apolitical and honest about such matters. Now, he is a socialist!"

Although in Madrid and Barcelona the SEU had at one time served as an outlet for students with social ideas, that was not the case in Seville. The Falangists in control there were not of the social reform wing but opportunists. A couple of years after the Madrid students began to reject SEU, Alejandro and his friends came to the same conclusion to form an independent student organization. They were enterprising about it. During the summer break when Alejandro was nineteen, they elected to spend those months traveling to all the universities to confer with other students. They had no organization and practically no contacts at the places they intended to go. They had no politics either, only the desire to have a student organization they would themselves run; but they were full of high spirits: it would be an adventure, something new.

Alejandro's father did not encourage him, but he found nothing objectionable in what they were going to do. Except the fact of doing it. "He thought it was a necessary activity, but he wished his own son were not the one to do it." The SEU was the domain of the Falange; it was right that a Rojas-Marcos should not submit to it. He lent Alejandro a car and gave him whatever money he needed. The students headed north. First to Salamanca and then to Santiago de

Compostela. In both places they met with students and discussed coordinated activities for the coming term. At the next stop, Oviedo, they were picked up by the police: things were tighter there and the ease with which they had made contact earlier had made them less cautious.

"But Oviedo's police was not at all hard on us. They thought we were just *señoritos* on a spree. Still, they called *Seguridad* in Madrid, and Madrid instructed them to send us down for questioning. We were told this was just a formality, there were no charges, and we were not under arrest—they were simply assigning a policeman to drive down with us to Madrid. We were to travel without a stop, however, except for unavoidable ones, and we were not exactly free—we were not to call or speak to anyone until *Seguridad* had questioned us in Madrid. Right there in Oviedo we began to bargain. How could we leave Asturias without eating a *fabada!* It was one of the pleasures we had come there for. We hoped, of course, to pass a message to someone in the city that we had been arrested. We carried on in this way until the police chief relented. He told the man who was to be our guard to let us stop at one of the restaurants on the outskirts of Oviedo and there let us eat our *fabada*."

They were foiled, but they still hoped to outwit their guard. When they finished their meal, they insisted he had to pay for it, since they were no longer traveling on their own but as guests of the police. Their guard objected—he had not himself ordered anything, he kept repeating—but he finally gave in. From there they were to drive straight to Madrid, except to relieve themselves, and when they learned that the guard was prone to motion sickness while in a car, they took the curves of the mountain passes sharply. They urged him to take a pill to prevent the car sickness, and it made the poor devil so groggy that at one stop one of them was able to call friends in Seville without the guard's knowing to tell them they were under arrest. They were having a grand time.

They arrived at *Seguridad* in Madrid at the Puerta del Sol at two in the morning. The attitude of the police there was like that of Oviedo's—these were privileged kids on a tear. Alejandro kept getting up at every lull and announcing that since he was not under arrest he was going on to his grandmother's place in Madrid to sleep. The police could call him there if there was anything else they wanted to know. Obviously, their questioner could not let them go until he spoke to his superior the next day, so they were taken to Pensión Pilar down the street where more honored clients were usually put up, rather than to the cells in the basement for the real offenders. The next day the students at Seville demonstrated and boycotted classes, the police released them in Madrid, and when they got home they received a heroes' welcome at the university grounds.

Alejandro is red-headed and fair, his hair and neat beard are curly, and his recollection of that first political adventure gave him an impish look. Whatever arrogance the youthful knowledge that he belonged to an elite had given him is gone now. We were sitting at a café-restaurant at the head of Sierpes Street in Seville, and he did not play up to the deference and scarcely contained excitement of the waiters. Nor did he glad-hand them or play the politician. Nevertheless, he was still the young man who enjoyed to the full the ironies of the situation even while he explained to me, as precisely as a sociologist, the nuances of the clients' and staff's reactions to his presence there.

This is a knowledge which he has had to use in political campaigning, for in addressing workers his very name is likely to be a disadvantage, whereas at the university he was only among his peers. The friends he made there were not entirely of the upper strata as at the Jesuit school, but these are the ones that he kept throughout the years that followed: they developed together in university politics. For a while after his arrest in Oviedo, he continued the same kind of activities. "Oh, we were still quite ingenuous. We questioned academic policies, we called meetings that were illegal, and we were always together working out our ideas. But we had still not read Marx or even met a Socialist or a Communist, and the political ideas we were developing were of the vaguest, most amorphous sort. Then in my last year I became, like everyone else, apolitical, concerned only with classwork and getting my degree."

That year and the one that followed, spent at the law school in Madrid at postgraduate work, was a pause in his life. He had the bad luck, he believes, to have gone to Madrid University in the lull between the student unrest and militancy of 1956 and 1965. There was no student movement, no opposition activities in which he could participate. He appeared to be just another privileged student, but he did not live off his father as *señoritos* did. He had paid most of his way through the university, both in Seville and Madrid, with his first business venture. He had heard that his father was helping some employees of his who had bought small farms and were unable to keep them going. His father bought the farms and animals at a price that would get them out of their debts, and Alejandro asked his father to sell him on two-year credit terms the ten cows he thus acquired. He sold the cows immediately, bought a delivery truck with the money, hired a driver, and went into milk distribution in Seville. It was very profitable, and Alejandro still has many friends among milkmen to this day.

His success did not sufficiently capture his imagination to convert him into a businessman. It was simply an outlet for his energies. In a few years, he was to demonstrate his business managerial abilities on a much larger scale, but for him the period dating from his last year at the Seville University until the time he broke with his family and became a Socialist, some three to four years, was one less of conformity with the life set out for him as a Rojas-Marcos, which is what his activities appeared to be on the surface, but of a desperate search, an inner life he shared only with his wife and two or three friends of his university days. "I became obsessed with the desire to find a political party of the opposition that I could join. I wanted to meet Communists and Socialists, I wanted to make contact with people who fought the national regime."

It could not happen in any natural way. No one ever approached him. Who among those who risked being beaten and tortured and jailed would trust a Rojas-Marcos? He would have to find his own way into that world. He sat in the café on Sierpes Street and shook his head about that time, twelve years ago, which had seemed a dead end in his life. No young man could have that problem now: there was no opposition party, not even the least tolerated like the Communist, that could not be easily reached. In another week, in July 1976, the objective he and his isolated companions had finally envisioned—a socialist party of Andalusian origin and interests—would come to fruition with its first open convention. They had arrived.

I had already met one of Alejandro's friends from his college days who is also one of the leaders of the Socialist Alliance. Luis Uruñuela did not come from as exalted a family as Alejandro, and there had been a period when the Church had offered Uruñuela an outlet for his social ideals, but his development was similar enough to Alejandro's to keep me from repeating it here. (There was one interesting point that we argued about. Uruñuela felt that I was skeptical about that part of their party's program that insists that Andalusia is as distinct a nation within the Iberian peninsula as Catalonia, Viscaya, and Galicia, and he spent a part of our evening trying to persuade me that the fact that Andalusia did not have a separate language did not matter. I finally pleased him by quoting Shaw on the United States' and England's being two countries separated by a common language.) I was also to meet, before I saw Alejandro again in his luxury apartment given to him by his father-in-law, some young men of the Socialist Alliance whose trajectories were as different from Alejandro's as were their class and place of origin. I like to call them the Boys of the Tele-Club.

They all live in Écija, a town of about 36,000 on the eastern rim of the province of Seville, which twelve years ago, before emigration to the cities and Europe began in earnest, numbered almost twice its present population. July is not a good month to visit Écija. It registers the highest temperatures in Spain consistently and is known as the frying pan of the nation. A week earlier, to everyone's surprise, the agricultural laborers who travel out each day to work the great *cortijos* went on strike (illegally, of course) and so successfully stopped the sugar beet harvest that they won a fifty percent increase in pay—roughly five dollars a day. A young newspaperman friend was driving out in a borrowed car to do a follow-up story, and I could not resist the chance. He also planned to set up a network of contacts to report each day on labor and political unrest, the information to be channeled through the Socialist Alliance (for some, journalism is an activist profession). Écija was his first stop. It was my last: I decided to spend three days with the Boys of the Tele-Club.

The Tele-Club (I have not translated it) is just what it says: a club for watching television. At least, that is what the Ministry of Tourism and Information thought in the mid-sixties when they had helped to sponsor it in Écija. Actually, they were unknowingly lending respectability to an activity of some teen-agers of the town, most of them pious members of a youth organization of the Church, who had already begun to wrest from the authorities an abandoned series of rooms surrounding an inner patio. All the boys hoped to accomplish was to set up a place where they could be by themselves, away from priests, teachers, and parents. They were all children of the poor of Écija (there are distinctions among their parents; those who held regular or irregular jobs or trades in town, and those who simply went out to work on the great landowners' lands and traveled as far as Jaén during the olive harvest) and they had no place to go. On the town plaza they had an example, the Casino, to which only the rich could belong. The town plaza is called *el Salón* because unemployed men gather there from early morning until nightfall hoping that some farm overseer in town looking for workers will pick them; but none lolled on the sidewalk of the Casino.

Behind the town plaza, at the end of a narrow paved alley, you enter the Tele-Club past a tall wooden gate-door. The entrance widens onto a patio over much of which a grape arbor grows. Off the patio are separate rooms for the office and bar and other facilities; some of the rooms, such as the lounge and discotheque, are part of a building that fronts on the town plaza. One corner of the patio is bordered by the stone wall of the principal church of the town, and although there are no windows in it, they know its old-line priest watches them. From the first, he gave the boys trouble. He did not approve when the young priest in charge of the local *Juventudes de Acción Católica* helped them get approval from the mayor to use one room in this abandoned little complex. The old priest was not pleased, but he did nothing to prevent them from committing that original sin. Only later, when he saw the things they began to do, did he first try to stop them altogether or at least to rein them in to the one room they had been given permission to use.

The fact is that the site of the Tele-Club does not belong to the municipality. It had been a cooperative of the old Socialist Workers Party and was confiscated by the Nationalists, as was the Party's *Casa del Pueblo*, now the town's court building. It should gladden old Socialists to see that those fourteen- and fifteen- and sixteen-year-olds of the Tele-Club retrieved it, in their own version of the Reconquest, for the working class of Écija. They found the place rotting and in disrepair, the patio overgrown with weeds and wild shrubs, littered with debris, its dry well the nests of rats. "God, the insects alone were enough to drive you away," said Antonio, a twenty-eight-year-old who is the oldest of the founders of the Tele-Club. "It took months before it was a place where you could sit down, much less hold dances or cultural events."

They had no intention of confining themselves to the small office. They went to work on the whole place: cleared the patio, filled the well, repaired and painted the rooms, installed toilets, and planted vines and ivy. On the second floor of the building fronting on the town plaza two rooms were piled up with furniture belonging to the Falange. "Stolen by them, probably," said Antonio. You could only enter them from the main building, and since they did not have access to that, they climbed up the back wall, entered through the windows, and lowered the furniture to the patio. The old priest went to the mayor. They were compelled to return the furniture. A month later, they sneaked it out again. Two or three times they were forced to promise to retreat to the one room first given them. But they held their first dances, and with the proceeds cleared their debts with local stores who had sold them supplies on credit. The whole enterprise was on its way to becoming the kind of success the old priest feared.

There has never been an official truce between the boys of the Tele-Club and the old priest or between them and the mayor. To this day the situation is a standoff. They have imposed themselves by their persistence and their maneuvering. In the middle of their first confrontations with the old priest, they applied to the Ministry for recognition as a Tele-Club. With the recognition came a TV set and official literature (they have never used it) and their objective of outflanking the mayor: he cannot take the risk of closing down a club "sponsored" by the Ministry. He can, of course, denounce it, and the Ministry has sent down inspectors to look into the Tele-Club. The boys welcome the inspector with photographers and friendly newspapermen, they explain the folkloric work they are doing, and the inspector always leaves delighted with the photographs and publicity that appear about him in the papers.

Throughout the years the boys of the Tele-Club have held dances and lectures and shown films, and they have done so according to their own ideas and notions. The club became a place where you can come and play records and dance in one room, talk or read in another, or sit in the patio and have a drink. You pay less for a Coca Cola there than anywhere else in Écija, and the old man who takes care of it keeps the place neat and some of the borders planted with vegetables. Given the nature of the young men who were moved to start the club, it was inevitable that they should look at Écija, then Andalusia, then Spain with critical eyes. Some of the more active are now Socialists in Rojas-Marcos' Alliance, but they are less concerned with building their party than with calling attention to injustices that need to be rectified. It was inevitable, for example, that the agricultural workers who went on strike first came to them for help and advice. They made no attempt to control them; they put them in contact with the Workers Commissions of nearby towns who are, in the main, organized by the Communist Party.

Two of them act as stringers for a Seville newspaper without pay, in order to get unofficial news disseminated. During the days I was with them, I saw them use this power—so negligible in other countries it would not be considered power—to pressure the local authorities into giving a hearing to real estate developers who hoped to build in Écija but were turned away summarily because they had not bribed the right people. They went to the mayor to "interview" him and then to his appointee in Bellas Artes, a committee that is supposed to pass on all new building to guarantee that it does not clash with the artistic appearance of Écija. The town is historic; the Visigoths, Romans, Moors settled here, and they all left much evidence of their civilizations. The real estate developers had been told that their proposed apartment buildings would interfere with a view of Écija's many church towers as one approached the city from one point of the compass. The developers showed the Tele-Club boys that they did not.

The Tele-Club stringers announced to the authorities when they went to pressure them that they were covering a story, but their real interest lay in creating jobs for the hundreds of unemployed construction workers in town. In this affair they were following the lead of a member of the town council named Zapico, a fellow socialist whose odyssey to that elected office is one of the best stories I know of how Spaniards maneuvered under Franco to crack the monolithic facade of the regime. Zapico and the stringers met with the developers in the lounge of the town's modest hotel and came to agreement on strategy. Over drinks and hors d'oeuvres everyone became expansive and talked politics and ideology. The construction people believed that Écija must break the hold of the great landowners on politics, and Zapico agreed. Their lawyer, who at Salamanca had studied under an important socialist theoretician, said, "But you are moderates, socialists like you would let the capitalists live." Zapico laughed. "There is nothing moderate about us. We are Marxists and we want to eradicate capitalism, but right now we are interested in jobs for our people."

Later that afternoon, the stringers told a couple of unemployed construction workers who dropped by the Tele-Club about all this. "What! Obstruct the view of the town—when what is needed is to set fire to the whole place!" one exclaimed. Before he and his friends went out to *el Salón* to spread the word, he added, "Let Bellas Artes come to my shitty home and see if they can see their fucking towers from there!" This contempt for the works of the Church is traditional with the poor of Andalusia (several at the Tele-Club were unimpressed by the socialists and reformers in the Church—"It took them two thousand years to discover Christ was a socialist?") and Antonio and Angel, the two stringers, enjoy such talk, although they are versed in Écija's history and are indignant that nothing is done to uncover the mosaics under the town plaza or the ruins that lie beneath the slum section of El Picadero.

For Angel, whose story I should like to contrast with Rojas-Marcos', such talk would have been particularly wounding only a few years ago. He came close to taking the final vows in the Salesian order, and owes to it a thorough-going education and his desire to do good works. He is twenty-six and was born in a poor family, but since his father was a soldier (after more than thirty years' duty, the father recently retired with the grade of sergeant) he was able to go to a Salesian school in Écija. He might have had to drop out at nine or ten and go to work, as did almost all the boys of his neighborhood, but at confession he attracted the attention of one of the priests. He cannot remember why now, but the priest talked to him about going on to the seminary the next year (he was nine then) where he would live away from home.

I quote him from this point on: I liked the Salesian school from the very first, I must admit. I liked the way some of the monks acted, particularly the one who spoke to me. I decided that I wanted to go to the seminary and I told him so. I had not been very religious. I had not cared to be an altar boy and the mass did not thrill me. What I liked about the school was that it gave me a chance to play at sports. Most boys are not eligible to go to the seminary until they are ten. I was nine, I must have been a good student. I was to have spoken to my parents and been ready to leave in September, but once I got home I was ashamed to tell them. It ruined my summer, for I did not dare go near the school to play as I did other summers and I did not go to church either.

I do not know what the priest thought when I returned in the fall to continue with regular school. He did not bring it up and neither did I, but before the year was up I changed my mind and told the priest I wanted to go. The seminary would cost my parents nothing. I spoke to them and they let me go. It was an honor for them, I suppose, though it meant I would be gone almost the entire year. The seminary was farther south, but that turned out to be in such a bad state that we finally were transferred to one in Huelva. I was caught up in it and I think I only missed home during my first week. From then on I was totally devoted to my studies and to the routine of the school.

They were not bad men, the Salesians, though I learned later that all of it, or a lot of it, was hypocrisy. The Salesians are a teaching order and their vows include that and also chastity and poverty. They are, in fact, supposed to teach the poor, but the Salesian schools around here are really for the middle class. The studies were serious and we worked hard—I was later to learn how superficial most education in Spain is compared to the seminary. I liked it. I had friends, I studied. By the time I was fourteen I had finished the *bachillerato*, which prepared me to enter college if that was what I wanted or could afford.

I stayed with the Salesians, of course. First, you do a year of novitiate, which consists of just that, being an apprentice in the order, a kind of testing period before you take your first vows to study for the priesthood. It is all a slow process, becoming a priest, but I went into it wholeheartedly. I did not even go back to Écija that summer, and later on we were not supposed to. I took my first vows after the year was up and elected to study philosophy.

We lived in the seminary and never left it, we wore soutanes, and I was so serious, so dedicated and devout that the Father Superior took me aside when I was sixteen and told me to take things less intensely. Once a week we went into Huelva in groups for the afternoon. I kept my head down and did not look at people. My philosophy studies were to last four years, then I was to renew my vows for three years and spend that time teaching in a school as the final test before being ordained. But I was such a good boy, so pious that when I was nineteen there were some in the seminary who said I was ready for ordination. They did not know—nor did the group of my intimate friends who shared all their thoughts—that I was already in trouble: I was masturbating all the time.

I could not stop, and on Thursday afternoons in Huelva I was attracted by the girls. I was also subject to a strange disquiet that I still cannot adequately describe. It seemed physical and yet it was not sexual. I would, of course, confess my masturbation, but my confessor took it lightly—do not worry, do not do it anymore. I had heard of a Salesian psychologist in Rome. He too came from Écija, and I decided that only he could advise me about my terrible problem. To me my disquiet and my masturbation were signs that I was not ready to renew my vows, as I soon had to do. I wrote to him and asked him if I should. No one knew about this. My friends and I shared everything but did not tell one another about our sexual feelings. That was my only problem, not philosophical or theological ones. I so lived my life within the order that I did not notice how it did not live up to its vows to teach the poor, the more obvious of the transgressions against the founder Don Bosco's ideals.

I waited for the reply from Rome and it did not come. The day for renewing my vows approached and I could not decide until I heard from him. Finally, I did not take my vows. Nor did I take the final examinations that would have qualified me to be a teacher, for I did not want anyone to think that I had taken advantage of the Salesian brothers in order to gain a career cheaply. I was that proud and also that ashamed. I went back to Écija and the letter arrived twenty days later. No one at the seminary had pressured me, not even the Father Superior. I said that I had to think it all over, that I was not ready now but that I would come back. A group of my friends cried. It was inconceivable to them that I of all the ones there should not renew my vows.

The letter told me that my problems would go away of themselves and that I should renew my vows. I learned that there had been a postal strike in Rome and that was what had delayed the letter, so I owe it to the working class that I did not fall into the trap. But I wanted to become a teacher still, and with my parents' help I went to the university in Sevilla. I did not last out the year—the professors were of a terribly low level, particularly in philosophy. I quarreled publicly for the first time in my life—I told a professor his class was a fraud. It had not occurred to me then that I could easily have passed, with the kind of education I had received at the Salesians, the state examinations for substitute teachers in elementary schools. I had made friends with a young Galician, who also had dropped out of a Salesian seminary, and we went off to an Andalucían country town to live among the poor.

One of the conclusions I had come to while waiting for that letter from Rome was that I would make a very poor teacher the way I was. Once during Holy Week at the seminary I had asked to be assigned to a school, instead of going home to my family, and I had been appalled to see that I could not interest those poor children in what I was teaching. What did I know of the world? I had lived apart from reality. The Galician and I rented an abandoned home. I thought only of living among the poor, but he had a purpose—to turn the house into a kind of school for the children of the neighborhood. First we had to clean it up, fight the rats, clear out the yard, and create a place where children could play.

We taught them too, but not like the Salesians. We did not sit them in a classroom and dictate to them. Some seminarian friends heard what we were doing and came down. They marveled—what a difficult thing! They were foolish, for in fact it was very easy, we had no problems. Still, it started a group of us discussing what we could do within the Church. This was in 1971 and there were already precedents. All of us were seminarians who had dropped out, and we decided to go as a group to the inspector responsible for the order's schools in Sevilla and Córdoba and propose that he turn over to us the poorest of the Salesian schools, the one with the worst students as well. We promised we should then renew our vows and work within the order. We were too late. All assignments for the coming term had been made. That was that.

I then took the state examinations for *interinos*, substitute teachers, for which you do not need a university degree, and of course passed them without any trouble. There are now so many of us qualified in this way to teach as substitutes that the scene in Sevilla when you go to apply for an assignment is one of absolute chaos—a huge mass of people fighting their way to one window. I worked hard to get there and I then held my arms to each side of the window and stiffened them to keep from getting plastered against it. Even then one person on his hands and knees crawled between my legs and shot up in front of me. It was that or no job—I do not blame him. The emigration office is right next to it, and when you first go there, you think the pushing, milling mob are people looking for work in Europe. Some persons get so disgusted that they apply for emigration instead.

I taught as substitute for three years at the low pay, always unhappy about the little I could do, but I was not about to go through years at the state universities to get a degree in order to become a *licenciado* and get a permanent assignment at higher pay. I knew of the St. Thomas Aquinas University in Rome, where they would recognize my three years of study in philosophy with the Salesians and thus complete the degree in two years. Actually, I did it in one year, from 1974 to June 1975. I had saved fifty thousand pesetas and my parents lent me another fifty thousand. The degree from Rome would be an ecclesiastical one, but I could easily get it confirmed in Spain by taking tests. In Rome there were many courses I never had to attend; I simply took exams and studied on my own. Some of it I knew from my time with the Salesians. But others, like a course in which we read the first volume of *Kapital*, I had not the slightest preparation for.

All the courses were in Italian, but I had learned this language in my first years at the seminary, for when I was twelve I decided that I was going to read all twenty volumes of the memoirs of Don Bosco, the founder of our order, and they were in Italian. I read only four. What foolishness!—but not really, for those four volumes dealt with his childhood and youth and Don Bosco was an extraordinary man.

Anyway, I read *Kapital* with a priest who spoke Italian with a French accent—and I with a Spanish. It was extremely difficult and not just because of the language. I had no concept, given the life I had led, of what a salary was, much less surplus value. But it was a valuable experience, for it gave me a start towards where I was already heading.

Where I was already heading. I remember one night during the year that I never completed at the University of Sevilla going to a lecture that another student told me Alejandro Rojas-Marcos was giving. It was the first such I went to. I knew that it was dangerous to go, but I was such a scholarly type that I taped it in order to review it later and think about it. The student who told me was pleased to see me there and warned me at the end that the police were outside. He said I should give him the tape and he supplied me with a blank one; in case the police picked me up, I would have nothing incriminating on me and thus could make up any story I wanted, for I had, as we say, no antecedents, no record. I walked alone out of the place telling myself that I must do so in a measured way, it would be the best defense when they picked me up that I was not running. I accomplished this so well that it came as an intense surprise to find myself suddenly two blocks away and out of danger.

That was what happened to me by the time I returned a year ago from Rome—there was not the slightest chance that I would ever return to the Salesians. I was out of that danger. I took the series of five examinations to get my permanent teacher's license, and of course passed them without any preparation. Such is the low level of expectation in this country. I got assigned to a school here in Écija, and have now been teaching for one year. There is so little I can do here. A structure has been set up in school, and I do not believe in forcing my views on children, nor do they have the kind of preparation that would make them have any demands on me. The parents show no interest either. I was able to get them to act about the teachers who hit the children, and this gave me an opportunity to talk to the children themselves openly. But that is all. Most parents only came to see me towards the end of the term, to ask me to please pass their failing kids.

I of course looked into the Tele-Club when I returned from Rome, and in September one of them—Antonio, as a matter of fact—took me aside and invited me to hear Rojas-Marcos in Zapico's home. I was tremendously impressed. No tape recorder this time. I joined up immediately and took on the task of reporting for the Sevilla newspaper. And a few other things. It is a problem. The trouble is I am in an action group, and unlike other parties of the Left, ours is not ready to give me the kind of theoretical preparation I need. And there is no time, either. We are making it all up as we go along.

And there is another thing—I am still a virgin. I am unable to act a role, and such a thing goes on with girls, they put on such falseness the moment you address them, that I am unable to play up to them. One of my great problems is that I am a perfectionist. I am looking for the ideal girl, and of course she does not exist. The logical thing would be to find a girl with whom I have a great deal in common and then develop together. That is the way I shall proceed. For all my worries about masturbating when I was at the seminary I never thought to observe what was going on around me. Recently I heard that one of the students who was there with me was dropped because he was a homosexual. He had been molesting the children he was teaching. I was shocked, but the fellow who told me said there was a lot of that going on. I was amazed, but of course it makes sense.

I stopped taking the sacraments and going to church soon after the letter arrived from Rome. I had been overcome with the absurdity of it all. When I was in Rome, I was not uplifted by the sight of the evidence of centuries of the Church's existence. All those symbols of religion filled me with loathing instead.

"Then you no longer believe in God?" I asked Angel.

"I have made no decision about that," he replied. "It is not so simple. I should have to erect a whole philosophical structure at the top of which there would appear the conclusion yes or no. I have put it aside as a problem. I do not even know whether I have the capacity to work through that philosophical problem. I certainly do not have the desire. There are so many other things to do. At least, now I am out in the real world."

In the sense that Angel meant it, Alejandro Rojas-Marcos was always out in the real world. Still, Alejandro was not only circumscribed by his class; another factor contributed to his isolation: in Seville almost everyone had to start anew. There were no old-timers around when these young men born after the Civil War came of age; liberal and radical intellectuals, trade-union and left-wing political leaders had not survived the revanche. There were scarcely any exiles either in France or Latin America from Seville. Everyone was caught in the city when it was taken by surprise the first day of the uprising in 1936. The same situation obtained in Écija where the regular Army was quartered; there was no fighting there as happened throughout the Andalusian countryside. The great anarchist movement of Andalusia was wiped out, and the *Casas del Pueblo* of the Socialist Workers Party were obliterated.

Historians have documented the horrors of what happened in Seville, but no one has told Écija's sad story. It was all on too small a scale, I suppose. The first day of the uprising only one man was killed. A worker who had been drinking all day headed for *el Salón* to find his friends. It was deserted. On the walls of the buildings were pasted posters declaring the state of siege. "What is this!" he yelled, and tore one down. "*Viva la República!*" He was shot down right there. I sat at the Tele-Club and listened to the stories of what happened in the following days and months from young men who had heard it from their parents and middle-aged men who had seen it as boys. "I was six and used to go out early each morning to deliver newspapers," said one, "and I would see the corpses out in the street. I would come home and vomit."

"And it was not just the Army either with their lists taken from *la Casa del Pueblo* of poor devils who at some time had put down their names there in hopes of being called for a job. No. It was the *señoritos* too, the sons of the great landowners. Any one of them could come to your house or pick you out at a street corner. You, you, you, come with us. And then your body lay in the street for a couple of days and your family did not dare pick it up. They took their good time about carting them away. And that priest whom they practically made a saint when he died—they even named a street after him—he went out in his cassock and also took his pick—you, you, you."

"Then when there were no more left to kill, they put us through the years of hunger. It was to their benefit to have plenty of hungry people around to work their fields for nothing. Everyone knows the *señorito* who said everywhere, 'They tell me the people are hungry, but I do not believe it so long as the benches in *el Salón* are still standing.' And those benches are made of iron—that is what he would have had us eat. That *señorito* is not so young anymore, he comes almost every day to the Casino in his fancy German car, but we know who he is and what he said; we know."

The people remember. The corniest of slogans from movements of social struggles—No Voice Is Wholly Lost; The Fight Goes On; We Shall Not Forget—all regain their original luster when the boys of the Tele-Club use them as the coins of their exchanges. The early Franco years appear then as a time when their parents, and they, too, paused, not so much to regroup their forces but simply to survive physically. There was the business of ordinary living to attend to. You scrounged. You went out to the *cortijos* after the harvest hoping to find a handful of wheat that had been overlooked or a few beets that had not been dug up, but more often you came home with grass and weeds. It was a long time before anyone had time or energy to think of founding the Tele-Club.

The business of ordinary living was on a very privileged scale for Alejandro Rojas-Marcos. He returned from his year of postgraduate study in law in Madrid with the notion that he would make contact with a clandestine party and put his law degree to good use. He was in love with a girl from a rich Seville family and she thought as he did. "I had no intention ever, from the moment I became active in college, to enter into any of the family businesses, but my father made me a fantastic offer. I was to manage the largest cement factory to be built in Andalucía after first making a tour of several European countries to learn how such businesses are run. It was a new enterprise for the family. It would be solely under my command. That promised independence of a sort. The trip would be our honeymoon. I said yes, and when we returned, I became director of the business at the age of twenty-five."

The family thought he was securely in the fold. He did his job well, so well that his position there owed nothing in practice to the nepotism that made the appointment possible. His father and his uncles showed their pleasure by appointing him to the board of other family enterprises. At one time he served on ten of these. There was no supervision of the organization or running of the factory; his family had only to look at the production figures and at the bottom line of the quarterly reports to know he was performing beyond their expectations. They did not know that he had instituted practices new not only to their businesses but to most in Spain. He equalized the pay of office and factory workers, he extended vacations and pensions to all workers, and he paid higher salaries than any company in the area. All this went unnoticed for almost two years.

There were only rumblings at first. His father heard at his club from other businessmen that Alejandro was paying his office messenger boys more than they paid their clerks. He laughed it off. Soon some of his uncles began to criticize him: Alejandro's practices were giving them problems with their old employees. At the same time, Alejandro had begun to appear in public as an unorthodox aspirant to elective office. He was dropped from some of the boards because he also irked them at meetings about how those businesses were run. There was no question that the cement factory was efficiently and productively managed. They could not change his practices there and they were not about to replace such an outstanding director, but soon the cement factory was the only business on whose board he sat.

The *Leyes Fundamentales* of 1966, a species of new constitution imposed by referendum, gave Alejandro the opportunity to run for the city council in Seville. The outside world knows the *Leyes Fundamentales* mostly as the document by which Franco finally declared Spain a monarchy—though he was never to allow a king to rule while he lived—and then designated Juan Carlos, rather than his father who was the legitimate pretender, as the heir to be crowned in the murky, distant future. (Throughout 1976, Juan Carlos was to need to dismantle this constitution, to which he owed the throne, in order to create some sort of representative government.) But the *Leyes* also instituted the farcical *tercio* in the *Cortes* and city councils by which one third of the members were elected by heads of families. This was done to give credence to the thesis that Spain was an organic democracy. It was also Franco's grudging way of responding to the new era of Spain's relations with the outside world and to the restiveness of the new middle class.

The *tercio* was not to be elected in ways in which we are accustomed. It did not mean that political parties could be formed to put up candidates or that platforms could be drawn up that in any way questioned the manner in which the country was ruled. Nor meetings and rallies called. Indeed, there was no chance, even within what it did allow, that an honest election, or the semblance of it, would be held. To vote in such an election meant you were bestowing legitimacy on the dictatorship, and everywhere the apathy of the eligible voters was notable. Nevertheless, Alejandro and his old college friends, who knew better what they were about now, decided to take advantage of the elections for the first *tercio* in Seville: Alejandro was put up as candidate for the city council.

To all appearances, Alejandro's candidature was the kind the *Leyes Fundamentales* encouraged; he was a young businessman with the right sort of family connections. True, he had not been approached by the Movement or any other leader of the Seville Establishment to run for office, but this was the first time the law was being put into effect and there were many small details for running the elections that had not yet been worked out. For example, the kind of campaign, and the duration of it, that should be permitted. When three years later Zapico decided to run for the city council in Écija, the campaign period had been reduced to four days; but Alejandro campaigned for more than two weeks and he was not held down stringently to posters and handbills passed by the censorship, as Zapico was later, but actually went around the city giving speeches without interference from the police. Who was to worry, anyway, that a Rojas-Marcos might not be doing the right thing? The ballot boxes could always be stuffed—and were. Indeed, such had been the zeal with which the local authorities tried to outdo one another in showing the people's support for Franco's *Leyes Fundamentales* that when all the referendum votes were counted it appeared that one hundred five percent of the country had voted.

Alejandro knew that the small number of supporters of the regime who would turn out for the elections would vote for him. He did not have to woo them. What he wanted to do was reach the workers. For two weeks he made the rounds of working-class neighborhoods, concentrating on the bars where men gathered afternoons and evenings for talk, a glass of wine, and television. Often he or the friends who were the nucleus of what was to become the Socialist

Alliance would pay the bartender to turn off the television set. "I would then jump up on the bar and introduce myself to the ready-made audience," Alejandro said. "First, I always apologized for the intrusion and for my name. I told them they were right to be skeptical of a Rojas-Marcos, to wonder why one would want to do anything for them. I told them there would not be much that I could do but that I would honestly try. Actually, my name helped me in that election, even with them. I have found that working people have accepted me more readily than people of my class. It is not the workers who send me anonymous letters or make anonymous phonecalls to ask me if in view of some public statement or the other that I have made I am going to give up my luxury apartment on Plaza de Cuba."

He was elected. "We decided that for three months I was to do nothing. The group of us was already acting like a party in the sense that we worked out together what my stands would be. Then after the three months were up, I began to question the measures and reports handed down to us. It was unheard of. I tried to point out where obvious fiscal corruption was taking place. At our suggestion, the press began to cover the sessions and they reported what I said. What a scandal! None of it pleased my family— except my wife, who is one of the few wives in the group of us in *Alianza* who completely supports her husband's politics—and certainly none of their friends. That was when I began to be dropped from the boards of various enterprises."

Alejandro did not serve out his term. He confronted the mayor with evidence of blatant corruption and resigned in order to make the point, as publicly as possible, that the city council was a powerless body. Alejandro's resignation was not a defeat; they were exhilaratingly aware that they had rent the smoothness of the regime's political surface in Seville. They decided that for the 1971 elections Alejandro should run for the national *Cortes* as a *tercio* representative. (All other representatives in the *Cortes*, and in the city councils, are, of course, appointed.) They had no hope of electing him this time. Alejandro was now notorious as a dissident, and the ballot boxes would simply be stuffed to defeat him. They planned their campaign accordingly. They gathered the 14,000 signatures needed to place him on the ballot with success. Then they ignored the four-day limitation for campaigning; they issued hand-bills without the approval of the censor; they again assaulted the bars of the working-class neighborhoods. Finally, Alejandro rented a theater and issued a call to the other candidates to join him in debate.

Only three responded, but the place was jammed. "I announced at the start that I would be reading a statement at the end. I said no more and turned the platform over to them. That gave a certain suspense to the evening. They accused me of all sorts of opportunism—I was not running for the *Cortes* to join in the glorious work of the Movement, etc. I would use the position for self-aggrandizement and so on. I did not reply to any of their charges, I simply reminded them and the audience that I had announced I had a statement to read. Here it is. It made their charges ridiculous: I was withdrawing from the campaign and said why. There was shocked silence. It was the first time such a thing had happened, and it made national news, unlike my denunciations in the city council, that our so-called organic democracy had been openly called a fraud."

His example did not go unnoticed. In Écija, Zapico had hoped to run for the city council in that election, but he found out too late that he was not inscribed as a resident of that city and had to wait until 1974 to emulate Alejandro. Zapico had only moved to Écija in 1970, but he took for granted that since he came there appointed by the Spanish equivalent of the civil service as an aide of the court (he maintains the dockets of all cases for the judges, an office that is less clerical than it sounds, for he is the man with whom lawyers and plaintiffs confer before a case comes up for trial) that he was already included in the town census. Zapico did not know Alejandro; he did not belong to any illegal party; he did not even know the boys of the Tele-Club. "Oh, if I had known the boys of the Tele-Club then, I would have definitely crushed the Establishment forever!" he exclaims. "I only had the Écija *fútbol* team to help me, but I outstripped all my opponents anyway."

Zapico accomplished something that Alejandro did not—the first truthful election report in Spain on the number of citizens who voted in an election. Peanuts, one might say—Écija is such a little corner of Spain—but something of a triumph during the Franco regime. It took much maneuvering and astuteness for someone like

Zapico, who had neither the money nor the friends united by political ideals that Alejandro had. But Zapico is a little man full of fun and energy whose arguments come fast on one another with such good nature that they at least neutralize opponents when they do not convince them. He had so little experience that he did not even know the formalities for entering his name on the lists, but the clerks at the court, who during elections are the overseers, helped him with these, for like everyone with whom he comes in contact, they had all become his friends. There were other factors that decide the elections that he had to learn posthaste; such as the practice of issuing dummy ballots with your name plus those of your sympathetic fellow candidates; the voters take these into the polling centers and deposit them in the ballot box rather than write themselves the names of the three men to fill the vacant seat. In a town where most voters are functional illiterates it was important to do this right.

He could not slip up in any way, for there were only four days allowed for campaigning following the last day of official acceptance of nominees. Zapico's papers were in order and the overseers accepted his candidature. This astounded the mayor. Until now, the mayor would ask some five friends to put up their names for the three seats usually vacant, honorary offices in effect, so that there had never been a contender like Zapico. If there were not more candidates nominated than offices to be filled, the election was not legal under the law. The three men intended by the mayor to sit on the city council were always listed first on the dummy ballot, for most voters did not bother to mark their ballots and in that case the first three names gained the vote. Should too many voters cross out the first three names, the extra ballots with which the boxes were always stuffed would take care of this.

Zapico loves to explain all the details of what occurred, for his election depended on how he maneuvered with all obstacles. His main problem at first lay in the dummy ballots; the mayor and his cohorts would never include him in the ones which carried their candidates. Their opposition to Zapico had nothing to do with his political ideas—they were unknown, perhaps even to Zapico himself—but to his effrontery in putting himself forward. By a series of maneuvers, which included knocking out one of their candidates because there were unsettled legal charges against him and by a dramatic announcement of withdrawal on the second day of the campaign leaving only three candidates running, Zapico outsmarted the Écija Establishment. Zapico had to appear on a ballot by himself, but he forced them to issue another for their candidates with only the three qualified candidates listed. And on the day of the election, he played his trump card. "There are only twenty-one polling stations in Écija and the entire *fútbol* team manned them as watchers—there was no ballot stuffing possible with them around."

Unlike Alejandro, Zapico was not allowed meetings and speeches. Even one of his posters did not pass the censorship. "For a Clean Écija," one of them read, meaning the open sewers in the slums, but since in Spain, as with us, clean also means uncorrupt, the poster was considered to be subversive defamation. Nevertheless, there was word-of-mouth knowledge that he was challenging the old guard. This made him popular. "Not that the people were going to rush out to vote—why should they? But there were the *fútbol* players at all the booths and they were not even going to be able to boost the number of citizens voting to the proportions that national dignity requires. You understand, that you never got less than eighty percent voting according to their reports."

As the day progressed, the local authorities became reconciled to Zapico's winning one of the seats; people were using his ballot although it contained only his name. "When I threatened to withdraw my candidacy on the second day, even the governor of the province called me to say that I could not do this, but now they had no time. They wanted to make a deal—that after the counting was done, I allow the number of votes for each man to be boosted proportionally, so that Écija would not look bad. I said absolutely not. I won overwhelmingly with 1,900 votes and my nearest contender with eight hundred, but they had to report that only six and a half percent of the eligible voters had voted. The first time in Spain. That ought to give you an idea of how many vote in places where no one is challenging the established order."

The boys of the Tele-Club knew Zapico's story, but they were delighted to hear it again. Zapico dragged me and two or three of them to the nearby city hall to make a point—to show us the unparliamentary and undemocratic nature of the city council. He led me into the meeting room of the council, a long, spacious room with a Roman mosaic, uncovered in Écija, embedded in the middle of the floor. It is roped off and takes up much of the chamber. The room shines with restoration newness, like some of the hotels of the Tourism Ministry, and looks unused and fake, like a medieval court in a Hollywood movie. At one end is the mayor's throne-like chair upholstered in red plush; it sits on a dais in front of a long, bare table. Along two walls, at right angles to this throne, are a series of lesser, though still imposing chairs, also in red plush, for the city councilmen. There are no tables in front of them, no place for papers or books, nothing. "You can see what we are expected to do here—listen and nod to whatever the mayor reports to us."

Again unlike Alejandro, Zapico has not resigned his seat. He is a gadfly. He joined every one of the five committees of the council, but of course has not been appointed chairman of any. He wants to be able to question everything, and does. He has brought debate to any proceedings in which he is involved. At first the only nay vote was his. There are thirteen councilmen and Zapico has on one occasion mustered six votes. He has won over entirely one of the councilmen, and he brought him along to the Tele-Club when they were on their way to meet with the real estate developers at the local hotel. As soon as they left, one of the workers there said to me, "Zapico is one of us, but that other one is the class enemy—he is just looking to take the major's place when we clear out the old regime." Zapico is less harsh in his judgments—after all, he himself came from the lower middle class and is now a socialist—but he is not fooled. As with the real estate developers, he makes his own position clear, and as for the others' motives, what matters to him is that they are working together for the while.

Zapico was, of course, the kind of man whom Alejandro and his friends wanted for their group: Andalusians without any ties to the old Left and who had thought through the problems of Andalusia for themselves; regionalists for whom socialism would break up the centrist rule of Madrid and allow these problems to be grappled with by Andalusians. Alejandro and his friends saw that they could not continue simply challenging the regime in elections in Seville; they needed a party throughout their region that would organize Andalusians on many fronts. Their slogan could well have been the epigraph used at an exhibit of Seville architects, showing while I was there, that attacked the plan of real estate developers to divert the Guadalquivir River from its path through the city. The architects, I was told, were also socialists of the Alliance, and the epigraph of their exhibition read: "If the rich Andalusian thinks only of Madrid and the poor Andalusian of Barcelona, who is there left to think of Andalusia?"

Before the Andalusians began to migrate in the last fifteen years to Europe looking for work, they went, for a century earlier, to the cities of Spain's north. (There was a period in the early years of the Franco regime when the police stood guard on the perimeters of the cities to turn them back.) There is, consequently, an undercurrent of resentment towards the Catalan and Basque industrialists who gained from this cheap labor pool, and it galled a member of the Socialist Alliance when I told him that at a Catalan Communist meeting in the industrial suburbs of Barcelona, I saw the green and white flag of Andalusia for the first time. Indeed, I had been told that it was there that it had first been raised in modern times.

"That is not true," he said with anger. "We were the first to bring it back. The Catalans, the Basques! Someday the Alliance will have to raise the issue. They have depopulated our country and made money off our people—we are going to present them with a bill."

After 1971, Alejandro and his friends began the organization of the Alliance. They traveled, whenever they could get away from their jobs, to other cities and towns in Andalusia. Secretly, of course. One friend put them in touch with another. That is how they got to Zapico and the boys of the Tele-Club in Écija. By 1974 they had a skeleton organization throughout Andalusia, and although like all parties of the opposition their meetings were clandestine, they formally set themselves up as a party. At its head are three secretaries, one of whom is Alejandro, but Alejandro, who is an eloquent speaker, is without question its leader. From his college days he was always known as a *mitinero*, an orator who can draw a meeting together.

He resigned the directorship of the cement factory, but he still had to make a living, for the Alliance did not have a single paid functionary. A group of architects in Madrid asked him to run their business for them, and they paid him sufficiently well for him to spend three days of the week there. But the traveling back and forth ate up most of the generous salary: a new kind of exploitation of the Andalusian, he says and laughs. When I saw him, he still was commuting up and down the peninsula, and lived with his wife and four children in the luxury apartment on Plaza de Cuba, the most modern and expensive complex in Seville. He enjoyed it, he is not a monkish convert to socialism, but despite its spaciousness, its balconies, its high ceilings, its marble floors throughout (except in the servants' rooms, but then they have no servants), the apartment with its dozens of paintings and overflowing bookshelves and stacks of lp's has the air of relaxed quarters for intellectual activists. On the long dining table was a typewriter with an unfinished sheet in it, and alongside were envelopes, some still not sealed, with a mailing yet to be posted.

His father-in-law does not regret giving them this stunning luxury. I might have said that he approved after I saw them run into one another, and that he was even proud of Alejandro, had Alejandro not explained later. The occasion was the café on Sierpes Street. Alejandro got up from his seat and walked along the aisle by the bar to greet a slim, middle-aged man who hurried towards him from the street with a delighted smile. Neither had called to the other, but their meeting and unemphatic embrace, done without the loud backslapping of the middle class, silenced the nearby tables, and the bartenders and waiters paused to watch them. It was a social drama they did not intend to miss: they would be telling stories about it for the next twenty-four hours.

The father-in-law asked about his grandchildren and his daughter. "About you I need not ask," he added; "I read about you everywhere." He smiled at Alejandro and brought up a hand and tapped his shoulder again. They laughed together. Everyone knew the event to which the father-in-law referred, and he seemed to be giving his approval with his gesture and laughter.

A day earlier Alejandro had appeared on the front page of every newspaper in photographs of the amnesty demonstration for which the *Coordinación Democrática* had obtained permission from the civil governor. The *Coordinación* was an enlarged version of the *Junta Democrática* which (as I explained earlier in my account of the Workers Commissions in Asturias) had been composed only of parties of the Left, and the Socialist Alliance had refused thus far to join the *Coordinación*. They believed (as had the young Trotskyist in Asturias) that the moderates and right-of-center parties now added to the *Junta* watered down the opposition program, and that the organization of the *Coordinación* perpetuated centrist rule from Madrid. For a while, there had been a question whether the Socialist Alliance would be permitted to appear officially in the amnesty demonstration, since it was being held under the *Coordinación's* auspices. But the Alliance had done much of the organizing to bring people there and it could not be left out.

The demonstration was an enormous success. The authorities counted on the summer heat to keep people away, and they held the line of march down to a few blocks along the river and restricted its duration to one hour. Fifty thousand people showed up and most of them were unable to complete the line of march; the hour was over before less than half of the thick mass could reach the end. The demonstrators found a way to stretch the hour given them: they grouped early in a small park across from the Hotel Cristina and applauded as each group walked up with its banners. There were truck drivers, feminists, factory workers, neighborhood associations, workers in the "plastic arts," waiters and hotel workers, and many more. My favorite banners: *Olé la Amnistía*; and from the Triana *barrio* across the river, a working-class, gypsy, bohemian neighborhood: *Triana with Its Gaiety Demands Amnesty*. I met Manuel Delicados, a seventy-five-year-old Communist trade-unionist returned from exile that week. "Forty years ago I helped to organize the last demonstration in Sevilla," he said, his eyes shining. "I have lived to see the first one now."

I walked between Paco, a literary critic who worked at a bank for a living, and Fernando, a poet who worked nights as a hotel clerk. Paco said, "Socialism in Andalucía will be so beautiful—it will have such a happy tone, a gay tone, the happiest tone!" An old woman dressed all in black, the traditional crone of Spain, left the sidewalk to join us, suddenly skipping and clapping and yelling, *"Libertád, amnistía, viva Andalucía!"* Fernando got out of line and ran ahead and then returned to tell us that the first row of the march was a stunning sight—all the leaders and organizers inching along and clutching a long banner the width of the street, huge black letters on white spelling out *Amnistía*. The photographs in the newspapers the next day all carried that first line of the parade. Prominent among those leaders whom the great landowners would have gladly seen shot down was Alejandro: he had made his own way to the opposition.

I said to Alejandro when his father-in-law left the café, "You have won him over too!"

"Oh no," he said. "He hates everything my wife and I think and everything we do, but he takes it very well, very well."

"As would an assured member of his class?" I said.

Alejandro nodded, and for a moment he enjoyed thinking about it like a disengaged sociologist. "But not my father," he said, remembering the cost of his own commitment. "He takes it very bad." He shook his head. "It would be too much to ask of him."

11

An Oriol Regás
Production

In a word association game with Spaniards during the last twelve years, you might have received as responses to Oriol Regás' name: *la divine gauche*, decadence, rebellion, frivolity, swinger, Catalan astuteness. Or from a Castilian supporter of the regime, simply an apoplectic growl. Oriol is Spain's only modern show business producer, though he has turned his hand to almost anything but the moribund theater; and his restaurants, his discotheques in Barcelona and Madrid, the great rock concerts he has produced, all gather about them an ambience that so irritates the people of the Bunker, thus named to identify them with Hitler's last stand, that they have been inspired, with no sense of irony, to bomb his restaurant Vía Veneto, a chic, expensive place, one of the half dozen in Spain that Michelin has deigned to award a star. There is drama about everything Oriol does, and the stories you hear about him all promise a glittering personage on the scale of the great movie stars, marvelously larger than life.

The first story I heard about him (you hear many in Barcelona and Madrid) belongs in a Buñuel film. The paternal grandfather who brought up Oriol and his younger brother and two sisters is dying. He is a Victorian patriarch of the meanest kind, tight-fisted, pious, cruelly dictatorial, and he has ruled their lives almost since infancy. He has never expended any affection on them. He has manipulated them as if they were one of the restaurants and hotels he owns, but whereas these enterprises have been a source of pride and profit for him, the children serve only as bitter reminders of his dead ne'er-do-well son who for a while was married to a woman the old man despised. The children are close and loving with one another, like children in a fairy tale, and they have spent many hours in the house of the ogre telling one another what they will do when someday the old man dies and they are free.

Oriol is twenty-seven, and it is ten years since he broke away from home, but two years earlier, when his grandfather first began to feel the end coming, he returned at the old man's call. Oriol has been helping him run his business, but the old man has not softened. He has, instead, become obsessed with the afterlife, and is paying more attention to the Church than to his business. The Church recipro-cates, and the afternoon he is dying the Abbé of Montserrat himself comes to the sickroom where the old man has commanded the children to remain with him. The Abbé enters saying, "You should be very happy, for tonight you will see the Virgin of Montserrat." The old man is not pleased—his eyes flash as when an employee has overstepped the bounds of his delegated authority—but he says nothing, for, after all, there is some reassurance in having the Abbé of Monserrat, the highest dignitary of the Church in Catalonia, administer the last sacrament.

The contemplation of this victory has probably given the old man the ability to hold out a little longer. He does not die until a few hours after the Abbé leaves, late in the night. The doctor who had waited in an anteroom comes in and confirms the event to the children and then leaves. They are alone with him in the bedroom. They are mute. Oriol is the first to approach the body. He pokes an arm and it does seem lifeless. The others come to Oriol's side. Each tests with a jab some part of the old man's body. Then, in a frenzy, they begin to pull at his beard, his arms, his feet. Only this way can they believe the old ogre is dead. Their desecration of the corpse is also a celebration—at last, at last, they are free.

I met Oriol soon after attending a concert he produced in Madrid, in February 1976, for Raimon, the Catalan protest singer. It was the kind of spectacle Oriol now prefers to stage. In October of the previous year, while Franco was dying, Oriol had staged a concert in Barcelona with Raimon, and it turned into a political demonstra-tion, as had all of Raimon's appearances in the past. Indeed, for this reason it had been almost eight years since Raimon had last been allowed to appear in concert or on television. The permission for the Barcelona concert had been obtained before Franco fell ill, and because during the month that Franco's life was prolonged the authorities were nervously clamping down on the opposition (each day throughout the peninsula one group or the other was rounded up and jailed) the usual response to Raimon was even more explosive. But by February of the following year, relaxation of political control and tolerance of the opposition was underway, and Oriol planned a series of four concerts with Raimon in Madrid, at a sports arena seating only 5,000 persons; Oriol knew he could fill a larger one, but this was the only one the authorities approved.

The first night promised to be the event of the season. Oriol does nothing by halves; he gave away tickets for almost the entire front half of the orchestra to the most prominent intellectuals and cultural figures of Madrid. Some flew down from Barcelona to be there. There were jokes that those who did not get free tickets left town to appear not to have been able to attend. The wide first row of the auditorium was reserved for the leaders of the opposition political parties and illegal associations like the Workers Commissions. You had to have spent some years in jail to gain one of those seats. Instead of 5,000, about 6,000 got into the arena. They brought with them Republican and red flags and banners calling for amnesty for political prisoners, and they turned Raimon's concert into a dialogue while he sang and a demonstration during the pauses between songs and during intermission.

Oriol presented Raimon starkly—a bare stage, a huge black backdrop, a chair, a mike. Raimon sang in Catalan, but this Madrid audience—all young, except for the invitees in the orchestra—sang along with him. From the very first song they made the Catalan experience their own. This song was *"La nit"*—The Night—an extended metaphor about the long night of fascism in Catalonia. "This night, this long night we all carry in our hearts . . . so many nights lost that will never return." Someone in the dark arena lit a match and held it up, and soon from the galleries down to the orchestra a somber Christmas tree bloomed.

During the second half of the program some in the balcony yelled, *"La policia!"* We had noticed as we approached the arena earlier that the tactical police was out in force, and now all of us in the orchestra could plainly see they had moved into the entrance-ways of the balconies, wearing their ominous bulletproof helmets as when they go into action. They held tear-gas guns. "Ooo—ooo—ooo," the young people in the galleries murmured in unison, like children full of mock fear. But the minutes the Tactical Police stood in the entranceways menacingly were interminable. Finally, they left. By the time the concert was over, the story of how Oriol had convinced the police chief to withdraw them—how at least some dozens of us in the arena owed our lives to Oriol—had begun to gather momentum. The next day the more liberal newspapers car-ried an account of that tense moment and Oriol's intervention. To the image of sophistication I had gained from Oriol's two Bocaccios, his café-discotheques in Barcelona and Madrid, was now added authority and bravado.

I was not, therefore, prepared to be introduced at a Madrid literary cocktail party to a scrawny little fellow, as undernourished-looking as any peasant boy up from Andalusia, and believe it was Oriol Regás. He wore jeans and an Indian cotton, fitted shirt, the kind of outfit working-class boys were buying with their first pay. They were not Pierre Cardins. They were not even pre-washed. Nevertheless, I said respectfully that I very much wanted to talk to him. "What's the matter with him?" he said to the friend who introduced us, and it turned out that I had inappropriately used the formal *usted* instead of *tú* to address him. It was his way of turning away attention, but he said, when I persisted, that of course we could get together, in a tone that indicated it was, as we say, no big deal.

He was never to change this modest tone in all the attempts we made by phone, or at other such encounters, to make a date, but it *was* a big deal. He gave me all his phones, and he was so busy (he lives in Barcelona but flies down to Madrid for thirty-six hours each Tuesday to see about the Bocaccio there) that often no one could tell at home or at his various offices where he was, though he left me as many messages along the trail as Hansel and Gretel. Besides the restaurant and the two Bocaccios, there are his offices where the concerts are planned, and when we finally spent a couple of hours together in his slapdash inner office, I learned that he was also attending the University of Barcelona and was entering his third undergraduate year to get a degree in liberal arts. He is married and has children, and he was that year very involved with his sister Rosa, who is the object of almost as much gossip as he, in a new publishing house. To all this I suppose I must add his love affairs, always very complicated and secret and about which everyone talks but he.

"You must not forget," a friend told me, "that Oriol, like the other children, speaks at length on the phone each day with his mother. Everything is checked with her. They are a real mafia, so close that they cover up for each other's adulteries, and anything one of them goes into has been discussed with the mother in Madrid. She may have abandoned them when they were infants for her titled lover [a highly unorthodox liaison, some say] but they are more loyal than if she had devoted her entire life to them. Nothing can pry any of them apart."

All of this adds to the glamour. It does not go with his office. Obviously no decorator has been near it. He smokes Rex, a cheap black cigarette, from a squashed pack on his person, and he is lithe and youthful for a thirty-nine year-old. He does not dramatize anything he says or does. He looks at you as if open to whatever is on your mind, but he is startled when your question is serious or intimate. He responds after a pause, as if looking for a truthful reply. Then he cocks his head and puts up his guard: he projects the quality always of having overcome an especially wounding hurt. As a result, you never ask him about the gossip.

"My grandfather was a monster," he said. "He was disappointed in my father who started out as a mildly political man, a Republican, and went into exile. My father came back in 1944 and was satisfied to be housed and fed by his father. He was mostly busy with his mistresses. When he and my mother broke up, and she went to live in Madrid, he was not concerned with us, and allowed our grandfather to keep us from her. Our grandfather had no affection for us, but it fed his ego that he made a home for us. He permitted our mother to see us only one day a month for one and a half hours on the last Saturday of every month, and he did not allow any variations—it had to be that day and at a particular hour when he was not home or she forfeited the visit for that month."

They did not live like the children of the rich. They were given nothing unnecessary for physical survival. One visiting day Oriol's mother brought him his first electric train. "It was a very simple affair, a small round track with two cars. But it was a marvel to me. I set it up immediately after mother left, and I was running it when grandfather came into the room. He walked deliberately across the room and stepped on it with all his big bulk and broke it. To this day I remember seeing his foot coming down on it as I watched helplessly from the floor."

Oriol's first great passion was motorbikes. He began racing them in his early teens and eventually entered races throughout Spain and Europe. He became amateur champion of Spain. He did not owe any of this to the grandfather. He knew early on that he would have to carry himself in any enterprise that was not his grandfather's. The grandfather paid for his schooling, and at seventeen, when he finished his college preparatory course, offered him only the opportunity to attend a school in Toulouse in restaurant and hotel management. Oriol accepted, but he continued his amateur racing and this caused a quarrel with the old man which resulted in Oriol's leaving the school.

"I did not care. He was as much a dictator in his business as he was at home, and there would have been no pleasure in coming back to work for him, which is what I should have felt obliged to do if I had continued in Toulouse with his support. I had just won a prize in Switzerland, which had displeased him, and I sold one of my bikes and thus had enough money—just enough to go off on an adventure with three other Spaniards to China."

"China?" I said. "Why did you do that?"

It was the first time he was to pause and think of an exact answer, and to say, also for the first time, "I am a romantic."

The other three Spaniards were all older than he, and their objective was so exotic that it was bound to appeal to an eighteen-year-old. They planned to buy a junk in China and sail it back to Spain. Oriol had to pay his own way there and all other expenses until they actually boarded the junk and started back. He flew to Hong Kong and there found they could not get into China proper. Instead, the junk would be built for them in Hong Kong, and they were to spend two and a half months there waiting for it to be completed. This delay turned out to be the best part of the adventure.

Oriol fell in love with a Chinese girl. "It was my first experience of love. That time in Hong Kong was marvelous. She took me to her family and friends, and I spent my time only in the real Chinese community. Not the fake one that tourists see. She was a great beauty and tender and loving. It was difficult for me to leave when the junk was ready, but I thought I would see her again. How? Somehow. Actually, I did see her again in Spain nine years later— she was totally changed."

The voyage back to Spain took eleven months. More than enough time to learn that he had nothing in common with the other three. It was not simply a matter of age difference. They were all Franco supporters, and two of them were Catalans who were also Falangists, the worst possible combination. Observing them taught him that he was a Catalan nationalist. During those long days and weeks, he learned to live with solitude and nostalgia and to bear homesickness. Catalonia became precious to him. Oriol looked carefully at me with his head cocked, to see if I could be trusted to understand.

In Barcelona he kept up his motorbiking activities. He had always maintained his amateur status, but there had been cash prizes that helped him do things his grandfather in the past would not finance. Now, he started a small business in helmets and other equipment for drivers, and began the first magazine in Spain devoted to the sport. In connection with the magazine, he took a trip to the United States. New York City impressed him. Everyone there seemed to be on the eleven-month voyage on the junk. "Each New Yorker is an individual, and they cross one another as if at a distance." He went to Washington, D. C., to see a maternal uncle, Victor Alba, who had once been in the Trotskyist POUM. He decided he never wanted to be an exile.

When he returned to Barcelona, he began to lose interest in motorbiking. He has never entirely given it up. He loves fast cars, too. (Someone had said to me, "Do not get into a car that he is driving.") Next, he started his first restaurant and then sold it and started another. "I was in all sorts of short-lived businesses between the ages of twenty and twenty-five." He sat around with friends, and the talk gave him business ideas for them. The friends always went into his ventures too, as backers. "That is how I have always staged things, with the help of friends," he said. "The only thing I know how to do is to stage things." He used the verb *montar*, which in his context also means to set up, produce, direct, mount. "It is the only contribution I can make."

He believes that his impulse to start things for which he had no solid experience is a romantic one. "I never worry in advance whether they can be brought off, and I throw myself into them completely and later never look back or regret them." (But they always pay off, everyone will tell you.) At twenty-five, for example, he dropped all the enterprises which had kept him busy, and went off with his motorbike for a tour of Africa. He drove from Capetown to the Sahara. "I am a romantic, you see," he said, and closed his eyes a moment at the recollection of that trip. "I know many people, I am very interested in others, but I have few friends. That is why I could go off on such a trip."

When he got back, his grandfather sent for him. He had not seen the old man in several years. "The old man was very sick, he wanted me to help him run his business. He knew that I had shown some capacity for it. I agreed, but I told him I expected a salary of five thousand pesetas a week." That was a lot of money in Spain in 1961, about one hundred dollars, but modest for a professional and certainly skimpy for a successful business executive. "The old man replied, 'Not only is sin an abomination to God in heaven, but also an undeserved salary.'" Out of pride, Oriol told his grandfather that he would work for his keep only. He did not know why he went through with this, for he was in love and should have been thinking ahead.

He had already met Ana, the girl he would marry. Her father owned a motorbike business, and he met her at a meet in which he took part. "I remember I first saw Ana seated on a jeep." Her family disapproved of him, and sent her to a school in Lausanne to put distance between them. It was a mistake; he takes up all challenges. Although he had begun to work for his grandfather, he would get on his motorbike at three every Saturday afternoon and race non-stop

to Lausanne. He once made it in ten hours and twenty-eight minutes. He would spend Sunday morning and midday with her, and
race back to Barcelona in time to work on Monday morning.

He could not, of course, keep up these trips on his no-salary from
his grandfather, but since he was actively in charge of his grandfather's various establishments, for the old man was too sick to leave
the house except occasionally, he was able to manipulate many
transactions and pocketed much more money than the salary he had
asked for. "I would discuss many things vaguely, particularly these,
and he was never too sure what was going on." Spanish businesses
are not run with strict bookkeeping or, rather, are run with several
sets of books. The grandfather was an old-fashioned businessman
who kept many of the details—such as the purchase and resale of
delivery trucks and company cars—out of the books and maintained
as many transactions as he could on a cash basis. "There were no
real records of these, and to make things look good, I would sometimes tell him of some windfall profit I had brought off. That kept
him happy.

"It was a good thing I kept for myself what I should have been
paid, for when he died he willed every penny to the Church." Oriol
had taken for granted that the four grandchildren would be the old
man's heirs, but he had not been planning on it. Still, it is shocking
when a Spaniard, no matter how autocratic and mean, disinherits
his family. "He was buying heaven," Oriol explained, "and there is
no end to that purchase price."

To prove himself he went into a frenzy of activity. Within a year,
he opened the restaurant Vía Veneto. It was a resounding success.
In another year, he started Bocaccio, the café-discotheque he later
duplicated in Madrid. Both of them were still running and still in
fashion in 1976. The capital for them came mostly from friends. He
started Bocaccio with ten thousand dollars of his own, but there are
two hundred shareholders in the business. The friends (and friends
of friends) were people he got to know well during the time when he
was managing his grandfather's business and courting Ana. During
the siesta and evening of weekdays he used to drop by the Stork
Club, the first gathering place for the *divine gauche* in Barcelona.
"At three in the afternoon people began showing up there, and the
conversations went on into the morning. Sometimes I did not leave

the place until six. There were many weeks I got through with hardly any sleep.

"They were fascinating people, especially to me who had no real profession or education. They had a gift for frivolity that was a kind of rebellion. It was from them that I got the idea for Bocaccio as the sort of place which would have an air of snobbery and decadence, but in their professions they were actually hard-working and serious—photographers, actors, writers, directors. The manner we put on was our way of being against the Establishment."

Barcelona was the only place then that could have nurtured Bocaccio. In the late fifties and early sixties, everything new in Spain's cultural life came from Barcelona—the movies and publishing houses, in particular. The police and bureaucracy were not as pervasive as in Madrid. It was Catalonia, after all, where even the good bourgeois did not identify with the regime. Barcelona is nearer Europe; it has always been more cosmopolitan. A little money had begun to flow into the old stultified economy, and the Catalans were readier to spend it. The swinging youth were eager for a chic discotheque, and the intelligentsia for a place to gather that had style.

Bocaccio's style is that of the *belle époque*—apt for a city that nurtured Gaudí—and its spaciousness is thick with carved mahogany and red plush. It has a wicked air. Only the foyer is brightly lit. No doubt, to allow the clients to show off their elegance or studied casualness before they disappear into the dark interior. Beyond this point, all is dim and glowingly red—a long bar and curved couches and black tables on tiers. The young men and women at the bar may be wearing expensive jeans, but they lean against it as bonelessly as a Toulouse Lautrec figure. The waiters are many, unobtrusive and attentive; you never light your own cigarette. All is playful self-consciousness.

Down a narrow, winding stairs towards the front is the discotheque. Its sounds do not filter up, but it is, of course, ear-shattering once you descend. You pick your way down, for along the stairs girls and boys are draped, and there at the bottom are the strobe lights and abandoned dancing. A famous poet who had taken a group of us there after dinner said after I returned from my tour, "How did you like the take-out counter?" The others did not understand English, and they wanted to know what he had asked the *yanqui*. "I told him any of those girls are ready to go home with him—or any of the boys."

Another poet, a woman, looked around bored. *"Esto se ha emputecido,"* she said, turning the noun "whore" into a verb. It was 1976, and already there was nostalgia for what Bocaccio had meant to them in the sixties. In a moment, one person after another came to greet her, and she brightened up. Our host said loudly to me, "She is beginning to like it better," and laughed; he was interrupted by the maître who had returned to tell him once more what an honor it was for Bocaccio to have him there: they had missed him.

I learned that it is a good idea to take a friend with you to the rest room, as women once did in public places, because its two diminutive urinals are so closely contiguous that you are inevitably thrown into an intimate relationship with whomever stands alongside you. I told my friend this when I got back to our table, and added, "It's all innocent play here, isn't it?"

"Yes, yes," he said, like a man who knows the real thing. Then added, "And no."

Some months later in Madrid, after the Raimon concert that Oriol produced, I went to its Bocaccio with another group of intellectuals, this time invited by Jaime Salinas, the son of the poet Pedro Salinas, who was reared in the United States when his father went into exile. Salinas is a publisher who introduced quality paperbacks in the sixties by bringing out the classics and European moderns until then not easily found in Spain. Although he is to be found at every literary cocktail party in Madrid, he never goes to cafés and restaurants that are in vogue, or almost never. "I haven't been at Bocaccio's in more than a year," he said, "but you will see."

We were, of course, led to the best table, and when the check came and Salinas began to search his pockets for a charge card, the waiter said, "Don Jaime, if you will sign it, we shall send you the bill." And he did not ask Salinas for his address. Though the service and the décor are the same as Barcelona's, its overtones are not. The difference lies in the clientele: they are not Barcelonans. There is no playfulness. If some come to take home a girl—or a boy—they are hard and furtive about it. Oriol may have given in somewhat to hypocritical *madrileños*: the urinals are full size and are a respect-able distance apart.

Oriol is never to be found at Bocaccio, though I suspect he keeps a watchful eye on its style of service; he does not like rock music because it interferes with conversation, and even at obligatory cocktail parties he draws into a corner by himself. He tried once more to explain why to him and his friends it had seemed important in the sixties to elevate the show of decadence and frivolity into an expression of rebellion against the deadly conformity and bloated piety of the regime. He had not been impelled by a desire for commercial success when he began to import stars like the Rolling Stones; he had meant "to show them." "But it was foolishness, after all," he said sadly. "I should have done something better than that to make a contribution, something of more value."

Not only does he not like rock, he does not dance. One has only to look at his offices at the top of a nondescript building in Barcelona to see he is not interested in elegance. There is not even a recep-tionist. The offices' four large open rooms are full of earnest young people, however, in ordinary jeans and blouses and shirts—like Oriol. They all seem to be working. A square place.

Oriol has traveled in the opposite direction to the literary intellec-tuals who, when he started out, had made Barcelona the center of departure from official culture. They were committed left-wingers then, but since they were, like almost all Spanish intellectuals, sophisticated, university-trained professionals of the middle class, they welcomed the restaurants and boîtes that Oriol opened in Barcelona. What he called frivolity had its place in their ambience; cafés where they could relax and also *épater les franquistes*. In turn, they may have infected Oriol with their social guilt, for now that Oriol is all energy and enterprise about cultural events that are socially useful, they are mostly bored and tired, though willing when the show has sufficient éclat, like Raimon's concert, to appear or sign statements of support.

Perhaps Oriol's social orientation has developed more naturally, more in tune with the mass of Catalans. He seems always to know what is needed, like a good showman. But he is in earnest; he considers himself a man of the Left. "No one on the Left knows how to stage these affairs—it is my only contribution." He tries to explain why he needs to do them. "After all, when you think about it, I am part of the system that I oppose—I make money from it."

The fact that he is back at the university majoring in history places him with the new young intellectuals in their twenties who are studying economics, sociology, anthropology, and who tell you that the literary intellectuals now in their forties have all burnt themselves out. Oriol says that he is studying history and getting an education in order to provide for himself in a private way; he expects this knowledge to help him through the hard years of old age. He may not be aware that he is already putting his new interests to use. Throughout 1975, he worked closely with his sister Rosa, who by 1976 launched as publisher a series of monographs. Issued as inexpensive paperbacks, the monographs are meant to educate a mass public. Each week a new one came out, and they could be found not just in bookstores but at every newsstand. *What Is the Bunker? What Is the Opus Dei? What Is Socialism?*—these were some of the titles.

The authorities in Barcelona had not allowed him in the spring of 1976 to launch a series of concerts of the *La Nova Cançó*, the group of young Catalan protest singers much in vogue but also equally restricted. After the opening night in Madrid of Raimon, the three concerts to follow were canceled by the police. His experience with the police chief who was ready to fill the sports arena with tear gas and smoke pots taught him, he said, that he must go straight to the top. He had, therefore, recently gone to Fraga Iribarne, the most powerful of ministers in the king's first cabinet and who now that Franco was dead was pushing most for democratic reforms. He got an appointment with him and arrived with a graphic presentation of his new project.

With posters and drawings and graphs, he showed the minister the series of mass lectures he proposed to hold. Each evening was to be devoted to an important subject to be expounded, as in the case of the monographs he had issued with his sister, by a leading authority in the field. They were to be held in a hall that could seat thousands. The audience would be provided with a complete bibliography on which to base further reading, and the hall would be lit for them to take notes. Oriol felt sure that they would be a success—what better way for the mass of people to make a beginning on the education they had been denied? The minister turned the entire series down.

Oriol had said early during our talk that although he knows many people, he has very few friends, and there was no point in asking him about the closeness that exists among the four children brought up by the tyrannical old man. Yet all the stories he told of his enterprises, once he stopped going off on his solitary adventures, seemed to me evidence of his reaching out for a larger family. Indeed, the restaurants and boîtes and rock concerts and the events he planned now were, I believed, attempts to create on the basis of new ties one large family in which he could be useful. The afternoon was ending, and the private extension rang. He answered it, and his voice became soft and low and he half turned from me as he spoke and bent his body in the effort to create a private corner for himself. There is still that, I thought.

I asked him when he hung up, "When did the girls become demythified for you?"

He was perched on the arm of a chair and asked me to repeat the question. This time I added, "After the Chinese girl?"

He plopped down into the chair and spread his legs and threw his head back and thought and thought. Finally, I said, "Never?" and he opened his eyes and looked at me with delight and trust. "Never!" he repeated with a different emphasis.

"Listen, we have to talk some more," he said, bringing me into his larger family. "This is the day I fly to Madrid and . . . Will you be in your hotel tomorrow night?"

I said I had to leave now, too. I was going to the mass meeting permitted the *Convergencia Socialista*. It was being held at the sports arena of the university, and it was to be the founding meeting of what until now was an informal association of independent Catalan socialists.

"So am I," he said, sure of me now. "I am taking a later flight to be there for the start of the meeting. I have told them they must not get carried away. They must not let it run beyond two hours. Stop while everyone wants more."

12

Catalan
Fathers and Sons

I was having lunch in Jordi's, a fine Catalan restaurant in Barcelona, with the literary critic José María Castellet and his wife, and suddenly became worried, like a good American, that I had been speaking too loudly and possibly wounding the political sensibilities of people nearby. "Not here," Castellet said. "This is Catalonia." And his wife added, "Even in the worst days, if you heard Catalan spoken at the next tables, you knew that you could say what you liked and that no matter how strongly they disagreed with you, no one was going to report you to the police." In Madrid, a friend had bid me good-bye when I left for Barcelona with: "*Adiós*, that is another nation altogether." I knew this—I had lived there for three months in 1964—but I was unprepared for the nationalist fervor that the Franco regime for so long tried to suppress. The day Franco died the shops ran out of champagne and Asturian cider, the traditional drinks for toasts and celebrations. On my second trip in 1976, even the tobacconists pointedly replied in Catalan when I addressed them in Castilian. *Visca Catalunya* (Long Live Catalonia) every wall said. And where they had more time to write, there was the slogan: *Libertat, Amnistía, Estatut d'Autonomía*. The Catalan Assembly, composed of parties ranging from slightly right of center to the far left, all still illegal, was the only genuine political force in the region, and it would not include any party, no matter how opposed to the regime, like the Socialist Workers Party, that was not of Catalan origin. Indeed,

220

independent, liberal socialists had only recently begun to organize the *Convergencia Socialista* to fill the vacuum of the Socialist Workers Party, and in the summer of 1976 held their first legal public mass meeting. The years of the Franco regime had served to unite Catalan worker and Catalan bourgeois for Catalan independence.

Foreigners with any interest in modern Spain know the special role that Catalonia has played within the peninsula. Along with the Basque country it was the only industrialized section of Spain, and George Orwell's *Homage to Catalonia* gave the world an uneradicable picture of the courageous working-class movement it produced. The unarmed anarchists of the FAI *(Federación Anarquista Ibérica)* and its trade-union CNT, along with the mass of socialists and Catalan nationalists, in 1936 forced the Army to surrender one barracks after another throughout the city, and then themselves attempted to create the revolution while prosecuting the war. Factories and services were collectivized for a while, and the rights and wrongs of the FAI's short and violent rule and the Republic's suppression of it and the Trotskyists' POUM created a debate beyond Spain's borders that has only slightly abated after all these years.

Overlooked by historians, or perhaps simply forgotten, has been the liberal, Catalan bourgeoisie whose enlightened tradition of democracy and regional independence had been one of the few forces within Spain that tried to lead the country into the modern world. It was shocked by the generals' uprising and then almost as much by the actions of the anarchists who dealt out summary justice to their class enemies. That these class enemies were not fascists and did not conspire against the Republic or against the autonomy that Catalonia had gained under it, seemed not to matter to the roving bands of anarchists enraged by the Army uprising. They thus managed to split sections of these bourgeois liberal families from one another, though they were people whose family ties were extremely close, and to inspire some to transfer themselves and their children to the Nationalist side. Mostly via France. Within the Nationalist camp they were an anomaly: Catalan nationalists who worked or fought for a supremely centrist regime that was not to allow them for many years even the use of their own ancient language.

I owe to the poet Jaime Gil de Biedma, a Barcelonan son of an old

Castilian family, my first introduction to a member of one of these professional Catalan families—Jacint Reventós, who married Jaime's sister. I had not heard of Jacint when Jaime, in the course of telling me about the courage and fidelity to liberal values displayed by the Catalan upper middle class, read me a letter written in September, 1936, by Jacint Reventós' father, a doctor who was the most eminent authority in Barcelona on tuberculosis. He was writing to his wife who had taken, as was customary each summer, Jacint, age eight, and his younger sister to the south of France. For Jaime Gil de Biedma, the language of whose poetry is economical and elegant, the calm, practical, affectionate, and intelligent tone of the letter writer is most moving, particularly since the doctor has no assurance that he will ever see his wife and children again. If the style is the man, it is also, in this fearful circumstance, that of his class as well.

"Beloved María," the letter begins. "Taking advantage of the chance to hand this letter to a person who will be able to give it to you personally, I am writing you a much longer letter than usual. This last July saw the beginning of a tragedy whose outcome for the while is difficult to foresee. Without any, to me, understandable justification, certain sectors started a revolt; and the reaction to it has simply opened the doors to an inferno. Everyone seems to have gone crazy; vengeance and rage predominate in some, in others fear and desertion. I do not really know which is in the right, for what has happened afterward seems to justify what initially appeared unjustifiable. In these moments of collective fury I am not sure if we shall be able to see each other again, and I should like consequently to plead with you and to caution you with respect to your conduct and with respect to the future and education of the children. In any moment of doubt that you may have about problems in relation to our children, I beg you to ask yourself: What would Cinto [the writer of this letter] advise in this circumstance? You know me well enough and are intelligent enough to guess it. Even when you do not think that you are doing anything blindly in this respect, take this into account before deciding. With the education of the children, and in particular of the boy, accustom them to the idea that life is not a big party, that to think so is an infallible prescription for living badly."

He tells his wife to ask of the children a certain discipline in their daily life, such as never to play before they have done their homework. The pronoun, when referring to the children, changes from the third person plural to the singular, unconsciously revealing that it is the boy Jacint that he is most thinking of. The boy must learn that he is to be responsible for his mother and sister as he grows up; he is to think of himself as poorer than he really is, and his father adds parenthetically, even when he may indeed be poor enough. He wants his son brought up as a Christian, and asks that she look to the family for help in this; the important thing being that he lead his life in the spirit of Christianity and not place any emphasis on pious observances.

"Let him not hold the slightest hatred towards anyone, whatever happens to me. Try to keep him from losing his Catalan roots and try, too, to have him continue being educated as a Catalan, since without these things he would be no more than a spoiled *international boy*." He is capable of irony: he adds that things may be so bad for so long that all this advice will have nothing to recommend it, but he insists, "Let him remind himself that he is Catalan and that he cannot be anything else. Do not let him lose contact with his cousins and everything will take care of itself."

He returns to the practicalities of the boy's education. If he is at all intelligent, he should be encouraged to pick one of the liberal professions. Should this prove to be too useless and excessive an effort, then let him not be a clerk or bureaucrat, for if he has inherited any of his father's spirit, he would suffer terribly. Let him rather be an engraver, a mechanic, any practitioner of the skilled trades. He points out that he can study for two possible careers with one course of study: training for a medical career can prepare him to be a laboratory technician; for engineering, a manual mechanic. "Do not worry that he may be forced to become a man before his time. Treat him gently but with spirit. Little sport. Let no endeavor seem too difficult to him at the start, nor should he be made the less of by any job. While he is an adolescent, let him lead a life close to home."

He then realizes that he has scarcely spoken of his daughter, but he excuses himself by saying that he little knows the means by which women achieve happiness or sorrow. "After all, I do not know if I have managed to make you wholly happy." So he expects that she will know much better than he how the girl should be educated. "If I do not see them again, love them for us both. I know you will do it, for love without boundaries nor reserves has been what has most ennobled your life."

He again returns to the theme of his son's education by telling his wife to ask for advice and help from various people. He names his brother Manuel first, and reminds her that since he would do the same for these men that she must not hesitate to go to them for support.

"And now some words for you, whom I have so loved in my clumsy and self-serving ways, but also with all the force of my soul. Would that you do not have to make use of the recommendations and warnings which I have given in this letter, and that together we could raise our children, but if it does not so happen, be sure that my last thought like my last affection is for you."

The letter is no less moving when one learns that he managed to rejoin his wife and children in fascist Italy, where they waited for him for several months, that he moved them all to the Nationalist zone, and when Barcelona fell returned home wearing the uniform of a captain in the medical corps. His son Jacint has not had to bear the burden of his father's advice not to hate those who harmed his father. Rather, he has had to exercise a subtler mercy: to understand how his father could be a good man and fight on the wrong side. It has been necessary for Jacint to do this because he had the example of his uncle Manuel, the brother who first came to his father's mind when he thought of those who could help his children. Manuel was an economist and lawyer, and he stayed in Barcelona and was never tempted to support the enemies of the Republic.

All Barcelona today seems to know what Manuel said to Jacint's father when dressed in his uniform of the Franco Army he arrived at the family home after the city fell. Manuel said, "Cinto, was it necessary for you to arrive in Barcelona in this masquerade costume?"

Some recited it to me as "dressed like a clown," but I have taken the wording from a remarkable little book, *Two Boys and the War*, published in 1974 by the sons of these two brothers. The cousins were born a year apart and were as close as their fathers. Except for the hiatus of the war, they continued, also like their fathers, to be as intimate, and it does not seem possible now that any political event will ever divide them as the Civil War did their fathers. Joan, Manuel's son, is the leader of *Convergencia Socialista*, a party solidly established by the summer of 1976, and Jacint, a surgeon, is an enthusiastic member working in its Socialist Studies Center to draw up the party's program for socialized medicine.

In their book, Joan and Jacint tell quietly and with precision, in alternating chapters, what they saw and felt during those years of war. They do not enlarge on the scenes in which they participated; they stick to what each personally knew. They seldom allow their adult knowledge and beliefs to intrude. The exceptions are revealing: Jacint recalling the rhetoric of Italian fascism during the months they waited for his father in Rapallo, and commenting, "Let us give thanks to God that being born Catalan we were given a language in which it is almost impossible to use the phraseology of an operetta hero." Or when Jacint defends Francisco Cambó, the richest of Catalan industrialists; he was also head of the *Lliga*, the party in those days of the Catalan upper class, and it was he whom Jacint's father went to visit at Rapallo when he got out of Barcelona. Cambó advised Jacint's father to go on to the Nationalist zone, and he had himself helped finance Franco, though with a measure of disdain. On Cambó's only trip to Catalonia after the war, he watched with Jacint's father the people of Badalona giving the fascist salute, and said, "Cinto, I shall not return until I can greet people with my hat." Cambó left Spain and died abroad in 1947.

Perhaps because *Two Boys and the War* is so restrained it has extraordinary resonance for Catalans. At its center is the tragedy of the Civil War that rent them and its prologue hopes that it will help a new generation to surmount this inheritance, but the unstated emotional currents of the book lead the reader to a more passionate conclusion. The Civil War was a tragedy because it brought to power a regime that tried in every way to suppress their Catalanism. Jacint said to me, "I remember at the Church school I was sent to after we returned to Barcelona that the prejudice against Catalan was so strong that we were punished for the use of even one Catalan word. At the start of each day, the first child in class to say something in Catalan was given a ticket and he could only escape punishment by passing it to another child when he heard him use Catalan. At the end of the day, the child holding the ticket was punished. How clever—to make us police one another."

True, the basis for their unity was always there, particularly in a family like the Reventós. Jacint's cousin, Joan, in his last chapter in their book, tells with what emotion his family greeted Jacint's father when he arrived in Barcelona at the family home. Manuel's famous question to Jacint's father, as Joan tells it, came only after the most affectionate embraces were exchanged, and once he asked his brother why he had arrived as if for a costume party, the women left them alone and closed the doors to the room. The two men talked for hours and emerged their old selves.

In a sense, this is what happened to all of Catalonia once the war ended. I sat in Jacint's living room and looked at one corner of framed drawings by Picasso who, from his intransigent exile, did not allow himself to lose his friendship with Jacint's father. Some of the frames contained letters from Picasso, and their margins were filled with affectionate drawings and doodles. Picasso extended his affection to the son, Jacint, and as each of Jacint's children was born, he sent drawings. But of course, the dialogue between classes and generations of Catalans has not been as forgiving, and in the prologue to their book, Joan and Jacint hope that they are not wounding the sensibilities of those of their fathers' generation who are still defending their old positions.

But Joan's and Jacint's generation are another matter. In Jacint's living room I met Antonio Plana Torrás, a fifty-year-old engineer with whom Jacint and I were going to the university sports palace for the meeting of the *Convergencia Socialista*. Plana had had to live the kind of forgiving advice that Jacint's father had passed on in his letter to his wife. Plana's grandfather had owned a papermill in Gerona that Plana's father managed, and when the Civil War broke out, it was one of the industries the FAI confiscated. "Since only my father knew how to run the place, they made him the Comrade Manager, but they harassed him at every turn. Once, on the excuse that he had filled a form in triplicate that should be filled in quadruplicate, they accused him of recalcitrance and threw him in jail for a week. Unfortunately, during that week one FAI band decided to storm the local jail, since presumably only enemies of the Republic were to be found there. They got carried away and shot all the prisoners."

The jail was in the middle of town, and Plana, who was eleven, remembers the horror he and his mother and his brothers and sisters felt when they heard the shots. They knew what must be happening. They were the only ones in their family living in Gerona—others had left for France to escape the FAI—and they lived in their big home, though most of it was used by the new collective as administrative offices for the papermill. In some ways this saved them, for the workers were not cruel; they gave them food. Yet food was so scarce that at night Plana would sneak out to the countryside to steal more. At night, too, he sometimes helped hide runaways in their attic, young men trying to get to France and from there to the Nationalist zone. Or Plana guided them up the mountains where there were good trails to the border. On occasion these young men were caught and executed, but they never said who had helped them.

"I was forced to join the Communist youth organization and when Franco won, to become an Arrow in the Falange." Plana laughed, and I asked him why the senseless execution of his father had not stood in the way of his present socialist ideas. He answered self-consciously, embarrassed to be made to sound like a goody-goody. "They were poor, illiterate people, and, anyway, injustices like that always happen in revolutions—they cannot be helped."

The memory of the poor, and how they were treated, lives on as guilt in Jacint Reventós too. In his book, he speaks a little of the period following the war's end, and tells about the terrible state in which his family found their house in town. During the war, Álvarez del Vayo, the Republic's foreign minister, had used it once as his headquarters while in Barcelona, and today on Jacint's bookshelves there is a copy of the original English Left Book Club edition of Orwell's *Homage to Catalonia*. Del Vayo had left it behind. But most of the Reventos' furnishings and furniture were gone when they returned. Jacint's mother learned that many of their belongings had been taken by servants in the area before the Republican government had requisitioned the house. She found out where these people lived, and she tried to convince her husband to accompany her wearing his uniform to bring the furnishings back. He refused. She went with Jacint and an older brother of hers who, though he had spent the war in Barcelona and done nothing, belonged to a peculiar fascist organization which allowed him to wear a special uniform.

They drove to the workers suburbs, and the people there were so terrorized that they offered no resistance to his mother's and uncle's search in their homes. The things they found were of little value. "The people did not protest and only most timidly when something was taken, but they looked at us with a mixture of fear and hate that I shall never forget." As if to even the score, Jacint then tells about the worse state of a family summer home in Lloret. The town had been "liberated" (his quotation marks) by Italian fascist soldiers. "I know that Italians are a lively people," he says, "but such had been the drunken parties and depredations of these liberators that not only was everything in the house destroyed but they still found evidence of vomit on the walls."

Since so much of Catalonia resisted until the very end, the two decades that followed the Civil War were especially difficult for the people of Barcelona. What it was like has begun to appear in literature. The two most vivid accounts are a novel by Juan Marsé, *If They Tell You I Fell*, and a memoir by Carlos Barral, *Years of Penitence*. The Marsé novel gives a panoramic view of the hunger, fear, corruption, and humiliation suffered by the poor of the city, as much at the mercy of Falangist thugs as of terrorist bands of anarchists. Barral's memoir is a witty, stylish recollection of the suffocating piety in which boys of the middle class were reared. Everything about their lives was much worse than even the exiles were saying it was, for these members of liberal professions were far away in Latin America, in the main, and were prey to nostalgia and to embittered comparisons of what life would be like in their Catalonia.

One such exile family from Barcelona from the same social strata and sharing the same ideals was the Trías Fargas family, whose two older boys were youngsters when the war ended. The father, Antonio Trías Bujol, was even more distinguished in the medical field than Jacint Reventós' father; he was Barcelona's most famous surgeon, ran a clinic, taught in medical college, and was a trustee of the Barcelona Autonomous University. Trías Bujol numbered among his friends Luis Companys, who was president of the *Generalitat*, the Catalan autonomous government; Negrin, who was president of the Republic; the poet Antonio Machado; in fact, most intellectual and political leaders of the time, though he himself was only a liberal Catalanist like Reventós. When Barcelona fell, he left for France in the same car as Machado, but his connections were such that he was not, of course, interred in a French concentration camp but traveled on to Switzerland where his two older boys (there were six children in all) were at school. Years later, these two sons, Ramón and Carlos Trías Fargas, were to return in their teens to study in Barcelona, but for the moment their father had to decide where to take his family—temporarily, of course, since most exiles felt that Franco would not survive the World War that was in the offing.

In his valuable little book *El nuevo pensamiento político español*, a collection of essays first published during the sixties, Juan Marichal points out what were to be the intellectual consequences of the exodus of Spanish intellectuals—the distinguished men who went on to Oxford, Princeton, Mexico City, and Buenos Aires, and the lesser academicians who fructified the universities of Latin America. He compares this diaspora to the 1492 dispersal of the Jews from Spain: the poor Jews stayed close in North Africa, the wealthy went as far away as Salonika; the Republican exiles without status remained in the south of France, while Mexico City became the Salonika of the professionals. The father of the Trías Fargas boys had hoped to go to Mexico, and that country did offer him a university post, but would not under its laws allow him to practice surgery, an income he needed for his large family which was accustomed to living well.

He went to Colombia instead; a backwater, but although it did not encourage immigration, as did Mexico, which was never to recognize the Franco regime, it allowed him to settle there and practice surgery, such was his fame and the influence of his friends. They were never happy in Colombia. The younger son, Carlos, from whom I got their story, remembers theirs as the typical life of exiles—the sticking place of their interests and thoughts was Barcelona. The xenophobic laws of Colombia helped them to achieve this—to aspire to a municipal judgeship, for example, one had to be Colombian by birth—but even the most liberal atmosphere might not have mattered. At holiday dinners in their home, there were always any number of other exiles and their toasts and conversations were punctuated with the phrase, "Next year in Barcelona . . ." like good Jews at their seders.

The life of these political exiles has been portrayed brilliantly by the Republican novelist Max Aub, who himself lived in Mexico City until his death, in a satirical long story called *The True Story of the Death of Francisco Franco*. Its hero is a waiter nicknamed Nacho who came from Guadalajara as a young man to Mexico City and found a niche for himself in a café-restaurant in the center of the city. The café becomes his life. He never marries, and his knowledge of the world comes from the round of clients on whom he waits and to whose conversations he listens. Depending on the hour, these range from clerks to literati, and from businessmen to political bureaucrats. He never takes a vacation in all his years there. He would not want to miss any of the exchanges at the restaurant, for his clients' talk has become the cultural medium in which he thrives. He would not think of going to Guadalajara even for a holiday.

One day the Spanish Republican exiles arrive and make the café the site of their regular *tertulias*, those prolonged, chaotic, free-floating debates, a custom with them in Spain. He cannot bear their manner and their noisiness. He is repelled by the exiles' harsh consonants, their lisping c's and z's, their hand-clapping and hisses to call him, the way they yell all at once, and worst of all, by their endless talk of the past. After eight years of this, he decides on a course of action that will make his life happy again: to kill Franco, so that the exiles will return and leave him in peace. He astounds the café's owner by asking for a leave, and with the money he has saved all those years, goes to Spain and with no trouble assassinates Franco at a public gathering and gets away easily.

Nacho takes his time about returning to his job in Mexico City. He wants to give the exiles a chance to leave. He travels in Europe, unimpressed, as he was in Spain, by what he sees. He hears that a monarchy has been established in Spain and quite leisurely goes back to Mexico by boat. He reports for work, and there they all are. They are still arguing as noisily about what might have been if the Republican government had taken a certain measure or if a general another course of action. If . . . if . . . if! He retires and goes to Guadalajara for good and decides that it has cost him a lot to learn that there is something very wrong with the world—or could it be that *café con leche* has turned humanity into idiots?

In Colombia, Carlos Trías Fargas remembers, there was much of this kind of talk at home. The mistakes that were made and would not be repeated when they returned. For, after all, they knew how to do things in Catalonia. If, say, a local plumber was called in to do repairs, his work was always found inferior. In Barcelona, his father would say, it would have been done right. Carlos was on guard, like any boy, about anything the older generation said, but their talk of Catalonia seeped in and he really expected something quite different from what he found when, at the age of twenty, he came to Barcelona to attend the university. He had been preceded by his older brother Ramón and a sister, both studying in Barcelona, but except for political repression, which did not particularly bother him, his notions of what it would be like were what he had heard from the older generation.

"What a depressing place Barcelona was," he recalled. "The fifties were a bad time, though those who had lived here said it was as nothing compared to the forties. There were no real activities going on—perhaps there were a few, but I did not know about them. A totally repressive society and yet a young man could go on a spree. The contradictions of a country like this—for years you could see lines of men at some spots on the Ramblas waiting their turn at the whorehouses. Also, despite my father's record, I had no trouble getting a visa to come. Once here, I was called to police headquarters in the *Barrio Chino* and asked if I had associated with Communists in Colombia."

He told the truth: he had not, for he had been apolitical there, put off by the Republican exile talk and Colombian xenophobia. He was never bothered again. He lived the life of the bachelor student, a quietist one: there was nothing to tempt him. His grandparents and other relatives were here; his father's brother had been in trouble in the forties, but there was a lull now. In any case, the reality of Barcelona had opened his eyes to all that was absurd and ridiculous in the liberal stance of his father, and he extended this feeling to all politics.

Even his uncle's troubles, bad as they were, were more a source of irony than of inspiration. His uncle was a surgeon too, not as eminent as his brother though certainly well established, but he did not have his brother's luck and did not go to South America. He stayed in the south of France, in the Carcassonne, and worked in a poor clinic. He got into some trouble with the Pétain authorities when he was suspected of treating Maquis, and so had to flee to Andorra when the Nazis occupied the south of France. His wife and children were in Barcelona, and as luck would have it, a daughter's nylon dress caught fire and she was badly burned. He risked returning to Barcelona. He was ready for any eventuality, but nothing happened to him. Whereas his brother, Carlos' father, was so noted as an enemy of the regime that his property was liable to confiscation.

Carlos' uncle remained in Barcelona after his daughter got well, and began to practice again at a small clinic. More bad luck: he was picked up by the police when two guerrillas talked under torture and revealed that he had treated one of them. He spent only a few months in jail. He owed his light punishment—his sentence could have been death—to another irony, that he had once treated Ramón Franco, the dictator's aviator brother, during the time Ramón had been an anarchist. A speaking platform had collapsed under Ramón Franco at a Barcelona meeting, and he had broken some bones and cracked a few ribs. Francisco Franco was then head of the military academy in the north, and he paid his left-wing brother two or three visits. He had met Carlos' uncle there and remembered him. Besides that, Carlos' father had served in Morocco as a colonel in the medical corps when Franco made his name there, and since Franco was always sentimental about his African buddies, this was another reason to let Carlos' uncle off lightly.

There was always something slightly ridiculous about the attitudes and fears of these old liberals. Carlos' father was finally persuaded by his wife in the sixties to visit Barcelona. A daughter was getting married in England, and the mother thought that on the way there they should see Barcelona. His father was certain the Spanish embassy in Colombia would not give him a passport to travel to Spain. (He had kept his Spanish citizenship, but his passport was valid only for traveling to other countries.) He had to answer political questions at the embassy, and he denied nothing, except when he was asked if he was a Mason. "I am not a Mason," he said, "but if you mean by that if I was a Catalanist and a democrat, I was and still am." That would do it, he thought, and so told everyone at home, but the passport was validated anyway. He even made a second trip to Spain in 1970 and died there suddenly.

Carlos' apolitical life style when he came to Barcelona may also have been a reaction to his brother Ramón's example. Ramón was ten years older (in 1976, he was head of a new Catalan party, said to represent banking interests) and he had always been very aggressively political. In Colombia, when he was only a university undergraduate, he had hired a hall and announced a lecture to be given by him. All his father's friends attended as a matter of courtesy, and Ramón announced at the lecture that he was a Communist and told his audience of old Republicans that they need not think that they would someday return to Spain to regain their old businesses and lands. It caused a scandal. Carlos was not about to emulate Ramón: he was skeptical of his father's grasp of Spanish reality, but he also loved and respected him.

Carlos' lack of interest in his father's ideas was a muted generational rebellion—muted because he was mindful that his father paid the cost of his studies for years. After Carlos finished in Barcelona, he spent the year 1958 in Dallas, Texas, taking a postgraduate law course. "It was the equivalent of an M.A.," he said, "and I spent all my time with foreign students. I left Dallas with the impression that it was the most right-wing city in the United States. One night at a party at a Spaniard's home, the police arrived because the neighbors had decided that our party was subversive—we had just been singing old songs."

He followed up this year with another at Oxford that was quite different. In England, the campus was full of lively political interest, and he attended conferences where the Spanish exiles spoke and confronted representatives of the Franco regime. "It was there, in this new atmosphere, that I first began to think about such matters. My studies, however, were terribly boring—I spent a year working on a paper dealing with the legal aspects of bills of lading!"

He returned to Barcelona to practice law with his brother Ramón in the magnificent old family building on the upper Ramblas. The building had come to the children directly from the grandparents because any property of his father's was liable to confiscation. Ramón, who had been frustrated in his medical studies in Colombia, was now losing interest in law, and soon left the practice to Carlos in order to pursue his interest in economics that, via work with the Urquijo Bank, has led to his present political activities. Carlos' offices are still in this building, once one of the grand apartment buildings of the turn of the century, with high ceilings, massive doors, and enclosed balconies. The good families of Barcelona have moved to the upper sections of the city, where Carlos and his wife and children live in a superb duplex; and he is happy to live his life within these physically bourgeois ramparts, although his politics, like those of Reventós and Plana, is much further left than those of the older generation.

Juan Marichal, while speaking of the intense ideological life of the Civil War, leans on Thomas Mann and Antonio Machado to affirm that the bourgeoisie has been the only class to transcend itself, and it certainly seems true of these Barcelona bourgeois. Perhaps their Catalanism and their close family ties help: what one of them does has its immediate effect on the others of their class. It is a closely connected world. Quite casually, for I had no reason to think they were even acquainted, I learned that Trías Fargas had introduced Plana to his Colombian wife. "We returned the compliment," Plana said to me. "We introduced Carlos to Rosa María."

Rosa María is ten years younger than Carlos and met him during her second college year, when he returned from Oxford. "It was his seriousness that attracted me," she said. "He was interested in ideas and actually talked to me about them, so different from the college boys who only flirted." Carlos had changed, and although his practice had no relation to politics, he met at a bank, for whom he did some work, a man who in his teens had been a member of the old POUM. "We talked, and I met others and in an unorganized way I began to engage in political activities. Some years ago when a young anarchist was going to be garroted, two of us went to Paris to hold a press conference to create publicity for his case. We just did it on our own, and although it was useful, activities of that sort can also be foolish. I remember going with a group of the opposition to Portugal to talk to the pretender Don Juan. What foolishness that was—all of us there in that hotel room speculating about what the prospects were for Spain now that the Salazar dictatorship was overthrown."

He has tried to make his profession useful to the opposition, but he is not a trial lawyer. It disappoints him that most of what he does in his office is to handle urbanization problems. "That means I represent people whose property has been confiscated for urban growth. Do not believe, however, in the regime's talk that their expropriating property is a sign of their liberality—it is never for any social benefit to the people or the community." Spain's modernity in the last ten years is at the stage that the United States, say, was at the turn of the century—the national and provincial authorities are simply ruthlessly clearing the way for speculators and industry.

Carlos is now a member of *Convergencia Socialista*, and he feels that at last, after years of being on his own politically, he is part of a movement that makes it possible for him to be less foolish than he believes he was. Even when the authorities first took note of him, his activity had been tinged with absurdity. He was driving his car and happened to come upon a political demonstration at the time the students had holed up with cultural leaders at the Capuchin monastery, when drivers were being called upon to honk their horns and create a traffic jam. "Since the newspapers would not print news of demonstrations, this was one way of letting people know there was resistance." A traffic policeman was rudely trying to get them to move on, and he spoke threateningly to Carlos in Castilian.

"It made me so angry to see that Catalan doing their dirty work that I said to him, 'Do not talk to me in that clumsy Castilian—it is not your language—speak to me in Catalan.' That did it. I was arrested." He laughed at the recollection. He was fined about four hundred dollars, and his driver's license was revoked. After several months, he was permitted to take a new driver's test, but he would not have passed it had not his secretary, in keeping track of his appointments, found out about this. Her father worked in the automotive department giving road tests, and she told him about Carlos. The father passed Carlos, but he told his daughter that he had received instructions from the police to fail him if it was at all possible.

That 1966 demonstration that Carlos stumbled on was an historic one for the student generation that was some ten years younger than Carlos. For many others, too. At the university the students had made the official student organization inoperative, and their meeting at the Capuchin monastery was called as a constitutional convention for an independent student organization. The work to set up this convention had been arduous; about four hundred delegates had been elected from the various departments of the different colleges. Important Catalan cultural leaders, like the poet Espriu and the painter Tapies, were also participating as guests. The Barcelona Capuchin order, whose independence from reactionary Church leaders was of such long standing that even in the worst days of the Civil War their monastery had never been in any danger of burning, let them use their auditorium for the convention. But once everyone was inside the police laid siege to the place.

The police demanded that delegates and guests surrender by turning in their identity cards. That meant that in a few days each would have to report to police headquarters to retrieve them and, even if not charged, all would have a police record that would prejudice their future. The convention voted unanimously to hold out, and did so for three days. The monks made them welcome in the monastery, fed them, and took them into their cells to sleep. They also managed on the first day to get more supplies through the police lines or the students could not have held out so long. Throughout those days, the convention not only adopted a constitution for the new student organization, they also held lectures and roundtable discussions. Espriu recited his poetry, the new Catalan protest singers gave recitals, and when the police broke in by force, the filled auditorium was listening to a discussion on urban planning led by prominent architects and the dean of the school of architecture.

The street demonstration that Carlos Trías Fargas unexpectedly joined was one that the parents of the students were holding to call attention to the police siege. Almost everyone who told me about the siege made a point to tell me about the parents also, as further proof of the liberality of the Catalan middle class. One of the students at *los capuchinos*, as that event has come to be known, now a professor of economics, was particularly thrilled about his parents. His father had never talked politics at home nor encouraged him in anything but to speak Catalan; his mother had, of course, been no more than a traditional Spanish mother. Yet they went out in their car that night, and when the police hustled the students out of the Capuchin monastery, he saw his mother across the street behind the police line straining to get to him. "She had come to protect me," he said, still filled with wonder at the great transformation.

This meeting at *los capuchinos* may have inspired the opposition movement, particularly the illegal trade unionists, to use the churches as meeting places. The opposition could not grow if it did not find a way to circumvent the total ban on meetings, for in trade-union actions it was essential to include the masses in all decisions. The Catalan Church was sympathetic; indeed, in the sixties the Vatican, in an attempt to placate Franco, had transferred the liberal Abbé of Montserrat to a post in Rome. And it was finally at a church in Barcelona that Carlos Trías Fargas got into real trouble. The SEAT auto workers went on strike in 1974, and each day held "lightning" meetings. To one of these, Carlos went, persuaded by a Communist friend to appear as speaker.

He was nervous about going because he knew there was some risk, but it bothered him more that he had nothing to say to these workers and little useful advice to give them. Still, they told him that his presence would give them heart, and so he went. He never got to speak. The meeting had hardly gotten underway when the church was surrounded by the political police. There were about four hundred workers in the church, and most of them tried to storm the police lines. Many were wounded, and Carlos' Communist friend was so badly beaten that he had to be taken directly to a hospital instead of jail. Forty of them, including Carlos, stayed inside long enough to call friends and warn them they would probably soon be jailed. They decided to surrender when the police called out with bullhorns that if they stayed longer the charges against them would be worse, whereas if they came out now, before the police went inside to get them, it would count as a gesture of cooperation.

It was a fearful moment for Carlos. He did not know if they would also be beaten when they walked out. He knew they would be jailed. He was crossing class lines from a world of comfort. I was listening to him and his wife Rosa María talk about that experience while we were sitting on the upper terrace of his duplex apartment. It is a splendid place, designed by Lluis María Sert, the architect whose stunning building for the Joan Miró Museum in Montjuich had just been inaugurated, and below us the terrace descended into a spacious garden of their own. Their children were down there playing.

"I was to learn a great deal from those seventy-two hours they held me incommunicado," Carlos said. "I learned what class differences really are. They questioned me—they hoped to get me and my Communist friend to admit that we were the chairmen of the meeting, since that could get us ten years while simple attendance at the meeting meant only three months—but they did not touch me. You could even say there was a certain formal politeness in the way they dealt with me. But they treated the workers miserably in every way, and they beat them."

They had all been booked at *Seguridad*, security headquarters down in the old city on Vía Layetana, and Rosa María, who had not known where Carlos had gone that day, began to call there as soon as friends informed her what had happened at the church. For her this was a new experience too; he had kept her innocent of much of his activity. But she knew she had to be careful. She could not say on the phone that she had known Carlos was at the meeting, only report that she had heard that he had been picked up on some unknown charge. On the phone they told her nothing, but she went down to *Seguridad*, as dreaded in Barcelona as in Madrid, and they said yes, he was there. She could not see him for seventy-two hours (her presence there was important because it put them on warning to observe this law), but she could bring him food if she wanted.

"The next morning I made him a little package of nice things and went down again to *Seguridad* to deliver it," Rosa María said. "The wife of one of the workers who had been jailed arrived at the same time I did, and she was carrying an enormous package. Although I did not know her, I said, 'But can he eat all that? It will spoil. Isn't it too much?' She replied, 'Oh, but there are the others, it is for them as well.' That was *my* lesson about class differences, and the next morning I tried to make up for my thoughtlessness the first day."

From the months I spent in Barcelona twelve years earlier, I knew what *Seguridad* had meant in the past: I used to cross the street on that block of Vía Layetana in order not to pass its ominous entrance with the *grises*, as the political police in gray uniforms are called,

standing guard. But now, the evening prior to my visit to Carlos'
home, I had had proof of how little the Barcelonan activists dreaded
it. Rather, of how they consciously defied it. Xavier Folch had
helped me discover this. Folch is an editor at one of the Barcelona
publishing houses and also a member of PSUC, the Catalan Communist Party, and it was interesting, also, to hear from someone of
his persuasion, tributes to the Catalan bourgeoisie. His own parents
had at the start of the Civil War immediately transferred to Burgos,
then the major capital of the Nationalist zone. Xavier was born
there, and the first time he was arrested some years ago and questioned, his interrogator had exclaimed when he saw his birthplace
on his record, "But your family is of the regime!" Xavier replied, "No,
my mother was never of the regime and from this day forth neither
is my father." His interrogator pointed out that Xavier had not seen
his father and could not possibly know. "I told him that as between
the regime and his son my father would choose his son. And so it
was. There is something very fine about these Catalan bourgeois
families—I know no one whose family did not stand by him."

I told Xavier that I had seen a notice in a paper that day about a
forthcoming meeting to form a Permanent Assembly of Catalan
Intellectuals, Artists, and Professionals, but it had not said where it
was being held. "That is never given and the police never know," he
said. He added that it would be a working meeting of no more than
fifty persons but that I could come. He gave me the address. It
shocked me—"But that is across the street from *Seguridad!*" I said.
He laughed. "Even after it is reported on in the newspapers," he said,
"the police won't know. That cannot happen in Madrid. Only in
Barcelona."

Carlos and Rosa María agreed about this when I told them. I had
gone to the meeting—from its windows you could see *Seguridad*—
and had read about it that morning in the papers. None of them did
say where it was held. "Even if the *grises* knew, they would do
nothing," Carlos said. "Not now." The Catalans had imposed themselves. For three decades they had not been allowed to dance the
Sardana, the national folk dance of Catalonia, but the regime had
had to give in. The first time I saw it, I understood why it was
banned, but this is difficult to explain when one is away from its
magic. The Sardana is danced in a circle with the dancers holding

hands, to music that is unvarying in its rhythm and beat; the circle slowly revolves to a series of intricate steps and at one point, its sole climax, the music rises an octave and the dancers, still holding hands, lift their arms high. And they go on and on and on, never changing their steps and only imperceptibly moving clockwise, and each time the music rises and they lift their arms, tears come to your eyes. A *madrileño* told me, "I envy them this dignity and controlled gaiety."

In just that careful, thoughtful, Catalan way, Carlos had chosen to join the *Convergencia Socialista*. His choice exemplified some of this spirit of family that the Catalans have developed under Franco: he was affirming his socialist ideals without taking an anti-Communist stance. Unlike Jacint Reventós who is irked in small ways by Communist behavior in united front activities ("They are admirable as individuals and they insist on perfect freedom of discussion, but always after everyone has said what he thinks, you find when the final position paper is published that all of that has been ignored and it says no more than what the Communists originally wanted"). Carlos will not even criticize the Communists in any way. He shakes his head and says, "No, we others have done some things, gotten arrested and jailed a few days—but they have suffered everything, beatings and years in jail, and are absolutely dedicated."

In any case, what worried Carlos those days was that the *Convergencia* had gotten its permit to hold their first meeting at an arena that could hold thousands and they might well not be able to fill it. They were a party mainly of intellectuals and professionals. Would workers come? He was eager for me to attend, and although there would be no tickets to the meeting—it was open to all without charge—he spent the larger part of a day obtaining me a pass to Row O which was being reserved for the press and honored guests. Reventós and Plana Torrás were impressed when they saw my pass; they did not know about Row O. I said I wanted to sit with them, and they thought there would be no problem. The problem would be filling the arena. "The city is full of our posters for the meeting, but they are so damned artistic that you can hardly tell what it is or where it is held," Jacint said. "If it is not filled, everyone will rightly say that our socialism has no appeal for the workers. Particularly the Communists."

We decided to leave early for the arena, as if that might somehow encourage others to attend. Plana was driving, and Jacint was free to talk about his interest in socialized medicine—his practical reason for being in the *Convergencia*. "Yes, you leave the philosophical questions to me," Plana said to him. I asked Jacint if he had operations to perform the next morning. He said yes, and I congratulated him on his professional calmness. He replied that he was not so busy any longer, because he was not getting many referrals: he would not pay the forty percent kickback the internists were accustomed to demanding. "You see why I am so interested in socialized medicine?—that forty percent should stay in the patient's pocket."

It was a depressing thought to have on top of his worries about the meeting. We passed one of the *Convergencia*'s posters, and Jacint said, "You see, it cannot be read." But we were nearing the new extension of the university and there seemed to be many cars heading in the same direction. We had to park a few blocks away from the arena, and we only got as close as that because Plana simply drove the car up on a sidewalk and left it there. Ahead of us, as we walked, were many groups, and although we made it to the arena a half hour before the meeting was due to begin, we could not get inside. Indeed, there were already a few thousand surrounding the building.

I pondered the correctness of using my pass to Row O. I could read Catalan, but I would not be able to understand the speeches. Should I offer it to Reventós? What about Plana? The problem was solved for me by the sight, across from the main entrance, of people like the singer Raimon, the painter Tapies, the critic Castellet, the editor Folch. They and others with them had been among the two hundred signers of the call for the meeting. They, too, had passes for Row O, but these were useless—even the entranceways were jammed. Everyone had come—the entire Catalan political family was there, eager to make the evening a success—and no one was leaving.

The design of the new university arena is modern. Above us were overpasses leading to the balconies arched like wings, and floor-to-ceiling glass walls curved around the outer corridors of the circular building. All these areas created a sense of space—now tested to its limits by the crowds—that was a hallmark of the new architecture. But the arena was not air-conditioned (typical, someone said, of Spain's uncompleted entrance into the modern world), and everyone repeated that it was like a sauna inside. At first, I thought this was just an expression people were using, but after an hour of conversation with all these friends, enough of the outsiders left to allow us, now on the upper level, to approach the *vomiteras*, as the balcony entrances were called, and the blast of hot air emanating from fifty feet away was enough to turn us back. At that moment, one couple struggled out of a *vomitera*, and their clothes looked as if they had fallen into a swimming pool. They were laughing and we cheered them.

The corridor between the glass wall and the cement inner wall of the arena is some thirty feet wide. After a while, we made a second try and managed to get in there but had to leave immediately. It felt like a sauna and, after all, the only thing we could hear from that drenched humanity inside was cheers. We stood on the overpass again, but careful not to stand in a direct line with any entrance, to avoid its hot, billowing breath, and looked at the people still elbow to elbow inside the corridor. The glass wall was totally steamed over, as in a veritable sauna. I watched the first young man to get the idea of writing on it with his thumb. He wrote: *Visca Catalunya.*

13

Galicia:

The Unknown Nation

On a sunny day, there is no happier landscape in Spain than Galicia's. Its green hills and pine-thick mountains rise joyously above flowering, cultivated valleys into which the Atlantic playfully enters, along this wavering coastline in the northwest of the Iberian peninsula, forming exquisite *rías*, fjords so peaceful that they are a vision of the good life. Nowhere in Spain, either, do people love their land as do the Galicians. Indeed, to be away from it is cause for an unappeasible *morriña*, an untranslatable Galician word that combines the feelings of inexpressible longings, homesickness, nostalgia, emptiness of soul, and even at home the Galician is subject to desolating attacks of it. *Morriña* is akin to but more intense than what American blacks used to call the blues, for it is inseparable from love of their nation and their patch of geography. Yet Galicia is a sad land. It was wounded in its very soul by what historians mistakenly call the Reconquest of Spain by Isabel and Ferdinand, its social and economic structure so disturbed and its development so frustrated that for centuries its men have had to leave it always meaning to return. First to other areas in the peninsula, later to the Americas, lately to all of Europe. It has become a truism that there is no place in the world where a Galician has not been looking for work.

In the middle of the nineteenth century a great lyric poet, Rosalía de Castro, who brought the humiliated Galician language back to honored life, gave us a despairing look at the condition of Galicia.

All her poems were a keening over its sorrows, and yet she managed, as if the short lyric form had no limitations, to be as precise as a modern sociologist. Here, without its music, is one of them:

> This one leaves and that one,
> and all, all go away;
> Galicia, left without men
> that can work you.
> You have, instead, orphan boys and girls
> and fields of loneliness,
> and mothers who have no sons
> and sons who have no fathers.
> And you have hearts that suffer
> long mortal absences,
> widows of the live and dead
> whom no one shall console.

My father left his widowed mother and younger sister at the age of thirteen. He had lived in one of La Coruña's mountainside parishes, a form of social organization in Galicia which dates back to pre-Christian Celtic times, and after a few years in Havana as a kind of indentured apprentice at a cigar factory, he ended up in the United States. When he became seriously ill at thirty, he returned to his parish to let its clear mountain air, sharp with the smell of pine and eucalyptus, cure him of his sickness. It did not; he died there. In 1965, I went to look at the place and was welcomed by cousins and other kin whom I did not know existed. To them I owe some knowledge of Galician peasant life. I returned twice in 1976 and again found Galicia such a captivating place that when I am blue now, I know I am suffering from its eternal *morriña*, although it is not rightfully mine to claim.

Real sadness belongs to my cousin Claudio and his wife Isabel, who have never left the parish of Miamán, and to his younger brother Gustavo and his wife Luz, who have left the countryside and made another life in the nearby city of Santiago de Compostela. All have prospered in a typically exceptional Galician manner, but they have not ceased to think of their lives as burdens which they have only been able to sustain with excessive, accursed work. Already in 1965, before emigrant work in Europe had begun to make itself felt in savings sent home and while Spain was still a preponderantly agricultural country, Claudio had cause to feel pride in having built the first two-story home in Miamán and Gustavo in starting his successful little restaurant in Santiago. Claudio and Isabel had worked so hard and been so frugal that ten years earlier, in the fifties, they had helped Gustavo get a start by advancing him the money to go to Venezuela to work in construction. Gustavo slaved there for several years, and with the money he saved returned to marry Luz and open his modest restaurant in a working-class section of the city. In 1965, they had two small children, and Claudio and Isabel an only son. This son was nineteen when I first met him; Claudio had sent him to Santiago to live with Gustavo while studying to enter the university. Claudio and Isabel, Gustavo and Luz, felt the only value their hard work had was, God grant it, the different lives their children would live.

Finding Miamán in 1965 had been an adventure for me. (I have told this story in *The Goodbye Land*.) No roads led you to it and within it there were only oxen trails. I hired a taxi in Santiago and we drove on the only highway between it and the Atlantic. I had learned from the tourist office in Santiago the name of the town on that highway which was nearest to Miamán, and I left the taxi there to wait while I walked three miles uphill through woods and rutted trails. Looking for my father's and grandmother's graves, I was referred to a house where I found second cousins. They told me about Claudio and where I could find Gustavo in Santiago. One Sunday, Gustavo took off a day from work for the first time in his life, leaving Luz to run the restaurant alone, and we went to Miamán for a dinner at Claudio's and Isabel's with all the nearby cousins seated on benches around a long rustic table. I was served an endless number of dishes and many bowls of Galician wine, and we were all extraordinarily happy. I think always of Breughel when I remember that day, but I knew even then that such pleasure was not only unusual for my cousins, it was unique.

In the winter of 1976, I went straight to Gustavo and Luz in the city. The restaurant had not changed—they had installed a gas stove, though Luz still used the wood-fired one as well—but they now owned the ancient three-story granite building in the old city that housed it. They had fixed some of its tiny rooms to rent to students. Gustavo had bought a secondhand Renault. Also, as investment, an apartment in one of the new high-rises and a ground-floor section in the same group of buildings, where they hoped to open a second restaurant. These last were not yet completed, but they did not mean to move to them. Their children were going to school, and during the last two years, they had taken off summer weekends and gone to the shore.

Although it was winter, when there is much rain and slushy snow in Galicia, Gustavo was able to drive me right to the door of Claudio's farmhouse. The highway to the Atlantic was still no grander than some county road of ours, but the moment we left the town on the highway, where in 1965 I had left the taxi, I could see changes in Miamán. First of all, the paved roads that traversed it, and also the many new two-story houses. The cultivated fields were larger now, too, the result of the land redistribution organized by the Franco government's agricultural extension service. When I first walked up those hills, I had seen only tiny garden patches—the *minifundios* that had helped keep the economy depressed. Now, there were plots as big as one and two acres. But the most striking contrast, other than the paved roads, were the tractors. In 1965, there had only been oxen to work the fields and pull the wagons. Indeed, in those days they were still using the implements of Roman days.

I exclaimed about all these changes to Claudio and Isabel, and Isabel threw out her arms to express the ineffable wonder of it. "If I could read and write, if I were not an ignorant old country woman," she said, "I would have written Franco a letter to thank him for what he did for us—the roads and the *concentración*, what beautiful things! I mourned for him when he died, more than some who went about crying."

She held out her hands towards me. "But, of course, they never taught me to write and I did not write that letter." She was small and thin and intense at fifty-nine, and the hands she demonstrated as useless for writing were so swollen with work, which began at the age of six, that they appeared to belong to a man twice her size. "Anyway," she added with a shake of her whole body, which she uses when a bitter grimace is insufficient, "there is only time for work here. Our life is slavery."

The land redistribution was being talked about in 1965 and did not get started until two years later. At that time, Claudio's twelve and a half acres were scattered throughout Miamán in fifty different parcels. Some were as small as one *ferrado*, which take eighteen to total two and a half acres, and some no larger than a *cuartillo*, which is a small fraction of a *ferrado*. In Claudio's home, there was a surveyor's map drawn by government technicians before they began the redistribution in Miamán, and I saw strips as narrow as a truck's path. I said to Claudio, "How did people keep track of them? How did you remember where each parcel was every spring?" Claudio stared at me in incomprehension: land, no matter how small, is something no Galician ever misplaces.

I wondered, given what I knew was the Galician peasant's strong feelings for his land, if there had been any problems in agreeing, on the voluntary basis that the redistribution was done, about the land which was to replace the separate parcels. Claudio said no. "The quality of the land was taken into account. After all, except in the mountains where it is rocky, the land in Miamán is all very much the same," he said with a show of reasonableness.

He took me beyond the yard's magnificent haystacks and kitchen garden to show me his land now near the house. It did not look like twelve and a half acres to me, and Claudio then said that there were another five parcels in different sections of Miamán. I asked him if the government surveyors could not have managed to group all his lands in this one convenient spot. "Well, no, not exactly," he said without irony or self-consciousness. "I wanted to keep the bottom land where I planted the wheat, and another piece of land where I always grew maize . . ."

Only a year earlier Claudio had bought from the municipality some pineland up in the mountain. It cannot be converted to farmland, but with his son Paco he timbers it and sells the wood to middlemen. He had also continued to maintain the *taberna* in their corner of Miamán (there are only one hundred twenty-five families in the parish), and besides sodas and wine and cognac, he sold enough items for the *taberna* to serve as a general store. He had even equipped it with a used television set. And, of course, he owned a tractor. Thirty-five families had bought tractors, and between him and Isabel they could name every one of them—they were such an index of prosperity. Their only disappointment since I had last seen them was Paco's inability to make the university, but that had turned into a blessing: he had married and stayed home and given them two grandsons.

In 1965, Paco used to say to me in Santiago, "Yes, I like Miamán, but my feelings about the countryside are romantic and folkloric—the life there is too hard." And when he did not make the university, he got a job as a traveling salesman that took him as far away as Vigo. It was not good, and after a year he took a test for a bank job. He failed. He came home for a few days to get over the disappointment and never left again. "I did not make the decision to stay—I just stayed."

He fell immediately into the routine of young men in the countryside: work all day and early evening and a walk after dinner at ten. It had been going on for centuries. "You make your way in the dark to the home of a girl you fancy and call out to her from the lane. If she comes out, you stand in the yard talking. You do not go inside, not until your intentions are serious and you speak to the father." Paco courted three girls at the same time, as a kind of insurance that each night there would be a girl who would come out and stand in the yard and whom he might persuade to go all the way. "It is a game all the fellows play," he said, now that he was a solidly married man. "You never know which girl is going to hook you."

Most Spaniards will tell you that in Galicia sex relations have always been saner and healthier than anywhere else in Spain. Illegitimacy does not bear any stigma for the child, and the worst the mother with a child born out of wedlock suffers is a narrowed choice of husbands: she may have to settle for a widower with children. In 1965, I learned that Claudio and Gustavo and I did not share the same grandfather: our grandmother gave birth to their mother a few years after my grandfather died, although she had not remarried. The same occurred with her daughter, Claudio's and Gustavo's mother: Claudio and Gustavo were not sired by the same man, Gustavo having been born out of wedlock after Claudio's father died. But courting is played along the old Spanish *macho* lines, although the girls here may have more maneuverability in the game, as Paco calls it, and although Galician women have always been the equal of men in even the hardest farm labor—indeed, they have often been the heads of families during the long absences when their husbands migrated to find work.

How Paco's wife, Clara, got such a good catch (Claudio in Miamán's terms is an affluent citizen and Paco is his only heir) is a mystery to the women in the ancient house of my second cousins where my grandmother was born. "Do you think Clara is beautiful?" each of the black-garbed women asked in rapid succession, and before I could reply they shrieked with laughter. Clara is handsome; her face has the definition of a Flemish portrait and she is trim and vigorous, but in Miamán beauty is prettiness. "Paco was a dumbbell in school," one explained, "and he is a dumbbell with women. The other girls were beautiful, and he let Clara hook him!" The word "hook" occurs so often in talk of marriage that it would seem that choosing a life partner is like making a living off the meager land: cunning and persistence and acquisitiveness come mainly into play.

Poor Clara. During the days I was with them, she got out of work only once. One Sunday afternoon Paco took her to the highway town with me to visit, for an hour, an aunt whose husband was dying of cancer. Clara stood all the while in the kitchen, which was crowded with the children and nephews and grandchildren of the couple, responding laconically when someone thought to ask her about her own children. Afterward, Paco was driving me to my hotel in Santiago, where I had an appointment with an elderly Galician scholar, and I was surprised when he let Clara off about a mile from home. "Aren't you coming to Santiago with us?" I asked. It had not occurred to either: excursions are not for women. But Clara smiled, and gently aping her mother-in-law's rough ways with Claudio, said, "He is very bad—he wants to be off alone." Paco smiled briefly; it was the closest they ever came to an affectionate exchange.

Claudio and Isabel, and Paco and Clara, get up at five three seasons of the year, at seven in winter. They are so busy until they go to bed soon after dinner that the only words they address to one another have to do with chores. They plant the twelve and a half acres with maize, potatoes, wheat, cabbage, and pasture; they have a small fruit orchard and a kitchen garden; and they raise cows for milk and to sell as beef. For their own meat, they slaughter three pigs a year, and sell the others. The hens are for laying, but they will occasionally kill one for the table. Except for salt, oil, wine, and rice, they produce all their own food, including sausages and cheese. Isabel remembers when they made their own soap.

Claudio opens the *taberna* for an hour at midday and for three hours in the evening. In winter, he and Paco cut down pines and bring them down to the lanes with the tractor. Before he owned a tractor and chain saw, they used ox-driven wagons with hand-hewn wheels, the work of a local carpenter. These wagons are still used for some jobs; they stand in the yard, along with the Roman plow, like magnificent antiques. Recently, a man showed up in Miamán interested in buying old things like these for his shop in the city, but Claudio would not think of selling implements which he can still use. On Sundays, Paco spends most of the day selling animal feed supplements from house to house in the parish. I went along with him in the rickety Mercedes Benz delivery truck that he bought secondhand five years earlier. He honks his horn at each clump of houses, and most often it is women who come out and carry off the hundred-pound bags on their heads.

All this is a simplified account of their work, and it glosses over the tremendous effort required for each job. For example, raising cows and pigs. When the weather is good, the eight cows and their calves are taken out to pasture, but in the winter months, the cows and pigs are kept most of the time in the labyrinth of primitive stalls that takes up most of the downstairs of the house. The pigs must be fed three times a day. Isabel and Clara cut *verdura* (cabbage greens) in a nearby field each day, chop it up, and add cornmeal of their own milling, stir in hot water from the cauldrons in the kitchen hearth, and carry pails of the mixture across the passageway that separates the kitchen from the stalls. They also bring in huge bundles of hay on pitchforks to the stalls and, when the feed gets low, the inferior, dried cornstalks stored in a shed in the yard. Milking the cows is Isabel's only moment of relaxation during the day.

In all the stalls and in the narrow yard between the lane and the house they spread layer upon layer of *tojo*, a kind of juniper that grows wild in the forest. It breaks down well with the excrement that the cows and pigs drop on it each day and creates a compost which is the bulk of the manure used in the fields. It lies underfoot all the time. As soon as you step out of the kitchen, you walk on the spongy mixture two feet deep. Everyone works at laying and gathering it when it is ready. The women sweep out the kitchen several times a day, but the floor is never clean. Isabel attacks the compost that inevitably gets dragged in and exclaims, "Filth, filth, filth!" and Clara smiles at me apologetically.

Since 1965, there have been two great changes in that house that seemed so rustically beautiful to me then. (It still does.) Upstairs, there is the long, bare room at the top of the stairs, with only the long wooden table and benches to adorn it, and beyond it are four bedrooms, two on each side of a corridor that ends in what is now the bathroom. In 1965, this last was simply a four-foot-square wooden room, bare but for a hole in the floor over the cow stalls. Now a flush toilet has appeared in it, a tiny washstand, a cement floor, and an open-ended pipe overhead that must serve as shower. In the kitchen, the only room downstairs that does not belong to the animals, there is now a butane gas stove with two burners and a small oven. Isabel uses it only to heat milk. The meals and the boiling of water in fifteen-gallon cauldrons are done on the hearth. This is raised six inches above the rest of the floor and takes up a third of the kitchen. It is roofed by a brick bell that slopes back into the chimney. There is room to sit under it and stretch your feet to the fire, the only heat in the house, but I was the only one who ever had time for that. From the moment they get up until they go to bed, no one ever stops or goes upstairs.

"Oh, Pepe," Isabel said to me. "This life is slavery."

I could not interview them. I simply talked family talk, but once I surprised Claudio and myself by asking which had been the happiest years of his life. The three years of the war, he replied. He had served with the Nationalists as an artilleryman with the Army of Galicia. Brunete, Belchite, Teruel, the fall of Madrid—those tragic engagements for us who had supported the Republic—were for Claudio years free from grinding care. I could not take that away from him with political arguments. I said nothing, probably because I should not have been able to convince him. In a moment, I thought to ask him if he had volunteered, and he laughed scornfully. "Volunteer!" he exclaimed, and shook his head, as if to say he was no fool. That made me feel only slightly better.

In Santiago the mood was still with me, and the moment that Antonio Fraguas, a sweet elderly man who looked like my Galician

Uncle Antonio in Tampa, Florida, arrived at my hotel, I told him all about my cousins in Miamán. Fraguas was a Galician folklorist and had taught until he retired a month earlier at the Pedro Sarmiento Institute, called the Institute of Galician Studies under the Republic. "It is all a result of the Civil War," he said. "Your cousins probably do not know why they are sad, but the war changed Galicia drastically. One could almost say that gaiety disappeared from the countryside. Galicia was a land of songs—the peasants sang in the fields while they worked—but that is all gone. That ambience. It is as if a blanket fell over everything."

Fraguas was what is called a *galleguista histórico*, a member of the *Galleguista* Party that had formed part of the Popular Front which won the elections in 1936. Theirs was a moderate party that had evolved from the turn of the century, following the resurgence of nationalist sentiment in the middle of the nineteenth century which Rosalía de Castro had symbolized. They were not separatists; they worked for a limited autonomy for Galicia, mainly concerned with asserting their cultural differences by bringing back into the schools and official use their language and history. Even the Republicans in Madrid did not take them too seriously. The Basques and Catalans gained autonomy without question—except, of course, from the Right—under the Republic, but the *galleguistas* were stalled at every turn. It was not until June, 1936, one month prior to the uprising by the Nationalists, that they had been allowed to hold a plebiscite to decide if they wanted autonomy. More than ninety-nine percent voted for it.

The Nationalists persecuted the *galleguistas* ruthlessly. Depending on the community, some were summarily executed, others jailed, and others, like Fraguas, proscribed. He was not allowed to teach or to continue with his studies. He was born in a modest family, but when the war came, he was principal of an elementary school and was studying towards a university degree. It took him fifteen years of persistent appeals to reverse this sentence, and when the Institute of Galician Studies was permitted to reopen, under another name, he began teaching again. A priest had helped save the library of Galician books by transferring it to a room at the university in Santiago. Galician could not be used in newspapers, books, or radio, and was frowned on in conversation. "It is not that an order went out to the police. If you spoke Galician to a friend, he would say, *Se ve mal*—it is not looked on well—not in public."

Five hundred years of this kind of treatment and yet the Galician language survived. For Galician nationalists their language is key to independence. They agree that reinstatement of the language in all spheres of life will not solve the problems of Galicia, but without it they would have no identity as a people. A social history of Galicia can be written by simply tracing what happened to its language since the days when Ferdinand and Isabel won the region, took the nobles they did not kill away to their court, and made Castilian the official language—castrated the nation, as Galicians say. The people of the countryside, however, never stopped speaking Galician. It was in the cities that the upper and middle classes took up Castilian.

The use of Galician took on a social significance that modified personal behavior. The castilianized middle class used it to speak to their servants and as the vehicle for off-color jokes. The peasant, convinced of his language's inferiority, never spoke it to a priest or a bureaucrat or simply to anyone who was dressed well. Even if a merchant replied to him in Galician he persisted in speaking his bad Castilian, as if to show that he was as good as anyone else. Sociologists believe that no more than twenty percent in Galicia speak or think in Castilian, but the poor's feelings about their own language is still widespread. When I returned from Spain in 1976, I told my Uncle Antonio, who at ninety was leaving in a few days from Florida to Galicia for his first visit in sixty years, that everyone now spoke Galician. He was not pleased. He grimaced and said, "I do not like that—it cannot be." In 1965, when I went to Miamán for the grand reunion at Claudio's home, one of my second cousins said to me, "After you left the other day, we were all wondering how it is that you understand Galician so well." I said that I knew a little French and Italian and that these plus Castilian helped me with the Galician. Behind me I heard another cousin exclaim to the others, "What is Galician to a man who is master of so many languages!"

In 1972, a Madrid publishing house issued a bilingual anthology called *Eight Centuries of Galician Poetry*, announcing in its very title the long history of Galician literature. In the thirteenth century, Alfonso the Wise of Castile chose Galician as the language most apt for the lyric and wrote his own songs to the Virgin in it. For a couple of centuries, to write poetry in Spain was to write in Galician. In the 1920's García Lorca, an Andalusian, paid obeisance to this lost tradition by writing a few lyrics in Galician. Galician poetry declined not because it lost its vigor as a form but for political reasons: the separation of Portugal from Spain caused a truncation of peoples who shared the same language and culture, and the conquest of Galicia by the Catholic kings and the ensuing uprisings laid the country waste. The Galicians, as one Castilian historian of the time put it, had to be tamed. The sixteenth and seventeenth centuries were a dark age for Galicia.

The return of the language among intellectuals and artists was again a political event. It came in the nineteenth century with the struggles for recognition of the area's depressed conditions. A present-day Galician Marxist like Xesú Alonso Montero goes so far as to say, "Yesterday like today, to write in Galician is to begin to break with the bourgeoisie." The most popular of contemporary poets, Celso Emilio Ferreiro, in his most quoted poem says in part:

> Proletarian language of my country,
> I speak it because I do, because I like it
> and want to be among mine, with my people,
> near those good men who for long have suffered
> a history told in another tongue.

Ferreiro was put off recently by an interviewer who asked him whether he continued to believe that social poetry (referring to the literary movement that was popular in the late fifties in Spain) should still be predominantly written in Galicia. Ferreiro told him he had made a mistake, that he (Ferreiro) was not the leader of social poetry in Galicia, as the interviewer had said, for "this form of poetry has always existed there. I mean by this that there it has not been a fashion [*moda*] but a permanent mode [*modo*] of understanding the question. To the point that protest already appears in the medieval Galician-Portuguese troubadors."

Starting with Rosalía de Castro in the nineteenth century, a whole new literature in Galician has arisen. Galician novelists like Valle Inclán and Emilia Pardo Bazán wrote in Castilian, as continue to do moderns like Corpus Barga and Torrente Ballester, but there is an

254

insistence, in their subject and outlook, on being Galician. Still, the test of *galleguismo*, of the push for autonomy that has increased rather than lessened under Franco, has been the use of the language everywhere and every place, not simply among one's own as with the peasants, but in every activity, and this has, of course, meant defying the regime.

An extraordinary man, now dead, serves as guide and example for them—Alfonso Castelao. A priest gave him the name of the Spanish crown prince at his birth, but he was always to prefer Daniel. He was born in 1886 in the coastal town of Rianxo, his father being a small wholesaler in fish, and when he was ten, his father, hoping to better himself, took the family to Argentina. They stayed four years. His father prospered, and when they returned to Galicia, Daniel was able to go to the university like a *señorito*. He studied medicine. It was his father's ambition for him. "I became a doctor out of love for my father," Daniel was to say, with the kind of self-deprecating humor that is typical of Galicians, "but I did not practice this profession out of love for humanity."

He left it because a hobby of his since his adolescence—drawings, "caricatures," he called them—overtook him. He began publishing them in a local conservative paper in Rianxo, and they immediately took the shape and context of everything he was to do in his life: simplicity, directness, humor, and an identification with the condition of the poor in Galicia as compassionate as Rosalía de Castro's. These were to be collected in a volume called *Nos* (We), and since then they have become everyone's visual image of Galicia. Most, like all caricatures or cartoons, carry a line or two of dialogue by the characters depicted, but often they are an illustration of a statement by Castelao. An example: a sea of people, who from the lower third of the drawing up appear as kerchiefs and round peasant hats, totally crowds the frame to its limits, with only two broken patches of earth in the foreground uninhabited; beneath it the statement: *In Galicia people do not ask for anything. They emigrate*.

For him art was the elimination of the inexpressive. One of the most beautiful and typical artifacts of the Galician countryside is its *hórreos*, tall enclosed corn-bins sitting on stilts that separate them from the damp of the ground by four or five feet. The bins themselves are often tall enough for a person to stand inside them, and their sides are slatted to allow the air to circulate freely and dry the corn. In 1965, my cousins proudly took me into their big one at the unshaded end of their yard, to show me their stored corn. I thought only of the *hórreo's* classic beauty. Castelao said, "An *hórreo* that through its slats shows only the sky tells more about hunger than an article in depth."

Castelao was to do the same with his prose. His book *Cousas* (Things) is a collection of short tales, some no longer than a page, taking as subjects some moments in the daily life of the poor, sometimes a whole lifetime. There is not an unnecessary flourish in his sentences, but there is always time for the visual detail that makes the story true. The prose of his stories is like the line of his drawings—a spare economy that encloses bulk and weight and illustrates a whole world. The critic Domingo García Sabell, attempting to find differences in the great common significance that Rosalía de Castro and Castelao have for Galicians, decided that Rosalía (in Galicia her first name is all one need use) always asked the radical questions about Galician existence and Castelao gave testimony. Indeed, a book Castelao began to write during the Civil War, *Sempre en Galiza* (Always in Galicia), has become the touchstone for Galician autonomists: they go back to it for confirmation or for a point of departure.

When Castelao began to publish his drawings, he also became active in a group called *Acción Gallega*, which developed in the following decades into the base of the *Galleguista* Party. Under the Republic he served in the *Cortes* when this party put him up as a candidate, and there rose to speak in 1931 when the new constitution was being voted on to ask for the same recognition for the Galician language that the draft constitution already gave the Catalan. His charm and eloquence gained him the adherence of Unamuno who, like Castelao, was impatient with many of the large empty phrases of the constitution. Unamuno was also a deputy, and he used to spend much time in the corridors of the *Cortes* irritated with what was going on inside. He told Castelao as much one day when they ran into each other there, and Castelao repeated a statement made by a Galician peasant at an election meeting that for Castelao was reason enough for participating in drawing up a new constitution for Spain. "This time the constitution must be written on sandpaper," the peasant got up to say, "so that afterward they cannot wipe their asses with it."

Unamuno laughed with untypical abandon. "You must go inside and tell them," Unamuno said. "That is the authentic voice of the people." But Castelao did not. He did not want to shock the deputies or alienate them. It took five years of sweet reasonableness (but pursued as obstinately as by any Galician peasant) to obtain from indifferent Republican leaders the plebiscite to vote in autonomy. Castelao was to remain loyal to the Republic and fight for it, unlike Unamuno. He was, of course, physically separated from Galicia from the start of the uprising, and before he went into exile, while the Civil War was still going on, he began to publish as newspaper articles the first section of *Sempre en Galiza*. They were an attempt to give himself and his people hope so long as the fight went on.

He starts writing the second section in 1940 in New York City. He is writing by the light of a window shaded by an awning, and the many windows he can see across the street from his make him lose the thread of his thoughts. He wonders whether inside them may be people of many other nationalities filling notebooks with their own complaints. "None of my neighbors across the way knows there is a nation called Galicia, and I cannot expect them to guess at my own existence. I am a son of an unknown country because no one knew how to give international fame and authority to our patriotic demands. For this, pardon our modesty or our desire to appear good in the eyes of other Spaniards, who never wanted to understand us. Are we again to begin anew?"

He was to continue to add to his book until he died in 1950 in Buenos Aires, where he spent his exile after a few months in New York. With the second section the book begins an examination of the past, the politics of *galleguismo* under the Republic, the problems of Galicia, the nature of the Galician—always the concern is the new beginning that will bring them independence and liberty. When he died, there were many to mourn him in Buenos Aires, for this is the most populous Galician city in the world, but in Galicia only a handful knew about him then. Between that time and now he has become a kind of father to the nation. His books—the drawings, stories, plays, political essays—have appeared in many editions, and there is no Galician political party that does not claim him. Late in

1975, the mayor of Santiago de Compostela, an appointee of the Franco regime, made the mistake of saying in public that Castelao has no relevance for the present, and in the summer of 1976, when I was there a second time, he was still apologizing for it.

I had come to Santiago again, primarily to see two men, one of whom was Domingo García Sabell, whose essays I had discovered in Madrid. "Oh, if Daniel were to come to life now and hear everyone speaking Galician and see the bookstores filled with our books, he would die once more but of delight!" García Sabell said to me. "*Galleguismo* is stronger than ever. They thought they had wiped it out, stamped it down, pushed it aside, and it has surged and surged. Even the bourgeois speaks Galician now. If you had said to me that the university students would someday demand that they be tested in Galician and that it would be done, I should never have believed it. Or that I would have two grandchildren both of whom would be speaking Galician . . . ah, indeed, Daniel would drop dead with joy."

One of the things that had attracted me to García Sabell before I met him was a long essay of his that I read in Madrid on Joyce's *Ulysses*. It piqued my curiosity: how did a *galleguista* who had lived all his life in Galicia, most of it under Franco, find time for the great modernist? How many Galicians could have read Joyce? "Oh, that is another thing—our translations! The first translation of *Ulysses* in the Iberian peninsula was in Galician, though only a group of chapters. Let me tell you, I sent a Castilian friend, a professor of philosophy at the University of Madrid, the translation of Heidegger by Ramón Piñeiro, and he told me it was better than the Castilian. Galician is a much more supple language. All that play of Heidegger's with prepositions and pronouns can be done in Galician but not in Castilian—it is too rigid."

García Sabell is himself an example to Galicians. He was a young doctor just beginning his medical practice in Santiago when the uprising came and Galicia immediately fell. He made no attempt then or later to leave the country. "A man is not a man if he does not live in the culture of his people, if he does not have roots in the place he belongs. I did not think of exile—I had a wife and two daughters, and anyway, I believed it was my duty to stay. The years have proved me right." But as the article on Joyce may suggest, he is a man of broad international culture: the footnotes and references in his essays are an index to the extraordinary breadth of his reading in medicine, literature, and philosophy. An achievement that is astounding not only because Spain was sealed off for many years under Franco but because he read them in English, French, German, and Italian while carrying on a full-time medical practice.

At first, given the difficulty of publishing in Galician, he wrote his essays and his anthropological study of hunger in Galicia in Castilian. But once books in Galician were permitted in the early sixties, he has published only in his native language. "In Madrid they tell me I should write in Castilian, that I would then have a national audience. I do not care, I am interested in my land and my people. It is for them I write." One might expect didactic simplicity from such a writer, patriotic subjects, exhortational pronouncements; but a good example of his work was the new volume of essays he handed me: besides articles on Rosalía and Castelao, it contained a one-hundred-twenty-five-page essay called *The Faces of Contemporary Eroticism*, and another long one called *Painting and Knowledge*.

He was sixty-seven, but he still worked a full schedule at the small clinic he runs in Santiago. I called on him unannounced, and in order to devote two hours midday, between the last of his morning patients and the first of the afternoon, to talk without interruptions, he passed up lunch and stayed in his office with me. I have never met a happier man. It is the hopeful state of *galleguismo* and his own varied work that make him so. When he first began as a doctor, he had hoped to engage only in research and teaching. Instead, the Civil War plunged him into a more rewarding life.

It was sometimes fearful. "I had begun my practice, but I had an appointment for later in that summer of 1936 to try for a chair in pathology at the University of Zaragoza. It was not to be. I was stopped by the uprising. I was a *galleguista* and tending towards a socialist political stance, but I was young, I was not a leader, nor well known, so they did not come for me. We tried in those days to stay at home and keep out of trouble. And so it was for me. Poor Antonio Fraguas went through the humiliation of being made to sweep the streets in Lugo. And others." But in a few months the first wounded from the Nationalist front began to be brought to hospitals in the area, and there was a call for doctors. Everyone but Sabell volunteered.

"That is when the threatening phonecalls began. Tonight we take you for a *paseo*, you son-of-a-bitch Red. I used to wait at home with a pistol nearby. I believed that I should not go passively but shoot as many as I could. I did not sleep the nights that phonecalls came. I decided that I must suffer my fears with dignity—that was the best I could demand of myself. I had no hopes of being unafraid—being a hero was out of the question with me," he said, and then laughed at himself. "I was saved from my sleepless nights before the year was out by the military draft."

He was assigned to a hospital in the province as a doctor's assistant. "I gave injections like a nurse and served under a doctor who knew nothing about medicine. I was being treated like Fraguas. It was a way of humiliating me to keep me working in that capacity. That is what they did to *galleguistas* who were not jailed or shot." After a while, he was transferred to a concentration camp just outside Santiago. There were hundreds of prisoners of war there, Republican soldiers and political prisoners, and he was the only doctor for them. "They needed a lot of care. Their conditions were horrible—many slept on the ground and they were covered with eczema and lice-ridden. That was a disagreeable experience for me, knowing what I should do for them and having practically no medicines with which to treat them. I improvised. I spent the rest of the war there trying to alleviate their ills without even the minimum hygienic conditions."

When the war was over, the concentration camp was broken up. Some were sent home; others went to jail. Sabell felt like a prisoner, but he was let go. He started his practice again, but for sixteen years he was not allowed to publish or lecture. He thinks it was good for him; it gave him time to read and to begin writing in earnest. He worked in the countryside too, and began research that led to his book *Notes Towards An Anthropology of the Galician Man*. "I found parishes in which the diet was comparable to that of the Nazi concentration camps." The book draws on the medical, psychiatric, sociological literature of many countries, touching on subjects as diverse as the experiments carried on at the University of Minnesota on malnutrition and a study on the relation between scientific thought of Leonardo da Vinci and his ideas of art. All of it is, however, in the service of the Galician, so that the book, presumably a study of the age-old diet deficiencies of the region, turns into an investigation and exposition of the national characteristics of his people. Without a single overt political statement—it was published in 1966, when the censorship was still quite strict—it subversively destroys the bucolic, folkloric image of Galicia.

Sabell's book explained many things to me about my cousins in Miamán. From the huge, heavy meals they served themselves to the premature baldness and lined countenance and emaciated body of Gustavo. The chapter that describes how a Galician deals with illness reminded me of Isabel explaining the virulent sickness that had laid her low for months since I had last seen her. Sabell tells that for the Galician an illness is always a presence from the outside that enters the body, one he first ignores, then fights, and finally surrenders to as the last cunning defense. "At first, all the bones in my back hurt," Isabel said. "But I went on working. I saw a doctor and he gave me salves. Then it was too much for me and I lay upstairs, stiff, stiff, stiff. For months I lived with my pain. I did not even think how the house was getting on. Until one day I said to myself, Let me see, I think it is gone, and I got up and walked. But it did not leave me entirely, as you can see."

In another sense, this is how the Galicians have suffered the era of Franco. And some of the results of malnutrition—distrust, skepticism—that Sabell believes are now traits of the Galicians, have helped them come through. The *galleguismo* that Castelao stubbornly insisted could not be expunged holed up while the fever raged. Sabell would get together at home with a few friends, and slowly there were contacts with Basques and Catalans. Sabell's home got to be known to the police. One day the police chief came to tell him that he had proof that on a particular day a meeting was to be held there; he even named some of the men who were coming. This was in the early sixties, and Sabell was less fearful than in the days of the uprising.

"I denied nothing," Sabell recalled. "I told him that there was no question that I was opposed to the regime and that I could not help talking about it to my friends. You might even think I am a Red.

There is nothing that I can do about that. Think about it as an illness. I am a doctor and I can tell you that I know of no cure for it."

Sabell was a Red only in Francoist terms. Like Castelao, though Castelao was particularly pleased by Galician Marxists—that they should be Socialists and Communists and not cease to be *galleguistas*. The condition of Galicia dictated a radical posture for the *galleguistas* and a *galleguista* posture for the radicals. The overwhelming number of Galicians, until the last decade and a half, were fishermen and farmers; they lived in pre-capitalist economic arrangements, particularly in the countryside, that kept most of the people working hard merely to subsist. There was almost no industrial proletariat, and the tradition of working together in the country parishes was a collectivist sentiment centuries old, the result of a common struggle not against an exploiting class but against a hard environment that for many reasons, not the least being the *minifundio*, made subsistence farming slavery. The backwardness, illiteracy, isolation of this mass of people made them unassimilable—despite the adaptability the Galician has shown when he has left home—and kept the very language of Castile from making any inroads for centuries.

Galicia now has a population of about two and a half million and as much as another million (though official figures halve the number) are working abroad. From the sixties to the present, Spain has stopped being a preponderantly agricultural nation, and in 1976 was the ninth industrial nation of the world. Some, but only very little, of this industrialization has come to the cities of Galicia, and it immediately created a militant proletariat. And it has become obvious to all *galleguistas*, Marxist or not, that the savings of the Galicians working abroad, which according to official statistics amount to at least fifty percent of the savings of all of Spain's emigrants, are not put to work by the banks to create jobs in Galicia but are invested elsewhere in the peninsula. Castelao in the later sections of *Sempre en Galiza* already announced that the Republic's constitution's limited autonomy should not in the future suffice Galicians, and his political heirs agree.

The *Galleguista* Party no longer exists. Instead, there is a group of parties which have evolved during the clandestine years into a kind of extra-official representative union, like that of Catalonia's, called the Galician National Popular Assembly. It rejects the Republic's hesitantly granted autonomy and calls for, besides the common demands of all Spaniards for democracy and political amnesty, "the substitution of all administrative institutions which are of a colonial character by ones that are proper to Galician reality; the formation of our own organization and bodies that will achieve: industrialization by means of a rational exploitation of Galicia's resources, the restructuring of the fishing economy, and the creation of an agrarian reform with the participation of farmers and fishermen; the investment of Galician earnings in the country and the control of the great corporations and monopolies that operate in Galicia; the power to determine and execute budgetary, commercial, fiscal, and tariff policies for Galicia . . ."

It is interesting that the Galician Communist Party is not part of this group because its program for a democratic rupture included starting off from the Republic's limited autonomy, and because many in the Assembly criticize the Galician Communists as Hispanicists and centralists, a charge that is not entirely fair. Even more interesting is that the demands quoted above serve as a fanfare for the climactic demand for "normalization of the language at all levels." It is stated flatly, for it needs neither rhetoric nor explanation for Galicians. The last two decades in Galicia have seen a surprising development: the defense of the language, not only of its use but also of its purity, has passed from the countryside to the cities that in the past first gave it up. I had seen the students in Santiago demonstrating for a chair in Galician history at their university, and I stood as in a jammed subway car at the rush hour to listen to a roundtable on Galician history led entirely by professors speaking in Galician.

Even from within the Church, which was always the central government's most efficient arm for weaning the people from their language and traditions, there has come a defense of Galician. Monsignor Miguel Anxo Arauzo, bishop of Mondoñedo-El Ferrol, issued in May, 1975, a pastoral letter in which he criticized the anti-Galician activities of priests in the past and urged the clergy to adopt with conviction the Galician language in all the works of the Church. "We are aware," he said, "that given the inferiority complex that many Galicians have with respect to their language, a

veritable catechism may have to be imposed to make them understand the human and religious values of their tongue, and that they
need not nor must not talk to God our Father in any language
different from that in which they talk to their mothers or fathers or
children. I sincerely believe that this catechism should free them
from the insecurity they feel about their language and firmly convince them that they are no less as persons for speaking the language
they learned as children."

Having gone first to Miamán to visit my cousins and then gone to
the city and seen the students and *galleguistas*, I had traversed
emotionally the political path that Galicia took under Franco. I left
Miamán sore with frustrated hopes that those dear to me there
would have gained some better understanding since 1965 of the
forces that ruled their lives. Indeed, my young cousin Paco, perhaps
bitter that he failed to become one of those university students now
so rebellious, was a staunch supporter of Franco. "There was always
enough democracy," he said to me. And in my presence he resisted
the liberalizing talk of the new parish priest, a son of Galician
peasants who did not wear his cassock, and played cards every
afternoon with his parishioners at a bar in the highway town. Only
with great effort was Paco able to contain himself when the priest
criticized Franco as a Galician who had done little for his own
region.

It hurt me, too, that it should be the old *galleguista* Antonio
Fraguas who in the city confirmed the statistics I already knew about
Galicia's countryside. Yes, he said, in your cousins' parish all the
land is still cultivated, but that is because their valley is one of the
most fertile in La Coruña. Everywhere else the peasants are leaving
the land untended. You cannot say that it is even going to pasture,
for scrubs and pines have taken over. In some places the new middle
classes are picking up the abandoned farms for a song and building
summer chalets. True, Claudio and Isabel were aware that in
Miamán all the new two-story homes, except theirs, were built with
money that emigrants saved while working in Europe, that fifty
percent of the old parish had moved away, that those who returned
from Europe most often went on to the cities to live, having learned
the value of a weekly salary. The *concentración* in Miamán had
made them happy, but they did not work any less. (They did not

know that the land redistribution achieved no more than a minor face-lift, and had no effect on agricultural production in Galicia.) They knew these facts, but they did not put them together; they were random factors in their sadness.

But when I returned by bus to Galicia in summer from Asturias, I recalled one puzzling bit of information I had gotten from one of Clara's relatives in the highway town, the afternoon we visited with Paco the aunt whose husband was dying. To make conversation, I commented on the charred patches of forest in the mountains overlooking their valley, and asked if the previous summer had been unusually dry. One of the men looked gleeful and said, "They say fires were set to protest." Paco looked away with a show of irritation, but an interruption made it impossible to pursue the subject. On the bus several months later, that moment came back to mind when we entered the western Asturian countryside, which had been part of Galicia until it was administratively removed from it in the nineteenth century, and I saw a small forest fire underway. As we drove towards the city of La Coruña there were more and larger and larger, the last one just outside the city billowing huge black clouds of smoke that made us close our bus windows.

The young Army draftee sitting next to me, on his way to spend his weekend leave in his country parish, got the same pleased look when I asked him about the fires as the man in the highway town during the winter. "It is very complicated," he said, but this time I persisted. True that it was a dry summer, he replied, but the fires always occur only on the lands of the *Plan Forestal*, a project of the regime's for replanting and scientifically developing unclaimed highland areas with timber: a laudable enterprise. But these lands, from which the peasants were now excluded, had for centuries been the common lands of the parishes, from which they collectively cut firewood and gathered *tojo* for compost. "They do not have papers to show that it is theirs," the soldier said, "but they are theirs. So they prefer to burn them down."

This was the first thing I checked with Xosé Manuel Beiras when I reached him in Santiago. He and Sabell were the two men I had come unannounced to see. I had read an article by Beiras on the problems of rural Galicia, and everyone had told me he was the most interesting of the young Galician economists, a professor, also, at the university and leader of the Galician Socialist Party. (No one had thought to tell me that he was also Sabell's son-in-law.) Beiras said I should not feel too sorry for what the peasants were doing to the *Plan Forestal*; the Plan was not helping the poor but simply planting pines for the paper companies. While driving out of the city recently, he had come across an example that he thought was telling. On one side of the road there was a sign announcing that the land beyond it was part of the *Plan Forestal*; it was all planted with pines. Directly across from it were peasant-owned lands; it was all planted with hardwoods. "It is the peasants instead of the government who have long-term plans," he said, and to make sure I got his point, added, "Pines are hard on the soil—they spoil it."

I did not have Beiras' address or telephone when I arrived in Santiago, and I was staying at the Hostal de los Reyes Católicos, a luxury hotel developed by the Ministry of Tourism from a magnificent fifteenth-century renaissance building, where the service and the furnishings are so elegant that they perhaps thought it too coarse to have a telephone directory in the room. After all, the telephone operators sprang to attention the moment one lifted the receiver. With some self-consciousness about asking for the number of a socialist at the Hostal, I gave her his name and explained that I did not have his second surname, always necessary in Spain when looking up a listing. "Do you mean the economist?" she asked brightly, and when I said yes, she answered even more eagerly than at first, "That will be no problem at all."

I tell this minor incident not to emphasize how popular Beiras was in Galicia (there is no need to labor that fact) but to show what became increasingly clear to me—that the slightest clue that one is a *galleguista* quickly breaks down social barriers. In Galicia, some historians aver, political differences in the past, in view of the pre-capitalist economic relations that obtained, have been not so much between classes as between the country and cities. And even that point of conflict was softened by the experience, like Beiras', of the town bourgeois children being sent to the country for days and weeks at a time in the care of servants. Beiras had no trouble identifying with the peasants—he could never feel the discouragement I did after being in Miamán—and neither did the other intellectuals I met in the cities. Unlike, say, American or Madrid intellectuals, when they say "we" they are not unconsciously referring only to the middle classes; nor, to take an extreme example, would they be capable of the "we" of American southerners who consciously exclude all blacks from the category of southerners.

Beiras was forty, which meant he was a child during the years of hunger, and although his father was only a shopkeeper, there were two servants at home. One of them was a young peasant woman from a parish a few miles from Santiago. He often went with her to her *aldea*, the name for country settlements that make up a parish, and stayed in her parents' home. Many upper-class families would send their children to peasants who rented lands from them because the peasants would invariably feed such children with the best fresh food, not for pay but to gain the good offices of their patron, so that he might one day extend them favors in getting them jobs or dealing with the bureaucracy. In Beiras' case, the relationship was more disinterested, and an incident he recalled added admiration to the affection that he felt for the servant girl and her family.

In Galicia, as throughout Spain, there was much contraband and black market dealings during the lean years, and the local trains were usually filled with persons carrying bundles that they hid when inspectors came through—or flung out the windows just before reaching their destination, since there were Civil Guards at all stations inspecting any suspicious packages. The same was true of all the roads leading out of the cities. The scarcity of bread was such that Beiras' father, when he could, would buy wheat on the black market and the servant girl would take it to her *aldea* to be ground at their crude mill, and bring it back to the city with her. She placed the wheat at the bottom of a huge basket topped with clothes she was going to wash in the *aldea*'s clear stream, and carrying it on her head with the aplomb of Galician women, she would walk with impunity with little Beiras past the guards on the outer limits of Santiago.

"One day, I remember, a guard made her stop and put down the basket," he said. "He made her remove all the clothes and thus uncovered the unground wheat on the bottom. The next thing I recall is the guard running. He was terrified by the woman's rage." She knew that the wheat must be hidden, but it had apparently never occurred to her that it could be confiscated. "She struck out at him and raised such a cry that his only recourse was to run. He never stopped her again."

Beiras' father was both a *galleguista* and a devout Catholic, and the latter helped protect him from the attention of the authorities. In any case, he was never an activist but spent his leisure hours reading his good collection of Galician history and literature. His mother taught them music. At home and in the *aldea*, Beiras spoke Galician, and without being told did not speak it elsewhere. But in those days their life was mostly spent at home. Beiras was not sent out to school; he was tutored at home. When the time came to prepare for college, his father and others like him prevailed upon a group of teachers to tutor their children as a class, and this led to the formation of a private school. All the while, their evenings at home were, due to his mother, musical. He was to become, when in college, part of a choral group that toured doing traditional Galician songs. From this has come his love of performance and the theater; he translated Anouilh's *Antigone* and Giraudoux's *Tiger at the Gates* into Galician. This resumé of his early years makes them sound privileged—and they were—and yet when he was ready for college, his family did not have the money to send him to Madrid.

The University of Santiago was a poor one. "A poor substitute for a poor university," he said. Though music and literature were real loves, he wanted to study economics, but there was no economics chair at Santiago. (Spanish universities cannot be said to have departments but a tenured professor or group of professors in particular fields.) He had to select law, and that was so badly taught that although he completed the course of studies, he got to dislike the subject and never practiced it. (All the gifted persons I met in Spain of Beiras' age found it difficult to get an education at any of the universities.) Beiras was able to keep up his many cultural activities—theater and the choral group—because, as he calculated, he could with one hour of study a day remain at the top of his class.

He began to make his own way. He became a teaching assistant in his last year, and he tutored and saved money. Then with the help of a new private foundation he went to the Sorbonne to study—at last—economics. That was when he first read Marx—in French, which he learned in six months. But to get his doctorate in Spain he had to go to Madrid, and to support himself he studied towards an examination for a job in government. He had to be in Madrid, also, to unearth statistics for his thesis which, for obvious reasons, he wanted to write on population changes in Galicia. The statistics had to be found in old files and copied out by hand, there being neither any rational filing of documents nor Xerox machines for reproducing them. But first he had to secure the government job, and he devoted six months to mastering the subject, only to find that the examination was all trick questions that caused him to fail miserably.

"I came out of the whole thing a neurotic," Beiras said. He was forced to return to Santiago, which still had no economics chair, and get his doctorate in political science. The research in Madrid did not go for naught; he wrote the thesis on population changes, and the Casa de Galicia in New York City gave him a prize for a study he did on the problems of rural life in Galicia. He has been teaching and writing ever since, but he wishes he could stick to that and research rather than be a political leader. His sensibilities are those of a literary man, and like Rojas-Marcos in Seville, he has none of the manners one expects of a politician. Climbing the stairs to his second-floor apartment in an ancient granite building near the Cathedral, I stopped and involuntarily exclaimed about the broad-planked raw wood steps, which reminded me of old houses in New England. I saw he took pleasure in them and in the new piece of cultural information I gave him.

We had returned from a long dinner at a modest restaurant, and while sitting at a table outside on the old granite pavement, I saw how ordinary Galicians felt about him when they greeted him. He also talked to me about the tendency of many left-wingers to give up on the peasants. Aside from the human question involved, it seemed to him that this view did not take into account facts that he knew as an economist: the peasant did not live in a world of "salaries" and capitalist relations, though he lived in a world in which capitalism was dominant. Nor did he think it was correct to say that the peasants were exploited by the *minifundio* they created, for again this was a pre-capitalist property which went hand in hand with an economy based on use values. What was needed, Beiras believed, was an imaginative strategy for bringing the peasants into revolutionary struggle, for the usual class struggle perspectives of Marxists not only did not apply but would be disastrous.

I took all this personally. In effect, he was advising me to leap out of my own confines when I thought about my cousins, and it had eased my feelings about them to hear him talk this way. I was to feel even better when we returned to his apartment. Besides his wife, Sabell's daughter, an upstairs neighbor, was there, the Ramón Piñeiro whose translation of Heidegger into Galician Sabell had praised. It took me a while to realize it was he—he looked much younger than his sixty years, he did not talk like an intellectual, and our conversation at first was about the methods the Franco political police used in questioning prisoners. I had started it by telling how the Catalan Xavier Folch had gained a kind of ascendancy over his interrogators by not allowing them to address him as *tú*. In this connection Piñeiro told me a story about himself that is worth repeating.

He had gone further than Sabell in those early clandestine meetings with Basques and Catalans, and had on two occasions crossed the Pyrenees to the French Basque country to confer on the course of action they would all follow once the Allies defeated the Axis, and Spain would, of course, be liberated with their help. He was studying for his doctorate in philosophy in Madrid at the time, and returned there after his second trip. It was 1946, but they still had not given up hope, and he was meeting at a café on Gran Vía with fellow conspirators when they were all picked up by the police. It seems that one of them, a Catalan, had been followed all the way from the frontier. Piñeiro was not suspected, and neither had he thought he was in any danger in those days, for he had not even taken any care with the clandestine literature and mimeograph machine he kept in his room at the *pensión*. But when they took his identity card at *Seguridad*, he knew his room would be searched and he would be faced with all that incriminating evidence.

Fortunately, he was not questioned for a few days. (He did not know then that the Basque government in exile had obtained the good offices of the French, English, and American embassies in behalf of the Basques with whom he had been picked up, and since the Spanish authorities were trying to appease the Allies for their past friendship with the Axis, they were being less precipitate with them than usual.) Piñeiro thought up a plan to save his friends. He himself had no police record, but the others had served jail sentences and one had had a death sentence commuted: any new charges could mean the end for them. Through a friendly guard ("There is always at least one," Piñeiro said) he sent a message to the friends arrested with him saying that he would take all the blame since the police would, anyway, have evidence on him. And then began the game with the interrogators.

He decided to talk about his trips to France, to name names, to give true details, but all about people beyond their reach. On his way to being questioned the first day, he saw an elderly socialist lady who had just been picked up being slapped by a guard. "She was a very refined person and I thought, Oh . . ." In the room where he was questioned, there were several men; they fired questions at him from all sides. "But sometimes they completely ignored me and talked among themselves, and that is when I became really nervous. Isn't that strange?" But when they gave him a chance to reply, it was they who were taken aback. Some of the clandestine people he named they had never heard of. They would look them up in their records, find that his stories about them were true, and bring him back and he would spring another name of some militant they very much wanted to catch. Finally, they realized that he was not giving them any account of clandestine organizations in Galicia, and they told him this was what they wanted.

"Do you think I would be so foolish as to tie up with people who were being watched?" he said, as if all his contacts were with people abroad. He explained once more that when he came to Madrid to study he happened to meet a Basque who was the one who took him to France. Who? they asked, and he named someone who recently had escaped from his guard while on a moving train in Bilbao. "I was in *Seguridad* for a month and I was so talkative that they never tortured me—they never felt the need." But he only implicated himself and those the police could not catch.

On the last day at *Seguridad* before being transferred to a jail to await trial, the head of the political police came to see him. He was in a good mood because Piñeiro had been cooperative. In a hectoring tone, the chief said, "There is something that does not make sense here. You are an intelligent man, you have talked because you realize that there is no denying the evidence we found. But being intelligent, why did you on your own search out people who do not have a chance? You do not believe in the United Nations and all that, do you? This regime is firm, as you can see, so why were you so foolish? Were you not drawn in by some organization?"

Piñeiro replied, "Well, one has ideals. If you do not like the regime, you have to do something, so I did what came my way." He was sentenced to six years, and the others were let go.

It seemed to me a story out of the fiction of Camus and Sartre, and I liked to think the experience prepared him for translating Heidegger. I had not known he spent four of those years in jail, nor that he had been a political activist, but I did know that since the fifties Piñeiro had been more responsible than anyone else for the diffusion of Galician literature. He was head of the publishing house Galaxia and editor of the literary quarterly *Grial*, and this was what we first talked about although I have left it for the end.

Piñeiro had astounded me on being introduced by saying how much he appreciated my book on Galicia. I demurred, saying he must be taking me for someone else—my work was not known in Spain. He then, with Beiras' help, found a five-year-old issue of *Grial* on the shelf behind him, and showed me a long article on my book with excerpts from it, both in Galician. My name was spelled Xosé.

I held the magazine in my hands transfixed with joy, and when I finally looked up at Piñeiro and Beiras and his wife, I hoped they would not think my happiness was due to an author's vanity. They did not. They knew that it was seeing my work in my father's language that brought tears to my eyes. I should not have worried, for later that night thinking about this welcome in my father's land, I remembered a letter I had received from the Centro Gallego of Montevideo, Uruguay, a year after the book on Galicia was published in the United States. They had somehow heard of it and were asking me how to obtain copies to display at their annual fiesta on Galician culture. They addressed me as "a son of our land."

Was this what I had hoped for from my Galician cousins? I had until then recalled only the sadness of my last meal in Miamán. Isabel had made us sit at the small table in the kitchen before starting to serve us directly from the hearth as each dish was cooked. I knew she would not sit down until the last, so I asked her, "Tell me, how would you like to live?"

She placed her heavy hands on my shoulders and said, "The way I should like to live is with less work. We could sell most of the land, raise just a few animals, and live off that."

I asked why they didn't do that.

She pointed to Claudio. "He is not a man for decisions. When Paco was studying in Santiago, there was a chance to sell most of this and buy an apartment there and have a little business like Gustavo and Luz. But he never decided."

She returned to her saucepans on the fire, and when she served the first dish, she shrugged and sighed and then smiled, as if to say she too was as enmeshed in the work as Claudio. "Eat, eat," she said. "That is what we do well here."

Before she sat down, she dared her worst prediction. "When Claudio and I die, these two are going to sell everything and go to the city and not work anymore."

Paco did not answer her, and it was not, of course, for his wife Clara to say anything at all.

This scene had stayed with me because I had turned Isabel's mood into a sociological phenomenon I had picked up in the city. I should have known it was her *morriña*. Earlier that day when she and Claudio and I had been alone, Claudio had gripped my forearm to make me listen. With a sudden outburst, he told me that I must keep my promise to return in a few months. He wanted to divide the lands he and Gustavo had inherited from our grandmother so that my sister and I would share them with them. We argued about it. At everything I said, Isabel shook her head emphatically—"No, man, no!" I came as close as I ever did to telling them what my views of property are; I said that the land belongs to the people who work it. It carried no weight with Claudio and Isabel.

"You must have this land as a remembrance of Galicia," he said, "so that it will draw you back to Miamán."

Postscript

Antonio Fontán is a prominent member of the *Opus Dei*, the Catholic lay organization that gave the Franco regime in the sixties its best technocrats. He is a Latinist and holds the chair in Latin Philology at the University of Madrid. He was managing editor of *El Diario de Madrid*, from 1969 to 1971, during its short liberal period, and this newspaper's closure under pressure by the Ministry of Information brought Fontán some notoriety. He is also Chairman of the Board of Cid, S. A., a thriving advertising and public relations agency, and in February, 1976, was meeting with individuals of varying political backgrounds to explore setting up an independent political party. Despite all this, he is a private person, and we first talked about things that most interested him, like the works of Mauriac and Bernanos. But I changed the subject because I wanted to hear from him, more than from others, whether he thought that the old guard, those who wanted to hold Spain to a *franquismo* without Franco, would make a transition to democracy impossible. "Have you not noticed?" Fontán said. "It is three months since Franco died and not even the newspapers mention his name."